T0328886

The Cambridge Companion to Arvo Pärt

Arvo Pärt is one of the most influential and widely performed contemporary composers. Around 1976 he developed an innovative new compositional technique called 'tintinnabuli' (Latin for 'sounding bells'), with which he has had an extraordinary degree of success. His music is frequently performed around the world and has been used in award-winning films, and pieces such as *Für Alina* and *Spiegel im Spiegel* have become standard repertoire. This collection of essays, written by a distinguished international group of scholars and performers, is the essential guide to Arvo Pärt, and his music. The book begins with a general introduction to Pärt's life and works, covering important biographical details and outlining his most significant compositions. Two chapters analyze the tintinnabuli style and are complemented by essays which discuss Pärt's creative process. The book also examines the spiritual aspect of Pärt's music, and contextualizes him in the cultural milieu of the twenty-first century and in the marketplace.

ANDREW SHENTON is Associate Professor of Music at Boston University.

The Cambridge Companion to

ARVO PÄRT

....

EDITED BY
Andrew Shenton
Boston University, USA

CAMBRIDGE
UNIVERSITY PRESS

CAMBRIDGE
UNIVERSITY PRESS

University Printing House, Cambridge CB2 8BS, United Kingdom

Cambridge University Press is part of the University of Cambridge.

It furthers the University's mission by disseminating knowledge in the pursuit of education, learning and research at the highest international levels of excellence.

www.cambridge.org
Information on this title: www.cambridge.org/9780521279109

First published 2012
Reprinted 2014

A catalogue record for this publication is available from the British Library

Library of Congress Cataloguing in Publication data
The Cambridge companion to Arvo Pärt / [edited by] Andrew Shenton.
    p.   cm. – (Cambridge companions to music)
Includes bibliographical references and index.
ISBN 978-1-107-00989-9 (hardback) – ISBN 978-0-521-27910-9 (paperback)
1. Pärt, Arvo – Criticism and interpretation.   I. Shenton, Andrew, 1962–
ML410.P1755C36 2012
780'.92–dc23
2012005155

ISBN 978-1-107-00989-9 Hardback
ISBN 978-0-521-27910-9 Paperback

For Nora Pärt

Contents

Figures, plates and tables

Music examples

Contributors

Marguerite Bostonia is Senior Lecturer in Music at West Virginia Wesleyan College, teaching twentieth- and twenty-first-century music theory, piano, and organ. She is also artist keyboard faculty in Community Music at West Virginia University, where she earned a Doctor of Musical Arts. Active for over forty years as church organist and director of music, she also assisted in pipe-organ and tower-bell renovations, learning bell acoustics from carillonneur and bell-founder Richard Watson. She has presented aspects of Arvo Pärt research on Russian bells and tintinnabuli at colleges, American Guild of Organist gatherings, and international conferences.

Leopold Brauneiss was born 1961 in Vienna. He studied at the University of Vienna (musicology) and the University for Music and Performing Arts Vienna (music education, piano), and received his doctorate in musicology in 1988. Since 1990 he has taught theory of music and piano at the J. M. Hauer Conservatory Wiener Neustadt; since 2004 he has been lecturer in harmony and counterpoint at the Institute of Musicology (University of Vienna); since 2006 he has held a lectureship in harmony, counterpoint and instrumentation at the Hochschule für Musik und Theater 'Felix Mendelssohn-Bartholdy' in Leipzig.

Laura Dolp is Associate Professor of Musicology and Coordinator of General Education Studies at the John J. Cali School of Music, Montclair State University (New Jersey). Her interdisciplinary research embraces a variety of topics, from the reception of Arvo Pärt to the work of the modern dance choreographer Mark Morris. Currently she is at work on a book-length study of the historical relationship between cartography and the musical score. Her articles are featured in *19th-Century Music*, the *Journal of Musicological Research*, *Naturlaut*, and *Muzyka*. She holds a BA from Mills College, an MA from Boston University, and a PhD in Historical Musicology from Columbia University. For more information see http://LauraDolp.com.

Jeffers Engelhardt is an ethnomusicologist whose research deals with music and religion (particularly Orthodox Christianity), the musics of postsocialist Eurasia (particularly Estonia), and music, human rights, and cultural rights (particularly in East Africa). Currently an Assistant Professor of Music at Amherst College, he is completing a book-length ethnography study titled *Singing the Right Way: Aural Piety, Orthodox Christianity, and the Secular Modern in Estonia*. His articles and reviews have been published in *Ethnomusicology*, *Journal of Baltic Studies*, *Yearbook for Traditional Music*, and *Journal of the Royal Anthropological Institute*, and he has contributed chapters to several edited volumes. He is co-editor of *Resounding Transcendence: Transitions in Music, Religion, and Ritual*, forthcoming from Oxford University Press, and is also at work on a project that explores musicians, social entrepreneurship, and peer-to-peer/web2.0 microfinance participation in Kenya and elsewhere. Jeffers holds a BM in Piano from the Oberlin Conservatory (1998) and an MA (2000) and PhD (2005) in Ethnomusicology from the University of Chicago.

Andreas Peer Kähler is a freelance conductor, composer, and pedagogue. He studied conducting and composition at the Universität der Künste in Berlin as well as in Sweden and Finland as a German Academic Exchange Service scholar. He was greatly influenced by Sergiu Celibidache, whose conducting seminars and lectures on musical phenomenology he attended. In 1980, he founded the Deutsch-Skandinavische Jugend-Philharmonie, and in 1990 he founded the Kammerorchester Unter den Linden and has given numerous concerts with both ensembles. As a guest conductor, he has worked in Sweden, Finland, France, Poland, Latvia, Switzerland, Iceland, Mexico, and Australia. He frequently performs for the Deutsche Oper Berlin's youth program "Klassik is cool!" The focus of his work centers on Scandinavian music, concerts for children, young people, and families, and the music of Arvo Pärt, whose friend and collaborator he has been for many years.

Immo Mihkelson is currently a freelance music journalist who, since the end of the 1980s, has covered a wide spectrum of music from pop to avant-garde in different Estonian language media (printed press, radio, and TV). For four years he was a music editor for Estonian Radio and spent ten years working for *Postimees*, Estonia's largest circulation daily paper. For Pärt's seventieth birthday in 2005 he produced a fourteen-part radio series entitled *Arvo Pärt: 70* (first aired on Estonian Radio's serious music channel *Klassikaraadio*). The series covered several aspects of the composer's life and work and was made in collaboration with the composer himself, who kindly shared his opinions and explanations with listeners. Recently he has been working as music editor for the Estonian central culture magazine *Teater. Muusika. Kino* (Theatre, Music, and Cinema). Mihkelson is connected with the International Arvo Pärt Centre in Laulasmaa and is currently working on a book which focuses on Pärt's life and work in Soviet Estonia from 1935 to 1980.

Thomas Robinson is a music theorist specializing in twentieth-century music. He received a PhD in Music Theory from the City University of New York, the Graduate Center, and currently is Assistant Professor of Music Theory at the University of Alabama. He previously held teaching positions at Queens College (CUNY) and at the University of New Mexico. His dissertation, entitled *Pitch-Class Multisets*, explores the theoretical and analytical ramifications of pitch-class duplication in a variety of contexts. At numerous international, national, and regional music theory conferences, he has presented papers on pitch-class multisets, the Z-relation, similarity relations, the music of Arvo Pärt, and the melodic analysis of popular music performance. He is also a practicing pianist, performing regularly in a jazz septet.

Andrew Shenton studied at the Royal College of Music in London, where he read for a BM degree at London University and was an organ scholar at St Paul's Cathedral. In 1991 he moved to the USA to study for an MM at Yale University and then for a PhD in musicology at Harvard University. Professor Shenton holds the Fellowship diploma of the Royal College of Organists and has toured extensively in Europe and the USA as a conductor, recitalist, and clinician. His two solo organ recordings have received international acclaim. He has been the recipient of numerous scholarships and awards including Harvard's Certificate of Distinction in Teaching and a Junior Fellowship from Boston University's Center for the Humanities. He is currently a member of the faculty at Boston University, where he directs the Sacred Music program, and Artistic Director of the Boston Choral Ensemble. His first book, *Olivier Messiaen's System of Signs* (Ashgate, 2008), won the 2009 Miller Book Award. Professor Shenton has written numerous articles, including most recently for collections published by Ashgate and Cambridge University Press. He is editor of *Messiaen the Theologian* (Ashgate, 2010).

Robert Sholl is a Lecturer in Academic Studies at the Royal Academy of Music and has taught at King's College, London and at the Royal College of Music. His doctorate, *Olivier Messiaen and the Culture of Modernity*, is currently being revised for publication. Robert is a member of the Theology through the Arts research group and editor of *Messiaen Studies* (Cambridge University Press, 2007). He has recently given papers on Messiaen at Washington, DC, Princeton, Brown and Boston Universities, King's College, London, the Royal Academy of Music, and the Royal College of Music. In 2008 he organized a major conference at the Southbank Centre on Contemporary Music and Spirituality as the first event in Southbank's Messiaen Festival. Robert studied the organ with Olivier Latry, and currently tutors for the Royal College of Organists. He has recently given recitals in the Festival de la Musique Sacrée at the Cathedral of St-Malo, at La Madeleine (Paris), Westminster Abbey, St Paul's Cathedral, and at Notre-Dame de Paris.

Benjamin Skipp is College Lecturer and Tutor in Music at Hertford College, University of Oxford, where he teaches a number of history courses, analysis, and practical musicianship. He studied at the Guildhall School of Music & Drama before matriculating at Christ Church, Oxford, where he took his bachelor's degree in Music. While a Junior Research Fellow at St. Peter's College, Oxford, he completed his doctorate on 'Late Minimalism.' His research is focused on the way that composers throughout time have taken a reductive or minimalist approach to musical material, and the way that these approaches have been received by critics and audiences. In particular, he has written articles, presented papers at international conferences, and spoken on radio on the work of Arvo Pärt. He is also a professional oboist who performs and teaches in the UK.

Plate 0.1 From left to right: Thomas Robinson, Laura Dolp, Andrew Shenton, Jeffers Engelhardt, Arvo Pärt, Leopold Brauneiss, Marguerite Bostonia. Canterbury, England, May 2011.

Acknowledgements

First and foremost, thanks are due Arvo Pärt and his family for their generous cooperation during the preparation of this book and to Eric Marintisch of Universal Edition, who was a gracious liaison.

I am greatly indebted to the many friends and colleagues who continue to provide support to my research and writing. I am especially thankful to my colleagues at Boston University for their good-humored encouragement of my work and the wise council of many, especially my indefatigable assistant Holly Reed. I am also indebted to Martin Wittenberg, who translated Leopold Brauneiss's essay and some of the appendices, and Triin Vallaste, who translated Immo Mihkelson's essay.

For this collection of essays I am profoundly grateful to the contributors for their willingness to turn spoken papers into readable ones and for their expertise in so many areas. Collectively, we wish to thank the staff at the International Arvo Pärt Centre, Micah Conti, Andrew Kohn, Aygün Lausch, and Linda Sabak.

Particular thanks are due to the Boston University Center for the Humanities for its support of the Conference at Boston University in 2010 and for a generous publication subvention that helped to make this volume possible, and to the following who kindly gave permission to use copyright material: Universal Edition, ECM Records, Madelon Rasz, Chicago Botanic Garden, and David Wright.

Finally, the contributors and I acknowledge the enormous amount of work done by Nora Pärt in support of her husband's music over many decades. We dedicate this collection to her.

Andrew Shenton
Boston, December 2011

Editor's notes

In preparing this collection for publication I have been guided by the following principles:

> Language: all translations are by the respective authors unless otherwise noted. The original language for quotations has been omitted unless the source is unpublished or the meaning obscure and subject to more than the usual degree of interpretation.

Because the contributors are an international group of scholars their essays retain their individual voices; however, grammar, spelling and punctuation conform to Cambridge University Press house style except where an original differs, in which case it is given precedence. Some titles of Pärt's works had been rendered entirely in lower-case letters as part of Universal Edition and ECM Records house style. For this volume they have been normalized with initial capitals where appropriate.

The psalms have two different numbering systems because the fourth-century translator Jerome used the Greek numbering (Septuaginta) for his Latin translation of the Bible, called the Vulgate. Traditionally psalms in Latin follow this numbering. Pärt generally uses this numbering when he uses Latin text and the more common Hebrew Bible number for pieces where the text is in any other language. This text follows Pärt's usage in his scores, and in the works list starting on page 203 offers parenthetical numbers for clarification.

Chronology

1935	Born on 11 September in Paide, Estonia.
1938	Moved to Rakvere, Estonia.
1945–53	Rakvere Music School, piano studies with Ille Martin; first attempts at composition.
1950–54	Rakvere High School.
1954	Tallinn Conservatory (formerly Tallinn Music School), composition studies with Veljo Tormis.
1954–56	Military service, playing oboe, percussion and piano in the Military Band.
1956	Continuation of studies at music college.
1957–63	Tallinn Conservatory (now Estonian Academy of Music), composition studies with Heino Eller.
1958–67	Sound engineer at Estonian Radio.
1961	Became member of the Estonian Soviet Composers' Union.
1962	Young Composers Forum Moscow, First Prize for *Our Garden* and the oratorio *Stride of the World*.
1967–80	Freelance composer in Tallinn.
1968	*Credo*, conclusion of his first creative period.
1968–76	Period of artistic reorientation.
1976	*Für Alina*, birth of the tintinnabuli technique of composition.
1976–77	Composed fifteen tintinnabuli works, including *Tabula Rasa, Cantus in Memory of Benjamin Britten, Fratres*.
1980	Emigration to Vienna; contract with the publisher Universal Edition.
1981–82	German Academic Exchange Service fellowship from the Deutschen Akademischen Austauschdienstes (DAAD), Berlin.
1984	Beginning of the creative collaboration with the CD label ECM; all authorised first recordings of major works with ECM.
1989	Classical Edison Award for *Passio* (ECM 1370).
1989	Grammy Nomination for *Passio*, 'Best Contemporary Composition.'
1990	Honorary Doctorate, Music Academy of Tallinn Estonia.
1991	Grammy Nomination for *Miserere*, 'Best Contemporary Composition.'
1991	Honorary Membership, Royal Swedish Academy for Music, Stockholm.
1992	Returned to Estonia.
1996	Honorary Membership, American Academy of Arts and Letters, New York.
1996	Honorary Doctorate, University of Sydney, Australia.
1997	Grammy Nomination for *Kanon Pokajanen*, 'Best Contemporary Composition.'
1997	Independent Russian Arts Award 'Triumph,' Moscow.
1998	Second-class Order of the National Coat of Arms, Republic of Estonia.

1998	Culture Award of the Estonian Republic.
1998	Honorary Doctorate, University of Tartu, Estonia.
2000	Herder Award, Germany.
2000	Nominated as 14th International Composer for the year 2000 by the Royal Academy of Music in London.
2001	Commandeur de l'Ordre des Arts et des Lettres de la République Française.
2001	Honorary Membership, Royal Academy of Arts (Académie Royale des sciences, des lettres et des beaux-arts), Belgium.
2003	Honorary Doctorate, University of Durham, UK (announced 2002).
2003	Borderland Award, Sejny, Poland.
2003	Grammy Nomination for *Orient & Occident*, 'Best Contemporary Composition.'
2003	Grammy Nomination for *Orient Occident*, 'Best Classical Album' (ECM 1795).
2003	Honorary Doctorate, Universidad Nacional de General San Martin Escuela de Humanidades, Argentina.
2003	Honorary Membership, The Royal School of Church Music, UK.
2003	Classic BRIT Award for *Orient & Occident*, 'Contemporary Music Award,' London.
2003	Composition Trophy C. A. Seghizzi for his choral work, Gorizia, Italy.
2004	Borderland Award, Sejny, Poland.
2004	Honorary Membership, Accademia Nazionale di Santa Cecilia, Rome.
2005	Musical America's Award 'Composer of the Year.'
2005	European Church Music Prize, Germany.
2006	First class Order of the National Coat of Arms, Republic of Estonia.
2007	Grammy Award for *Da Pacem*, 'Best Choral Recording' (Harmonia Mundi 097401).
2007	Honorary Doctorate, University of Freiburg Faculty of Theology, Germany.
2007	International 'Brückepreis,' city of Görlitz, Zgorzelec.
2007	Baltic Star Award, St. Petersburg, Russia.
2008	Austrian Medal of Honour First Class for Science and Arts.
2008	Sonning Music Prize, Denmark.
2009	Lifelong Achievement Award of the Republic of Estonia.
2009	Honorary Doctorate, Université de Liège, Belgium.
2010	Baltic Image Enhancement Award, USA.
2010	Grammy Nomination for *In Principio*, 'Best Classical Contemporary Composition' (ECM New Series).
2010	Lifetime achievement prize at the Istanbul Music Festival.
2010	Honorary Doctorate, University of St. Andrews, UK (announced 2009).
2011	Grammy Nomination for Symphony No. 4, 'Best Classical Contemporary Composition.'
2011	Classic BRIT Award for 'Composer of the Year,' London.
2011	Ordre nationale de la Légion d'honneur.

1 Introduction: the essential and phenomenal Arvo Pärt

ANDREW SHENTON

Arvo Pärt is by all criteria an extremely successful composer. He has composed many pieces that have garnered both critical and popular acclaim, and he has received prestigious commissions and worked with some of the greatest musicians of our time. He has received numerous honors and awards, and the diversity of these accolades demonstrates the breadth of his appeal, from the 1989 Grammy Nomination for *Passio*, in the 'Best Contemporary Composition' category, to a Classic BRIT Award for 'Composer of the Year' in 2011. His audience is diverse and international, with performances of his music and record sales all over the world. His hugely popular recordings have been used in both film and television, including Oscar-winning movies such as *Fahrenheit 9/11* (2004) and *There Will Be Blood* (2007), and have also been appropriated by the general public and used in video pieces on social media platforms such as YouTube and Vimeo. His ability to transcend genres is demonstrated in musicians as disparate as Björk, Keith Jarrett, Radiohead, and Lupe Fiasco, all of whom cite him as an influence. His music has had a profound effect on many visual artists who draw inspiration from what they hear; it is frequently choreographed to great effect (as seen, for example, in Helen Pickett's 2011 work with Boston Ballet), and is being used in pioneering work with people with learning disabilities and with palliative care for the sick and dying.

Around 1976 Pärt did something extraordinary and unexpected: he developed an entirely new technique for composing music, which he called 'tintinnabuli' (from the Latin word for 'sounding bells'). The technique is seemingly simple, comprising just two musical lines, one of which moves in largely stepwise motion and the other which moves through the notes of a principal triad. What is remarkable is that the method can offer such rich possibilities for compositional variety, all within a music that has broad aesthetic appeal. It is rare for a composer to create a new compositional system and even more rare for such a system to produce music that has such enormous popular and critical success.

The purpose of this book is to elucidate the essential and phenomenal traits of this remarkable composer and his music. The essential part deals with the interrelation of Pärt's biography and compositions, and continues with discussions of how to analyze and understand the tintinnabuli technique. The phenomenal part deals with the spiritual qualities of his music, its relationship with musical modernism, and its extraordinarily diverse appeal. It is not aimed at the academic, rather it is written for those who love Pärt's music and who want to learn more. What is presented here is a summary of important work that has already been done on Pärt and his music, new opinions and ideas from a group of distinguished writers, and suggestions for further exploration of this remarkable man.

Pärt was born in Estonia in 1935. He received his musical education first at the Children's Music School in Rakvere, then at the Tallinn Music School for a brief spell before being drafted, and finally at the Conservatory in Tallinn, where he studied with the distinguished Estonian composer Heino Eller. From 1958 he worked as a sound engineer on Estonian radio, and became a member of the Estonian Soviet Composers' Union in 1961. During this early period he composed music for more than fifty films and plays. In 1980 he left the USSR and, after a short stay in Vienna, settled in West Berlin before eventually returning to Estonia in 1992.

Throughout the 1960s Pärt composed art works using serial and collage techniques. In 1968 his *Credo* for piano, chorus, and orchestra caused a political scandal. It is not a liturgical creed; however, its title was interpreted as a gesture of defiance and the piece was banned in the Soviet Union for more than a decade. Following this, Pärt went into a self-imposed period of reflection until 1976, composing very little. Pärt claims that during this time he studied the music that was available to him, including plainchant, Guillaume de Machaut, Franco-Flemish music, and Josquin. As a result of this study he made an observation which was important to the development of his new style: "I have discovered that it is enough when a single note is beautifully played. This one note, or a silent beat, or a moment of silence comforts me."[1]

At the time Pärt's mature works were composed, musical modernism had left composers with the possibilities of myriad techniques at their disposal, but with no prevailing style. Composers found many solutions to the dilemma, including turning to music of the past, fusing music of different styles, mixing different styles into collages, randomizing music with aleatoric procedures, and by resorting to minimal use of materials. Pärt disconnected himself from modernism by turning not to the immediate past but to medieval and renaissance music. In an interview in 1999, he made a declaration that is key to understanding his musical technique: "I am tempted," he said, "only when I experience something unknown, something new and meaningful for me. It seems, however, that this unknown territory is sooner reached by way of reduction than by growing complexity. Reduction certainly doesn't mean simplification, but it is the way … to the most intense concentration on the essence of things."[2] Far from being simple, tintinnabulation is a process that affords a large and subtle range of consonance and dissonance, which Pärt uses to negotiate tension and relaxation on micro- and macro-levels. With this innovative technique Pärt has managed to create an authentically contemporary music.

Pärt came to prominence in the early 1980s due to the release of recordings of his music on the ECM label. This encouraged live performances of his work in many different countries, where it met with critical and popular acclaim. In a review for *High Fidelity* in September 1980, critic Robert Schwartz summarized the mood of the moment, observing: "Pärt's emotional intensity, his quiet strength and simplicity, his meditative rapture, had brought a fleeting moment of repose to our hectic lives."[3] In an essay for the *New Yorker* in December 2002, Alex Ross noted that several people have described to him how the "still, sad music of Arvo Pärt ... became for them, or for others, a vehicle of solace." Ross comments that "one or two such anecdotes seem sentimental; a series of them begins to suggest a slightly uncanny phenomenon."[4] These reviews have continued to this day and continue to emphasize the 'otherworldly' and 'transcendent' properties of this music.

What, then, is the enchantment of Pärt's music? At its most basic level, reduction to the simplest musical means allows us to construct our own meaning. There are clearly many ways of hearing Pärt's music made sensible by our individual responses to what we hear. This encourages strong personal reactions, typified by the American poet Rika Lesser, who wrote to Pärt: "Yours is the only music I've ever wanted to live inside. Sometimes I wish the music would stop, congeal, erect a lasting structure around me, one that was silently vibrating and resonating, enclose me. Forever."[5] This book explores Pärt's highly individual approach to composing and seeks to explain the quality of intimacy his music produces with his large and appreciative audience.

The tintinnabuli style is extraordinary in that it constitutes a fully developed new compositional style occurring late in the twentieth century. It is, however, not without its critics. An article written in 1993 by David Clarke explored some of the contradictions of Pärt's music, and suggested that "Far from signifying the resolution of the conflicts of modernity, this music is in fact symptomatic of a deepening crisis."[6] Clarke examined the simplicity of procedures and material of the tintinnabuli style and acknowledged that "compared with other such ventures, Pärt's tintinnabuli style ... appears a far more synthetic integrated and authentic compositional voice."[7] Clarke believed that in order to circumvent modernism's critical agenda Pärt has to "convince us of the validity – the contemporary meaningfulness and truthfulness – of the musical materials he has remortgaged from the past," and concluded that "It might be conceivable, then, to regard Pärt's music as the fragile growth of a few small flowers on the wasteland modern art has refused to reseed. We should not be fooled, however, into believing that spring is on the way."[8] Pärt's huge success since 1993 suggests that Clarke's slightly cynical view was misguided, because Pärt *has* managed to convince us of the validity of his musical materials, and he has done so repeatedly. These chapters evaluate Pärt's success, noting how unusual it is for the music of one composer to evoke the same positive response in so many people, and they address this phenomenon while at the same time locating Pärt in the broader intellectual current of the late twentieth and early twenty-first centuries.

Although Pärt is given much media coverage, there has been comparatively little scholarly attention paid to him and his work. His wife Nora commented on this in 1999, noting: "We've been in the West for twenty years now. Since then there have been a growing number of texts on Arvo's music but very little of it is musicologically founded. In effect, almost nothing. This deficit in musicological methodology is always smoothed over by biographical or personal information which cannot necessarily be linked to Arvo's music directly. Naturally, you can always connect ideas – biographical or not – with Arvo's music. Yet the meaning of the music is purely musical. Arvo is predominantly concerned with musical forms and structure."[9] The authors of these chapters tackle some of the important questions regarding Pärt's music: why is analyzing it so difficult if its structure is so simple? How can we talk about spirituality, in its broadest sense, in the music of a Christian composer? How can we account for its broad appeal? It is not easy to talk about any type of music, because it resists confinement by mere words. It is harder still to talk about music that has spiritual or theological content since, in order to do so, we must move away from vague description and invoke extra-musical discussions including philosophy, theology, history, and cultural studies. In addition, writing about a living composer is a fascinating enterprise since we assume we can go directly to him for answers. Pärt has resisted this, claiming not to be interested in such things, and has repeatedly asserted that people should find their own truth in his music. The contributors to this collection aim to help the reader find this truth.

All of the writers of these chapters have met Pärt and are advocates of his work. Conferences at Boston University in the United States (March 2010) and at the Southbank Centre in London, England (September 2010) organized to celebrate Pärt's seventy-fifth birthday, and a subsequent event as part of a conference on Baltic Music in Canterbury, England (May 2011) provided an opportunity for the authors of these chapters to get together and discuss Pärt's music. Pärt was himself present for portions of the latter two of these events. Pärt has supported this volume by granting interviews, allowing me access to archive material in the International Arvo Pärt Centre in Estonia, and by suggesting some of the contributors to this collection. He has not intervened in or influenced any of the chapters except to verify facts regarding his biography.

The contributors hope that this *Companion* will be read by those who enjoy Pärt's music but who may have little or no musical training, so every effort has been made to present a readable and comprehensible anthology and to provide sufficient explanation and additional resources for the interested reader. There are many points of connection between the chapters, which can either be read consecutively as a narrative or as individual pieces. We aim to provide information that helps to get to the inner life of both the composer and the music.

The contributors are internationally recognized scholars and performers who bring a range of skills and disciplines to their contributions. The first two chapters deal with Pärt's biography, starting with a chapter by Immo Mihkelson, a longtime friend of Pärt, who discusses the early years during the period when Estonia was part of the Soviet Union. Using personal reminiscences, formal and informal interviews with the composer, and archive material, Mihkelson draws a picture of Pärt's early career as a student, as a professional sound engineer for Estonian radio, and as an emerging voice on the Soviet and international musical scene. Mihkelson contextualizes the ideological pressure, restrictions, and prohibitions Pärt faced during this period, and traces his training at the Estonian Conservatory with Heino Eller through his emergence as a composer with an international reputation, with reference to works such as *Nekrolog* (1960) and *Credo* (1968). Observing the distinctive mark left by his work as a sound engineer (which had musical and social ramifications for Pärt as a developing musician), Mihkelson details Pärt's relationship with the Estonian Soviet Composers' Union and provides interesting information on his work as a composer of music for film and stage. Finally, Mihkelson describes Pärt's interest in early music during his period of reflection between 1968 and 1976, and how this came to have a profound effect on the development of the tintinnabuli style.

Jeffers Engelhardt situates Pärt in the soundscapes of twenty-first-century life, detailing the extraordinary influence his music has had on a diverse range of musicians. Engelhardt accounts for this success by outlining and contextualizing important biographical events in Pärt's life. Starting with the personal and compositional crisis following *Credo*, and the harassment and persecution he endured prior to his emigration from Soviet Estonia in 1980, Engelhardt describes Pärt's intensive and disciplined study of early music between 1968 and 1976. For the period from 1980 to the present Engelhardt concentrates his discussion on the relationships that were beneficial to Pärt's development, including those with the publishing house Universal Edition; the recording company ECM and its founder Manfred Eicher; and with several musicians and groups such as Paul Hillier, the Hilliard Ensemble, Tõnu Kaljuste, and the Estonian Philharmonic Chamber Choir (EPCC). Through detailed discussion of such works as *Passio* and *Kanon Pokajanen*, Engelhardt describes these collaborations and their effect on Pärt's music. A further section deals with Pärt's public return to Estonia in 1992 and his reintegration into that musical scene. Engelhardt concludes with a summary of Pärt's activities at age seventy-five, noting especially the way Pärt has used his music to address political and moral issues.

The second pair of chapters investigates in detail the tintinnabuli technique that Pärt devised. Leopold Brauneiss, another longtime friend of Pärt, discusses the basic mechanics of the tintinnabuli style. Brauneiss suggests that the essential elements of Pärt's tintinnabulation can be viewed as musical 'archetypes,' and he discusses how this idea is connected on a deep structural level with visible forms, shapes, and events, as well as imagined ones. Concentrating on what he perceives as the timeless and exquisite beauty of these structures, he talks about specific musical features such as scales (the melodic lines) and triads (the 'sounding bells') employed by Pärt, as well as more advanced techniques such as mirroring (moving pitches on vertical and horizontal axes from a central note), parallel movement (used to create multi-voiced textures from a single line), and finally multiplication (the mathematics of addition and subtraction to musical figures). Brauneiss draws his examples from well-known pieces such as *Spiegel im Spiegel* and also from more recent works such as *La Sindone*.

Music theorist Thomas Robinson's detailed chapter gives an overview of possible methods of analyzing the tintinnabuli compositions to answer the fundamental question: How does it work? The first part of the chapter examines how traditional analytical techniques can be applied to this innovative music and what may be gained from the application of five distinct analytical methods: style analysis (a comprehensive descriptive technique); musical hermeneutics (which seeks to find expressive meaning in music); Schenkerian analysis (a method that examines hierarchical levels of structure and how harmonies are prolonged at a deep structural level); pitch-class set theory (which enables systematic enumeration of pitches and the relationships between them); and, finally, triadic transformation (a technique inspired by the work of theorist Hugo Riemann, which provides tools to look at transformation of triads).

Because tintinnabulation is such a radical new technique it requires a radical new approach to analysis. In the second part of his chapter Robinson turns to minimalist music and how the two principal processes at work in this kind of music can be fruitfully applied to Pärt's music. He explains the multiplicity of events that can result from these two processes (called 'rules of the game,' and 'machine set in motion'), using examples from *Sarah Was Ninety Years Old* and others. Many tintinnabuli pieces use text, and for Pärt text-setting is itself a process that can be quite sophisticated. Robinson dissects the processes by which the text leads the music and vice versa, and he acknowledges that Pärt's tonal system is not truly a return to tonality as some might claim.

Despite the inherent problems of judging a work of art by assuming artistic intent, I contend in my own chapter that there is enough information available in statements made by Pärt to be able to compile a rudimentary philosophy of his tintinnabuli style. While Pärt has been very clear that he wishes people to find their own answers in his music, his comments, collected from many sources and some published for the first time here in English, present remarkable insights into his creative process, tintinnabulation, text-setting, and thoughts on subjects such as spirituality and time. This chapter also discusses some repertoire not covered elsewhere in the volume, as suggestions for further listening.

As previously noted, the tintinnabuli technique is named after the Latin for 'sounding bells.' Marguerite Bostonia's chapter examines how the mechanics of bell-ringing influenced this technique, and takes a practical look at how bells have directly influenced Pärt's music. Bostonia notes that, far from being a simple simile or metaphor, 'tintinnabuli' is a "fully engaged metonym: a figure of speech in which the name of an entity is borrowed to define another, where both share innate characteristics, musical and spiritual." Bostonia defines these musical and spiritual characteristics in both bells and the tintinnabuli style by referring to different types of bell-ringing, especially the Russian tradition with which Pärt is most familiar. A technical discussion of the harmonic series of bells shows why this label is apt for Pärt's musical language, the melodic and triadic lines of which share the sonic profile of sounding bells. It also explains Pärt's conception that the melodic M-voice and tintinnabuli T-voice are conceived not as two separate parts but as one sonic whole, characterized most succinctly by Nora Pärt in the formula "1+1=1."[10]

The final three chapters deal with the notion of spirituality in Pärt's music, his relationship with modernism and minimalism as movements, and his popular appeal and varied use in the marketplace.

Much has been written about the spirituality of Pärt's music. Robert Sholl delves further into the subject, providing a unique take on the ways in which the discussion of the spiritual or religious content in Pärt's music can be constructed, articulated, and evaluated. Situating his argument in relation to the idea of 'modernity,' Sholl examines Pärt's tintinnabuli language and relates it to a discussion of cultural and musical narratives of death, mourning, enchantment, and embodiment that inform Pärt's musical search for God. Drawing on comments by contemporary composer James MacMillan and writers such as Jeremy Begbie and T. W. Adorno, Sholl furthers the arguments of critics such as David Clarke, suggesting that "the music of Arvo Pärt once again breathes life into the corpse of modernity."

In a wide-ranging chapter, Benjamin Skipp discusses Pärt and his music in relation to two key issues, minimalism and modernism, noting that these labels, along with 'holy minimalist,' need to be fully explored and defined in order that we can begin to understand what is so valuable about Pärt's music. Skipp begins his discussion with an exploration of Pärt's 'style' and how it fits into general notions of what is 'modern' or 'postmodern.' Using examples from the pre-tintinnabuli works as well as the more familiar tintinnabuli ones, Skipp suggests that the music Pärt composed after 1976 resists the label 'modernist' and is generally situated as a counter-modernist reaction. Skipp explores some of the criticisms of minimalism in general and of Pärt's approach in particular. The term 'holy minimalist' Skipp finds particularly worthy of discussion since the addition of the term 'holy' implies a language of faith at work and this can hinder empirical discussion of the music. If we can accept that Pärt's music is sacramental (possessing a sacred or mystical significance, bestowing grace) what are the qualities of his music that ask for interpretation in this way? Pärt is an Orthodox Christian who uses specific religious texts, but whose music is perceived as eclectic, spiritual, and mystical. Skipp explores the notion of tintinnabuli as an 'antidote' to modernism and minimalism, labeling it as "an indictment of the detritus of contemporary living," and he describes its transformative potential using the example of *Spiegel im Spiegel* in the film version of Margaret Edson's play *Wit*. Skipp concludes that enjoying and appreciating Pärt's music at whatever level we do as individuals allows us the possibility of being a 'sacral community,' and that this music offers us a "release from the confused plurality which characterizes the postmodern."

No discussion of Pärt would be complete without an acknowledgment of his extraordinary popular and critical appeal. Laura Dolp examines the "vernacular meanings" of Pärt's music, recounting the way it has moved from a carefully controlled image to an object of extensive free-market forces. From his initial involvement with ECM Records Pärt has been branded in a certain way, and his early success and eventual long-term appeal is attributable to the themes with which he was branded, and a comprehensive strategy to market him to a diverse audience. From the debut album *Tabula rasa* in 1984 to the most recent compositions and recordings, Dolp traces the fortuitous partnership with ECM Records. Led by their founder and director Manfred Eicher, ECM does not consider itself just a recording company but one where music, title, and image are all involved in the design process and eventual product. This approach was foundational in the creation of Pärt's public ethos and is evidenced by Dolp's examples from the *Passio* and *Kanon Pokajanen* albums. Dolp describes Pärt's success and accounts for it by describing reception of his music in the western press and lately the prolific use of his music in film and new media. Attributing this in part to its "non-intrusive formal clarity," Dolp concludes that his marketable identity is rich and complex and that this complements his music.

The appendices include several short speeches by Pärt himself, published for the first time in English. There is also a short essay by Andreas Peer Kähler about the phenomenological effect of Arvo Pärt's music on listeners as well as an analysis of its special requirements for orchestral musicians. Kähler's starting point is a quotation from Saint-Exupéry's *Little Prince* about the desert landscape and the radiation from silence, which he associates with Pärt's "self-imposed asceticism" as a key to understand his music and its idioms. The main part of the essay is a reflection about the relationship between musicians and Pärt's music: about the psychological impact of being alone with few sustained tones, about practical questions (the right Pärt 'sound', using vibrato, how to tune, and so on), and the challenges that professional musicians face when charged with performing this extraordinary music.

Each chapter has its own suggestions for further reading and, since this text is the first major work about Pärt in English for many years, there is a comprehensive bibliography of studies in many languages about Pärt and his music. A discography is not provided here for reasons of space and because this information is readily available online.[11]

The tintinnabuli music of Arvo Pärt invites us to accept it as a point of departure for a new or different spiritual experience with music that is elegantly simple, deceptively complex, visceral, and remarkable. Perhaps the best thing to do is simply to listen to it. We hope, however, that this book will encourage active rather than passive listening, and that readers will gain new insight and understanding into the music of the essential and phenomenal Arvo Pärt.

2 A narrow path to the truth: Arvo Pärt and the 1960s and 1970s in Soviet Estonia

IMMO MIHKELSON

Estonia, a state in the Baltic region of Northern Europe, is an important part of Pärt's development as a composer. His experimentation and musical formation took place there, and it is where he went through the most significant changes in his output before emigrating to the West. Tintinnabuli music was born in Tallinn, the capital city. In a small apartment, Pärt composed such well-known works as *Für Alina*, *Tabula rasa*, *Fratres*, *Cantus in Memory of Benjamin Britten*, and *Spiegel im Spiegel*.

It is important to analyze the beginning of an artist's creative path to analyze in light of what follows. During the period of artistic maturing, discoveries, and emergence, every new detail can potentially have an influence that becomes decisive and long-lasting. Exploring the circumstances and conditions in which a composer most intensely develops his musical language gives us an opportunity to see the many crossroads at which he had to choose a path, and to understand how his choices determined the rest of his life and, for our purposes, the music he wrote.

Arvo Pärt lived in Estonia during a time when the country was under four different political regimes. He was born in 1935 during the first period of Estonian independence (independence was declared in 1918); he started elementary school when the German military had seized power; his musical career started under Soviet rule. Currently, he lives in Estonia, which restored its independence in 1991.

The Soviet era was the most significant, since its rules and context of living surrounded Pärt during his most formative years as a human being and composer. This is the era when he received his musical education, went through important periods of experimentation, and achieved his first goals. When Pärt's music was first internationally recognized in the early 1980s, Pärt was very often compared to other Soviet avant-garde composers such as Alfred Schnittke, Edison Denisov, Sofia Gubaidulina, and Andrei Volkonsky. It is immediately assumed that the conditions and environment in which these composers lived and worked were identical and, therefore, that it is possible to apply the same standards when analyzing them.

In Pärt's case, there are several additional factors to be taken into account in order to understand how the foundation of his music was laid. In occupied Estonia, situated on the outer edge of the socialist empire, the influence of the ideological pressure was slightly different than in the capital of Moscow, for instance. The Soviet regime had had a relatively short time to influence people, and the strong undercurrent of the previous cultural environment was still clearly present when Pärt started his career as a composer. For musicians, the degree of artistic freedom was somewhat greater than in Moscow, but politics and ideology, and resistance to them, are not the only factors relevant here. A number of other components specific to the time and conditions are also important.

There has been a vast amount of research undertaken on the post-Stalinist Soviet Union. The features specific only to Estonia during that period have been examined much less. Therefore, the argument that Pärt's musical path navigated a unique, once-in-a-lifetime maze of opportunities might come as a surprise. Pärt made choices based on his beliefs and ideals, some of which differed radically from other musicians around him. There were many external restrictions and prohibitions, and Pärt often tested them. It was his conscious choice to stay true to his goals even when it brought suffering and poorer living conditions. Due to these conditions, the path of Pärt's musical searching was at times extremely narrow. But there were many situations to learn from as well.

The beginning

Arvo Pärt was born in Paide, in the center of Estonia, and grew up in Rakvere, in the north. Both of these are provincial towns away from the cultural centers of the country. For Pärt, the most influential event during his childhood was the foundation of the Children's Music School in Rakvere in 1945. This music school was one of four founded outside of Tallinn, and it followed the model of the music schools founded all over the Soviet Union. During the years after World War II, the teachers who worked in music schools and other schools carried on the societal and cultural ethos of the pre-war independent Estonia. This had a definite effect on the formation of the young Pärt's worldview.

When Pärt was 9 years old, he started to study piano at the music school, a popular activity at that time. Later, he was active in the school's dance orchestra and accompanied singers who performed at festive events. By the time he was a teenager, Pärt's social status was already intimately connected with music in the eyes of his fellow students. With these experiences behind him, the decision to continue his musical education in Tallinn after graduating from high school was made without hesitation.

In the fall of 1954, Pärt passed the entrance exams for the Tallinn Music School (which, at the time, was an intermediary step between the Children's

Music School and the Conservatory, which in the Soviet music education system is the highest level of training). He was only able to attend school as a composition and music theory major for a few weeks before being drafted into the army. This was during the time when Estonian men were allowed to serve in the Soviet army in the Estonian regiment situated just a few dozen kilometers outside Tallinn. Since Pärt was a musician, he was chosen to play in the regiment's orchestra, which made his army experience more bearable. Sometimes he was given the opportunity to attend symphony concerts in Tallinn. He also attended a workshop for novice composers in the Composers' Union led by Estonian composer Veljo Tormis (b. 1930).

Because of ill health (which was ongoing for some time), Pärt was released early from the army – instead of serving three years, he served only two. The Estonian regiment was disbanded at that time, so if he had served his full term he would have had to do so in some other part of the Soviet Union far away from Estonia.

In the fall of 1956, Pärt reentered the Tallinn Music School and started studying composition with Veljo Tormis, who had just graduated from the Moscow State Conservatory, the most prestigious music school in the USSR. At the Tallinn Music School, Tormis founded a creative circle that aimed to "broaden the minds of students in every possible way."[1] During the first year, the circle actively made contacts with communities in Estonian Radio and the Conservatory, as well as with well-known musicians. Pärt took part in the circle's activities, although not systematically.

In the fall of 1957 a total of 144 students were enrolled in the Tallinn Conservatory. Prospective composition students could apply to the Conservatory only every other year (alternating with music theory students) and, although it was the year for music theorists to apply, a rare exception was made for Pärt, who started that year.

Heino Eller (1887–1970), 70 years old at the time of Pärt's entrance, was the most prominent among the three composition professors at the Conservatory.[2] Eller was as notable a composition professor in his arena as was his contemporary Nadia Boulanger in Europe. His students formed a large and influential group among Composers' Union members and were very supportive of each other. One of Eller's talents was to preserve every student's individuality while, at the same time, helping to strengthen their technique. Pärt's composition lessons took place at Heino Eller's home, which was located near the Estonian Radio building. In 1961, when Pärt did not take the exam in his polyphony class, his expulsion was discussed at the Conservatory, and only when Eller forcefully intervened was the matter dropped.

In the 1950s, the ten most gifted students were listed in the Conservatory's annual report. Pärt was the only composer in that list in 1958 and 1959, and this represents a significant accolade since the qualitative level of conservatories in the Soviet Union was assessed by the number of students who won various competitions or achieved other notable success. In the context of the Cold War's cultural battles, the results of international competitions were given a symbolic meaning, since they were used to demonstrate superiority. In 1961, in her speech at the party congress in Moscow, cultural minister Yekatarina Furtseva stressed that young Soviet musicians had participated in thirty-nine international competitions in 1960 and won twenty-seven of them (at thirty-five of the thirty-nine competitions they received the second or third place).[3] Although Pärt was listed among the top students, in many ways the Conservatory distanced itself from his success during the following years because of contradictory reactions to his music. For example, the rector of the Conservatory at the time was Eugen Kapp, a board chairman of the Composers' Union. Kapp was also a member of the Communist Party and had expressed a hostile attitude towards Pärt's orchestral piece *Nekrolog* (*Nekroloog* in Estonian) at a Union meeting.[4]

Working for Estonian Radio

In various biographies of Pärt, the fact that he worked for Estonian Radio as a sound engineer in the 1960s is mentioned only in passing. Pärt himself has talked about that period of his life only very briefly. Later, he has admitted that he did not enjoy this job since he did not like the music he recorded.

Since the recording process is central in contemporary practices of disseminating music, and taking into account the fact that Pärt is always very involved in the recording process of his music, it is important to talk more about the years he worked as a sound engineer and the experience he gained. Based on Pärt's own remarks, although infrequent, about this work, it could be argued that it shaped his attitude towards music more generally:

> This influenced me in one very odd way. The flawless quality of the sound captured brought me to the other end of the extremes: to the essence of the music, since external cosmetics does not say anything about substance.[5]

Initially, Pärt recorded his music himself but gave it up as early as the beginning of the 1960s (with a few exceptions), and he has since established a strong relationship with ECM Records, who produce almost all the first official recordings of his works.[6] One could argue that this was the moment when he started looking at his music differently – from a distance:

I heard that music only through loudspeakers, and when I did not like something in its orchestration or timbre, all I had to do was to work the mixer and filters until I did like it. Sometimes when I entered the studio and heard how this music sounded unmediated, I was extremely disappointed. I realized that I needed to make changes in the score. This strange situation accompanied me almost the whole time I worked in the radio. There was no correlation between the music sounding in the concert hall and on the record. My impressions of music had always been influenced by the fact that I was recording it. For that reason, I later needed to learn much more about the orchestra and orchestration.[7]

During the recording and editing processes, the music came from large studio loudspeakers, and usually it was rather loud. This also left a distinctive mark:

It was superb equipment I worked with at the time, but somehow I started to drift away from this noise and abundance, mess and chaos. I felt that it was too much. Then I realized that I needed to look for music someplace else. I bought a tape recorder. The quality of sound I got from it was just like from the kitchen radio. The real music will get across even with sound quality like this. It is not about the timbre or cleanness of the sound … If the essence of music is able to reach the listener even through this medium, it is enough for me.[8]

Working as a sound engineer definitely broadened Pärt's musical mind. He had access to the radio's sound archive, including tapes that had been prohibited from being played on the air. Although the collection had only a limited amount of modern Western music, it was still the best of its kind in Estonia at the time. Local musicians who had been given a rare chance to travel to the West brought back records, and it became common practice to lend them to the radio station to be copied. This was appreciated by the music editors in the radio archive.

When Pärt first started his work in the fall of 1958, he became one of five sound engineers (*toonmeisters*) working at Estonian Radio. Everybody needed to do everything: record in the studio and broadcast live from concert halls whenever needed. The music varied from entertainment and traditional music to symphonic music and opera. Young, talented composers were hired as sound engineers in hopes that they would be better prepared for recording serious music by Estonian composers.

Despite Pärt's comment, the recording equipment was comparatively primitive and, therefore, the more creative the sound engineer with the placement of microphones and operating channels on the mixer the better the result of a recording session. Editing took place by cutting and splicing tape in order to gather the most successful takes into a whole. This editing work was quite often done by a sound engineer.

Arvo Pärt was fortunate to work in radio during the years when the independence and importance of sound engineers were at their peak. The sound engineer was both a technician who set up microphones and a producer who judged the artistic quality of the results. In the studio, the sound engineer's opinion trumped the editor's, who had made the initial choice of whom and what to record. When the separate job of 'technician' was created in Estonian Radio and the whole recording policy was reformed in the mid-1960s, the importance of sound engineers started to decrease. Although Estonian Radio began testing stereo broadcasts in 1961, the music recorded in its studios was still captured monophonically at the time Pärt left the job. It is possible that this repeated exposure to a monophonic sound source had an effect on Pärt's compositional processes.

Pärt was also lucky because he was allowed to work full-time while studying at the Conservatory. The same year that he graduated from the Conservatory and was granted a job at Estonian Radio (in the Soviet educational system, it was mandatory to accept the job that was given to you after graduation), the rules for students who studied and worked at the same time were changed, which would have eliminated the chance for Pärt to work in radio.

There is another aspect during Pärt's period of radio work which has been overlooked but is important. Let us call it a social aspect, which has several facets.

Estonian Radio was at the center of the local musical life at that time. It employed the most important symphony orchestra, a professional mixed choir, a light-music orchestra, and various smaller ensembles formed by members of all of these collectives. Most of Estonia's best musicians worked for Estonian Radio or had recording sessions there, because it had the only recording studio in Estonia at the time. Due to his job, Pärt got to know all of these musicians – their skills and personal characteristics. This came in handy when Pärt the composer needed to achieve a certain sound or understanding of his music during the rehearsals preceding a premiere or recording sessions.

Sound engineers belonged to a subdivision of the music department. Pärt was a frequent guest in the music department. He is remembered as cheerful and a great communicator by his colleagues there. Often he played the piano for everyone's pleasure. There were active musicians as well as composers and musicologists working in the music department. All of those who have worked there have described the atmosphere as extraordinarily supportive, friendly, and creative. This environment was at the core of Pärt's social life at the time.

A young Soviet composer

The continuation of the Soviet occupation in postwar Estonia brought along the effects of a new war. The Iron Curtain constructed by the Cold War hid behind it a major part of the rest of the world and caused isolation. The change was sudden. The fiercer the ideological struggle was internationally, the stricter and more intense became the ideological oppression locally during this period.

In Estonia, this change brought along reforms in cultural life that followed the model of all Soviet republics. A state concert agency was founded that organized concerts, many musicians got jobs in the new orchestras, and composers were gathered into the Soviet Estonian Composers' Union, which was a subdivision of the Soviet-wide organization and received instructions from Moscow.

In their creative work, all composers were obliged to follow the methods of socialist realism, although nobody really understood during these years exactly what these methods were. The same way that artists were recommended paintings and sculptures from Moscow as examples created by well-known artists, during the Stalin era composers were given a list of recommended works that they could use as models.

At first, the new political system did not impose itself as forcefully as in later decades. The young Pärt, who was fond of cinema, watched films in Rakvere at a theater which retained its name from the prewar period. The name of the local paper, until 1950, was neutral: *Viru Sõna* (The Word of Viru). Then it was renamed *Punane Täht* (Red Star), which had obvious ideological connotations. Around that time, all movie theaters were given Soviet names as well.

A sudden and somber change took place when in March of 1949 over twenty thousand people from Estonia were deported to Siberia, Pärt's uncle's family among them. None of them came back, just like numerous other deportees who died far away.

The art community, scared already, was given another shock by the Party's meeting in Tallinn in March 1950, which, in accordance with Moscow's orders, heavy-handedly imposed the new rules on the creative communities. This is how the reality of the cultural battles of the Cold War arrived in Estonia. Three composers were imprisoned, some were expelled from the Composers' Union, and ten lost their jobs. The accusations against the composers were not always clear, but the usual complaints were 'formalism' and 'prostration in front of the West.' These were considered betrayals and were duly punished. A human life cost nothing during the Stalin era, so any discord with the government could have been fatal. Pärt's composition professor Heino Eller was among those composers who were targeted in this witch-hunt.

All 'formalists' lived in fear of persecution, and other composers, not accused, were scared as well. Extreme tight-lipped caution was characteristic of the entire generation, and it was definitely in the air in the summer of 1958 when Pärt, who had just finished the first year of his composition studies at the Conservatory, presented his First Piano Sonatina during a meeting of the Composers' Union.

At that time, Stalin's photos and busts had already been removed from almost all of the public institutions, and the signs of the so-called Khrushchev-era thaw were apparent. In the local newspapers from 1956 onwards, young composers had the opportunity to read translations of articles by prominent composers such as Shostakovich and Kabalevsky, and they found encouragement in what they read. As a result, Eino Tamberg (1930–2010) and Jaan Rääts (b. 1932) started to experiment with form and sounds in their works. Pärt and his compositions entered into the new wave when it was already in full swing.

A new generation started to take over the music, film, literary, visual arts, and other artistic communities during these years in the Soviet Union. They were curious about what was going on in the West, and they tried to take advantage of the knowledge and freedoms available and to make their mark. Among other things, these young artists were connected by the absence of extreme fear.

Officially, an internal generational difference between artists never existed in the Soviet Union. It was disavowed. There was only an ideological battle with the West and some young people who had strayed from the right path.

It is widely assumed that Pärt ended up on a blacklist because of his dodecaphonic piece *Nekrolog* for orchestra, written in 1960, but actually it happened earlier. In December of 1958, the board of the Composers' Union of the Soviet Union met for ten days in Moscow. The meeting was dedicated to the music of young composers. Seven from Estonia were sent to Moscow; Pärt, although not yet a member of the Union, was one of them. The resolution of the meeting mentioned Pärt's neoclassical piano piece *Partita*, along with works by Alemdar Karamanov, Edison Denisov, and Andrei Volkonsky, as non-recommended models ('formalist experimentation') for composing music. In the summary of the same meeting, more precisely in the critical notes sections, there are some generalizations about the deviant young composers, including "deficiencies in the ideological and creative development … undervaluing the national-folkloric music … [and] inclination towards certain 'modern' tendencies."[9] In Tallinn, the reaction to the resolution was very much the same as later reactions to Pärt's *Nekrolog* and *Credo* – in official documents, *Partita* was disavowed and Pärt received cautious, reserved treatment.

In general, though, Pärt was lucky to start his career during a time that favored young people. Both Union-wide and inter-Republic events were organized for young composers. They received many commissions, their work was covered in the media more than had been usual before, and there was communication within the USSR with other composers. This was exactly how the so-called Soviet avant-garde, despite all the restrictions, came to life in the 1960s. One of the important members of this group was Pärt.

One example of the extraordinary attention given to young composers' work was a composition competition that took place in 1962 and that is often referred to in Pärt's biographies. The competition was announced in August 1961, and in all of the Soviet republics, including Estonia, a highly qualified committee was formed to organize the competition. The main goal, as publicly announced, was to introduce and promote music by young composers. Over one hundred works by thirty-three young Estonian composers (younger than 33 years of age) competed in the local first round. The Union-wide rounds followed, and six Estonian composers made it to the finals.[10] The Estonian press called the results a triumph for Estonian music. All these composers received a great deal of attention, especially Pärt, and this brought him into the cultural mainstream for good.

Who is not with us, is against us: the Composers' Union

Pärt became a member of the Composers' Union in September 1961, when he started his fourth year at the Conservatory. Again, he was lucky, since just a few years later the rules for becoming a member were made stricter by the officials in Moscow. Becoming a member at that time meant that Pärt had a wider perspective and better conditions for his work.

The Estonian Soviet Composers' Union was a subdivision of the Union-wide institution that grouped together thousands of Soviet composers. Rodion Shchedrin, one of the most successful Russian composers who started his career during the 'youth wave,' has most aptly described the essence of the Composers' Union as a Stalinist organization founded in order to keep composers under strict control with a carrot-and-stick method.[11]

The local subdivision reported more to Moscow than to the local cultural ministry or to the Central Committee of the Estonian Communist Party. The Union-wide Music Foundation paid for composers' retreats and spa trips as well as scholarships. If someone was disobedient, there were plenty of ways to discipline them, including the cancellation of travel grants and scholarships.

Being a member of the Composers' Union had many perks for Pärt. In 1963, he was given an apartment in the brand new Composers' House in Tallinn; that same year he was given a chance to participate in the Warsaw Autumn Festival, which stimulated his ideas and thoughts. The Union was responsible both for compensating Pärt for his work (although technically the money came from the Cultural Ministry) and allowing a piece of music to be performed. Not being connected with the Composers' Union meant that it was practically impossible to have your music performed in concert halls.

Pärt, however, was rather a nuisance to the organization, since after he had composed the orchestral piece *Nekrolog* (1960) his music had been earning fierce criticism from Moscow. These complaints always included the disapproval of certain officials for work that, according to Moscow, was not done well enough. On the other hand, some other pieces by Pärt received a lot of praise, which balanced out the situation. In the early 1960s, the Estonian Composers' Union, despite having only sixty members at that time, had a much more significant position in the Soviet Union than in the following decades.

When Pärt became a member of the Composers' Union in Tallinn, one-third of the members were under 33. In the same union in Moscow (which included such composers as Alfred Schnittke and Edison Denisov), young composers comprised a much smaller minority, and their voice was not taken into account at all. It was the older generation's Union, and many of the members were war veterans. The situation was different in Estonia. Although, according to documents, one-quarter of the members had participated in the war with the Red Army, most of them were in fact forcefully drafted into the occupying army. Being on the side of the winner was a foreign sentiment in Tallinn. A few members had even fought in the German army. There was only a handful that belonged to the Communist Party, and this number grew very slowly. And, at least at the beginning of the 1960s, the Composers' Union had frequent difficulties in fulfilling set plans in terms of the number of patriotic works.

At the meetings, Pärt's new works brought out the most contrasting of opinions. Looking at the minute books of the meetings, it becomes clear that the attitude towards avant-garde music did not always follow generational lines. In general, the Composers' Union had, in the opinion of musicians themselves, a friendlier atmosphere than other artistic unions in Estonia at that time.

Film music: a separate corner

Moving picture and sound are two sides of the same coin both in film and theater. If a film director says that music added a lot to a film, a composer can say that it is completely different to listen to that music with and without moving pictures. These moving pictures provide an entirely new dimension for the music. But one can also find a kind of very poor music that has no effect whatsoever without the moving pictures. And in its scarcity there is the richness that is created in a synthesis with the moving pictures. And if in the visual side, there are so-called empty spots that leave room for the music, then this duo starts to breathe a new way.[12]

Film music and stage music form a significant part of Pärt's Soviet-period oeuvre (more than fifty films and plays). Pärt, however, has frequently stressed that this part of his work is less and less important to him, especially after he started composing in tintinnabuli style.

"At one point, music received no attention at all, it was cut like some sausage," Pärt said later about the handling of his music in films, mostly referring to the last-minute cuts made for by censorship reasons.[13] It is still likely that working with films has influenced his later works, as Pärt has admitted himself: "This should leave a mark after all. It is somewhere there but it needs to be found."[14]

The production of films in Estonia was reorganized after World War II according to Soviet models. A new practice of film music commissioned from local composers was introduced. The film music scholar Tatyana Egorova argues in her book *Soviet Film Music* that the film music composed in the Baltic states in the 1950s differed greatly from the other Soviet film music in terms of its Europeanness.[15] In her in-depth research she mentions the film music composed in Estonia on only a small number of occasions, and Pärt's film music only once in connection with Georgian films. This fact shows vividly what an insignificant role the Estonian films played in the wider arena. Only a handful of films made in Estonia by Tallinnfilm made it to the Soviet-Union-wide distribution network.

The first film Pärt wrote the score for was the 30-minute *Õhtust hommikuni* [From Evening to Morning], produced in 1962 by Tallinnfilm. This was a graduation film by Leida Laius (1923–96), a director graduating from the Moscow Film Institute, where she studied along with Andrei Tarkovsky and many other well-known directors. Laius made art films, a genre still new in the Soviet Union. She, like other directors of the same generation, brought a new approach to the symbiosis of moving pictures and music in the Soviet cinema.

Pärt, already locally well known as a musical modernist, worked hard on the commission. The score that he prepared was very much in the style of his *Nekrolog* and this made the Soviet officials cautious again, since Pärt apparently had not learned from his 'mistakes'. Meanwhile, he applied his new style and real aspirations in a number of film scores. In an interview with the Italian musicologist Enzo Restagno,[16] Pärt describes a situation in

1963 when he introduced one of his film scores influenced by dodecaphony to Luigi Nono, who was visiting Tallinn. Nono was most amused by the fact, as Pärt explained it, that while this kind of music would never be allowed to be performed in a concert hall, there were no problems with it as a film score. The score was for Elbert Tuganov's puppet film *Just nii!* (Just So!), which criticized Soviet bureaucracy.

In Pärt's opinion, the medium of film was like another country where those in power did not apply the same rules to music as they did to concert music.[17] It was therefore possible to experiment and use new sound techniques in film music, as evidenced by the work of Pärt's allies in Moscow: Schnittke, Denisov, Gubaidulina, and Volkonsky. Pärt's scores were mostly for 10- to 20-minute-long animated and documentary films, but also for a few full-length feature films. Hence, for Pärt, it was mostly a short but very intense period of work.

Since the Soviet film industry had to follow the rules of the Soviet planned economy, which made the deadline very tight, the score had to be composed and recorded in a very short period of time – often within only a few days. If the deadline was not met, the whole team working on the film was left without a bonus for their work.

The film's budget determined the size of the ensemble for the score. In most cases there were ten to twelve musicians, and for most of Pärt's scores the conductor was Eri Klas (b. 1939), a good friend of Pärt. There were several occasions where the film score was recorded in the radio studio at night and Pärt himself was the sound engineer during the session. Pärt was one of the most productive film music composers in the 1960s and 1970s in Estonia. He was highly valued for his film scores, although this was a local recognition only.

On the concert stages of the 1960s

In the early 1960s, when Pärt's music was first performed in various Estonian concert halls, the arts – architecture, fashion, and music among them – underwent major changes. The concert life in Tallinn had burgeoned and was now active and diverse. This influenced the music composed and performed in Estonia. Almost all of the concerts were organized by the State Philharmonic Society of the Estonian Soviet Socialist Republic (ESSR), which was founded in 1941 and connected to Goskontsert (the State Concert Agency). Goskontsert had a monopoly on the promotion of all concerts by foreign performers.

In the early 1960s concerts in Tallinn included performances by classical guitarist John Williams, Peruvian singer Yma Sumac, performers from Cuba, Brazil, India, Mexico, and Bali, as well as Hungarian Roma singers, popular singers from Georgia, African dancers, and Chinese traditional musicians. Almost all well-known Soviet musicians (Oistrakh, Richter, Gilels) performed in Estonia during these years. Music by composers such as Debussy, Ravel, Poulenc, Hindemith, and Messiaen appeared in the concert programs – music that only few years earlier had been on the non-recommended list. Works by Johann Sebastian Bach were relatively often performed, even sometimes his works with religious texts. By the middle of 1960s, there was a sharp decline in this kind of global and varied range of performers appearing in Estonia, and concert life stabilized although the size of audiences decreased.

The works: the 1960s

It is very hard to detect crucial influences and personal discoveries that bring along new perspectives without the creator's own explanations. Notoriously laconic, Pärt has given some hints over the years but this is not enough for a complete understanding.

Pärt first started to compose during his high school years. In 1954, when he entered the Tallinn Music School, he showed one of his piano pieces, *Meloodia* (Melody), to composition teacher Harri Otsa (1926–2001), who commented that it had an "unadulterated style."[18] What Otsa meant by this was the absence of motifs from traditional music and of a Rachmaninov-influenced sound. The community of Estonian composers, being frightened, diligently followed the models of socialist realism by composing works that were, in the words of a common slogan from the time: "socialist by content, national by form," emphasizing the latter part of the slogan. The scarceness or absence of folkloric elements was conspicuous. Complaints about the absence of these elements accompanied Pärt from the beginning of his career as a composer and continued until the end of the 1960s.

The fact that Pärt himself has named Tchaikovsky as one of his early influences is natural. From the end of World War II until Stalin's death in 1953, Russian music, especially Tchaikovsky, was frequently played on the radio, to the exclusion of other music. During this time the teenage Pärt would ride his bike in circles around a loudspeaker on a post in Rakvere market square listening to the symphony concert broadcasts. Radio was the main source for information about music in general, and the young Pärt wrote down every single name and work that he heard mentioned in radio announcements, filling one sketchbook after another.

Without doubt, important inspiration for Pärt's work came from his discussions with other composers from various Soviet republics, especially from Moscow. For instance, Pärt has recalled that it was at the

Russian composer Edison Denisov's house in Moscow where he first heard Webern's music on a record.[19] In Estonian Radio's sound archive, which had the best music collection in Estonia at the time and to which Pärt had easy access, there was no recording of dodecaphonic music in 1960. This compositional style was often mentioned though, along with abstract art, in Estonian-language newspaper articles that criticized Western society.

Heino Eller gave to Pärt two textbooks on dodecaphony that he had received from his former student Eduard Tubin, who had emigrated to Sweden.[20] Pärt, following the textbooks, started to compose dodecaphonic music without any audio examples or previous knowledge about the style. In an interview given decades later, Pärt noted that when somebody hears that in a faraway land people dance on one leg, traveling to this land and observing it is not necessary in order to imitate this kind of dancing.[21] So it was with his composing twelve-tone music.

The orchestral piece *Nekrolog*, completed in the fall of 1960, was one of the most significant milestones in Pärt's oeuvre in general. During the specific time and under the specific circumstances, composing this kind of work was a public defiance of the socialist rules for the creation of art. In a more general sense, *Nekrolog* gave a signal about the direction of Pärt's spiritual quest and formed a backdrop for the rest of his music.

> This piece was the starting point of my explorations. Searching for truth. Searching for purity. It is searching for God, in fact. What is really going on? What does have a meaning after all? This is like the end and the beginning all in one.[22]

The limits of what was allowed and what was not most certainly influenced Pärt's music during his Soviet creative period. The more he attempted to transgress these limitations while following his ideals, the more forcefully the system hit back and tried to discipline him, largely through harassment. Soviet officials were often satisfied when somebody went through the motions of making corrections and changes; however, Pärt did not do even this, and most of his problems with Soviet authority stemmed from unwavering commitment to his ideals even under duress.

The Soviet restrictions and rules were in constant change and they cannot be applied to the whole Soviet period mechanically. For instance, *Nekrolog* did not meet the standards at the time of its completion and was for several years a transgression so severe that it put Pärt's career as a composer in danger. But at the end of the 1960s the local board of the Composers' Union held serious discussions on whether this work should be sent to the festival of war and patriotic music taking place in Riga.[23] By this time the previously rejected piece could possibly be representing the classic example of Soviet music.

Pärt's vocal symphonic work *Maailma samm* (*Stride of the World*), first performed in October 1961, was in a way seen as a redemption after sinning with *Nekrolog*. This work won the first prize almost a year later at the all-Soviet Union composers' competition. Since on the surface it seemed like an ideologically correct piece, *Maailma samm* was the most aired of Pärt's work on the radio in the 1960s. In fact there were ambiguities in the text by Enn Vetemaa that appealed to the Estonian audience, and Pärt hinted sonically that the style that he used in *Nekrolog* was still part of his musical conception.

The prohibition of dodecaphony disappeared unnoticed sometime in 1963–64, when the methods of ideological control were changed in Moscow. After that, many Estonian composers, some from the older generation as well, proudly announced that they used elements of this compositional technique in their new works.

One of the most important events that strongly influenced Pärt in the 1960s was the Warsaw Autumn Festival, which he attended in 1963. Founded in 1956, this annual event is the largest international Polish festival of contemporary music and the festivals had an obvious connection with the burst of CIA-backed modernist music all over Europe. Pärt and Veljo Tormis were the first Estonians who, as members of the Soviet Union Composers' Union's delegation, had a chance to witness the performances of the new modernist works. After returning to Estonia, Pärt and Tormis shared their impressions and introduced the records they had brought back from Warsaw at a meeting of the local Composers' Union. All of this awakened significant interest for the festival. The activists of the Students' Scientific Society at the Conservatory even managed to attend the festival without needing permission from Moscow. Starting in 1964, groups of students and professors from Tallinn visited the Warsaw Autumn Festivals with the help of the youth tourism organization Sputnik, which specialized in exchange tourism in the Soviet Union. One of the foreign composers attending the 1963 Warsaw Festival was Luigi Nono. Pärt and Nono met at the festival and then, barely a month later, Nono and musicologist Luigi Pestalozzi unexpectedly visited Tallinn. The same trip also brought Nono to Moscow, where he attempted to have closer contacts with the innovative composers. According to the memoirs by Edison Denisov and Alfred Schnittke, the reception of Nono and overall attitude towards such kinds of contact were radically different in these two cities.[24] In Moscow, the Composers' Union's officials attempted to prevent the meeting between Nono and the young experimental composers, and diminish the possible influences of his visit. In Tallinn there was no such intervention. Some newspapers published overviews of Nono's visit after he had left Tallinn, and Nono presented his music to a large audience in an evening TV program. In the Composers' Union, Pärt's *Nekrolog* was introduced, along with works by various other Estonian composers, and it received a lot of praise from both Nono and Pestalozzi.

A couple of months later, Pärt's orchestral piece *Perpetuum mobile* (dedicated to Nono) was first performed at the Estonia Concert Hall. The following year, 1964, was one of the most productive in Pärt's career as a composer. It was the year he became interested in collage technique, which he utilized in his works until the end of the 1960s – until the (in)famous performance of his *Credo* in November 1968. For Pärt, these collages, using contrasting musical material, were about not only form but something much more serious and connected to Pärt's spiritual searching, as he has explained:

> I was like skin that got burnt and I needed a skin graft. One piece of new skin at a time. New live tissue was needed and planted on my burnt spots. They were my collages and these pieces started to grow together after a while. They formed a new skin in a way.[25]

During 1964, Pärt also experimented with serial technique (which uses a series of values to manipulate musical events), sonorism (an approach to music that focuses on the specific quality and texture of sound), and aleatoric music (a term coined by Werner Meyer-Eppler in 1955 to describe sound events that are "determined in general but depends on chance in detail").[26] For the score of the short TV-film *Evald Okas*, Pärt used tapes played backwards, which he manipulated, with records performed in different tempi. In addition to his personal musical language, a pursuit for timeless depth in music was a distinct feature that set Pärt apart from the rest of Estonian music in the 1960s. Since *Nekrolog*, whenever Pärt was portrayed in the all-Soviet Union press or in the Estonian media, a parameter of seriousness was almost always featured.

In 1966, Pärt's kidney disease led to several surgeries and to a near-death experience. The Second Symphony and Cello Concerto "Pro et contra," both using collage technique, were completed during his acute illness, and both were first performed at the end of 1967. They do not yet fully demonstrate the new and evolving worldview first seen in *Credo*.

In September 1968, when Pärt finally agreed to talk on a radio program (he had been avoiding interviews and so this was the first time a wider audience had had a chance to get acquainted with his way of thinking), it became clear how spiritually focused he really was now.[27] His answer to a question about how he understands progress in art is revealing: "Art has to deal with eternal questions, not just sorting out the issues of today … Art is in fact nothing else than pouring your thoughts or spiritual values into a most suitable artistic form or expressing them in artistic ways."[28]

He added that wisdom resides in reduction, throwing out what is redundant. He spoke about "the one" that is "the correct solution to all fractions, epochs, and lives."

Ivalo Randalu, the interviewer, did not air one part of the interview with Pärt because it contained material that would guarantee a ban from airing on the radio in late 1960s Soviet Estonia. He hid the tape with the edited-out section, but it is now available. Randalu asked about Pärt's most important paragons: "Of course, Christ," answered Pärt without hesitation and continued: "Because he solved his fraction perfectly, godly."[29]

It was much later that people realized that this radio program *Looming ja aeg* (*Creation and Time*), aired on Pärt's thirty-third birthday, contained a key to understanding his *Credo* in its many meanings and also explained some of the nuances in Pärt's later music.[30]

The performance of *Credo* in November 1968 once again put Pärt in the spotlight. The Christian subject matter was a problem for the Soviet authorities. As Russian music theorist Yuri Kholopov put it: "God and Jesus Christ were bigger enemies to the Soviet regime than Boulez or Webern."[31] Sometimes what immediately followed has been called a scandal, but in fact it is similar to the previous situation with *Nekrolog*. But whereas the issues around *Nekrolog* circulated for a couple of years and even reached the media and documents, the aftermath of *Credo* was suppressed and kept hidden from the public sphere.

The board of the Estonian Composers' Union, together with a guest from the Communist Party, discussed this 'problem' three months after the concert but they did not succeed in convincing Pärt to denounce his standpoints and purpose of the work. Under these circumstances, it took courage to stay true to one's convictions. Practically everybody who was active in the cultural and public spheres had made humiliating compromises and compliances as forced by the system. Some suffered from it, some did not. Pärt was disobedient and got punished. *Credo* vanished from all of the official reports and lists of Estonian music. Again, just like in the mid-1960s, the newspapers, following the Communist Party's ideological guidelines, started to avoid Pärt's name. Pärt's music was rejected in the concert halls, and radio was cautious with it for a while. But he was not expelled from the Composers' Union. He was pushed aside, and he himself withdrew from the public.

Credo marked the beginning of a substantial inner change, a long quest, in which external factors and environment did not play such a part as in the early 1960s. During the eight years from 1968 to 1976, only two works were completed: the *Third Symphony* and the vocal-symphonic *Laul armastatule* (*Song to the Loved One*) (which Pärt was dissatisfied with and later withdrew from his official list of works).

Significant changes also took place in his private life. His marriage to Nora provided him with important support and encouragement. The desperate searching of this period has been compared to pilgrimage through a desert without knowing whether there will be another side to reach. Then Pärt, on a sunny morning in February 1976, wrote down a piano piece that was later titled *Aliinale* (*Für Alina*). Tintinnabuli – the style, the personal philosophy, the technique – was born. Pärt had reached the other side.

A way out: early music

Pärt's interest in early music accompanied him throughout his years of reflection and was also one of the cornerstones for tintinnabuli. Pärt claims that his interest emerged before he composed *Credo*.[32] He and fellow composer Kuldar Sink started to gather information about the music originating from the pre-baroque era: relevant literature, scores, and recordings. In their music history classes at the Conservatory, this period was very superficially introduced, without any decent musical examples. Early music was thought to be inferior to later music, and, because the majority of it was religious, it was often rejected on the grounds of its subject matter.

In 1966 the first serious attempts in Estonia to perform vocal music from the renaissance were made. In the same year, several foreign performers gave concerts in Tallinn with early music as part of their programs. An important event was a concert in Tallinn by the ensemble Madrigal, directed by Andrei Volkonsky, at the beginning of 1968. Volkonsky later claimed that it was he who inspired Pärt to move towards early music. The fact that Madrigal attracted a large audience was a clear sign of early music's popularity. The radio started to air more and more early music. In Dorian Supin's documentary *24 Preludes for A Fugue*, Pärt describes how he studied Gregorian chant, which he heard for the first time on the radio, and tried to play the melody line on the piano but felt that he could not get access to this laconic music.[33] A maturing period was needed. Slowly and with fumbling steps Pärt was moving towards finding a new expressive style for his music.

Around 1970, Pärt met Andres Mustonen, who was 17 at the time and also, like Pärt, had a tape and record collection of early music. After Mustonen had entered the Conservatory to study the violin, he founded the early music ensemble Hortus Musicus in 1972. Soon Hortus Musicus concerts became hugely popular. The ensemble became well known across the Soviet Union and made numerous recordings for the record company Melodya. After Pärt had developed his tintinnabuli technique his music began to be played again, and Hortus Musicus was an important partner in reestablishing Pärt's reputation.

The end of the 1970s: departure

The environment of Soviet society affected Pärt relatively little during his tintinnabuli period. He was not expected to contribute Soviet music to the planned economy. In comparison to the 1960s, things were significantly different. Pärt did not challenge the cultural officials any more (with one notable exception in February 1979 at the Congress of the Estonian Composers' Union). His personal quest for truth did not depend on the external factors at the time, since Pärt was more occupied with overcoming the problems of his inner life.

As in the early 1960s, Pärt's first performances attracted a bigger audience than was usual for other composers. And again, most of the audience was young. His new music spoke to the next generation as well. The cultural life of Soviet Estonia was becoming multifaceted and, compared to the 1960s, serious music was pushed more and more to the side. The global popular music explosion in the second half of the 1960s had its impact too.

At the end of the 1970s, the ideological pressure of the cultural sphere was strengthened even more. The 1980s, when Pärt was already living in the West with his family, were hopeless and dark years of stagnation for the Estonian culture. Fortunately, this no longer had any effect on Arvo Pärt's music.

Further reading

David Caute, *The Dancer Defects: The Struggle for Cultural Supremacy During the Cold War* (Oxford University Press, 2003).

Peter J. Schmelz, *Such Freedom, If Only Musical: Unofficial Soviet Music During The Thaw* (Oxford University Press, 2009).

Valeria Tsenova, *Underground Music from the Former USSR*, trans. Romela Kohanovskaya (London: Routledge, 1997).

3 Perspectives on Arvo Pärt after 1980

JEFFERS ENGELHARDT

Arvo Pärt is everywhere these days, a cosmopolitan persona of global renown, a genre-transcending artist at the center of multiple musical worlds, an icon of contemporary spirituality, and, since the early 1980s, a figure around whom narratives and meanings of contemporary European experience have coalesced.[1] Pärt is everywhere no less through his globe-trotting travel schedule to attend performances and recording sessions or to accept awards and recognition than through the dozens of performances of his work each month around the world. His perennial Grammy nominations, the ubiquity of his music in the soundtracks of mainstream and independent cinema, his established place in the canon of late-twentieth- and twenty-first-century musicology, and the evocative power of his name and sound in all kinds of musical and media milieux are what make the Pärt phenomenon.

To make this tangible, I will begin by elaborating on Pärt's presence in the soundscapes of twenty-first-century musical life. According to the International Arvo Pärt Centre website and Universal Edition, there were (based on licensing and part rental data) sixty-three official Pärt performances worldwide in March 2011, ranging from England to Estonia, Italy to Ukraine, New Zealand to Venezuela, and many places in between. Expectedly, there were handfuls of classic tintinnabuli pieces such as *Tabula rasa* that month, but there was also significant breadth to the music that was performed, including older, pre-tintinnabuli works such as *Nekrolog* and *Credo*, monumental large-scale works such as *Passio* and *Kanon Pokajanen*, and new music such as *Silhouette*. Beyond this impressive number of performances at major venues (and what were, most likely, scores of undocumented performances elsewhere), what is important to note is the non-essentialized Pärt sound here, in contrast to the tintinnabuli music of 1976–78 (*Cantus in Memory of Benjamin Britten*, *Für Alina*, *Fratres*, and *Spiegel im Spiegel*) that dominates other mediations of Pärt. Audiences want to hear lots of different music by Pärt, and musicians and presenters want to stay in touch with his contemporaneity, making it their own as well.

Outside of concert venues, Pärt's symbiotic relationship with the recording industry means that the breadth of his work is easily accessible to consumers. There is often a lag of only a few years between the completion of a major work and its release on ECM Records or another major label: Symphony No. 4 in 2010, *In principio* in 2009, or *Lamentate* and *Da pacem Domine* in 2005, all on ECM, for instance. Pärt's commercial success beyond the niche classical market creates vital revenue streams for boutique labels such as ECM and multinational conglomerates such as EMI and Sony, which helps explain the proliferation of 'portrait,' 'tribute,' and 'best of' albums that capitalize on Pärt's persona and a label's catalog. Other projects such as ECM's *Alina* release in 1999 (consisting of three different recordings of *Spiegel im Spiegel* and two extended performances of *Für Alina*), or the commemorative edition of the 1984 *Tabula rasa* recording ECM released in 2010, push this trend further by building on Pärt's penchant for new arrangements. This monumentalizes the intimate association of Pärt, the producer Manfred Eicher, and ECM, and attempts to make the familiar once again novel in an appeal to consumers new and old. As this feedback loop between Pärt's work and the recording industry makes clear, it makes sense to think and write about this side of Pärt in the language of popular music studies. Given Pärt's experience as a recording engineer and his involvement in the recording process, it can be fruitful to consider how Pärt might approach composing with an ear already towards the eventual mediation of his music via recordings.

Since the early 1990s, directors and music editors for film and television have ineluctably been drawn to the popular currency and evocative potential of Pärt's sound, so much so that some suggest that using Pärt's signature tintinnabuli works is clichéd, the sign of lazy direction and music editing.[2] Whatever the case, the marriage of Pärt and moving images in films such as *Lessons in Darkness* (Werner Herzog, 1992), *Wit* (Mike Nichols, 2001), *Heaven* (Tom Tykwer, 2002), and *Fahrenheit 9/11* (Michael Moore, 2004), among dozens of others (not including Pärt knock-offs in dozens of film scores), gets at something vital about Pärt as the 'soundtrack of an age' (to borrow the title of a 2010 conference on Pärt in London).[3] The 'natural' invocation of Pärt in particular cinematic and televisual moments of spiritual intensity, nostalgia, tragedy, mortality, and remembering, to name a few, is how culture works and is continually made and remade. This shows how the self-reinforcing dynamics of representation, affect, convention, and marketing in sound and image engender the practices and texts that become culture. Pärt's sounds work at these moments because they resonate, and they resonate because they work.[4]

Observing how Pärt is regularly translated into social media echoes this resonance. There are countless examples of photomontages and short video pieces on social media platforms such as YouTube, Dailymotion, and Vimeo that use *Spiegel im Spiegel*, *Fratres*, *Für Alina*, and other early tintinnabuli as their soundtrack. The similarities among pieces such as *Ava &*

the Magic Kingdom (2009) by Vimeo user FotoNuova and *Snow Games: Quiet Winter Toboganning* (2008) by Vimeo user Kurt_Halfyard in terms of style, content, ethos, and visual aesthetic are compelling.[5] Here, *Spiegel im Spiegel* seems to iconically evoke or represent nostalgic adult imaginings and commemorations of middle-class American childhood pleasures – the surprise trip to Disneyland and backyard sledding on a snowy day. For FotoNuova and Kurt_Halfyard, the two different recordings of *Spiegel im Spiegel* they use bear a non-arbitrary relation, shaped by circulations of *Spiegel im Spiegel* in other media, to the ethos and affect of the visual content. Beyond questions of motivation and intention, the significant similarities in these pieces as they circulate publicly points to the iconic qualities of *Spiegel im Spiegel* and tintinnabuli style that are recognized in social media and cultivated in various markets.

Pärt's resonance reaches into music scenes beyond the world of Western classical music he inhabits. Björk, who thought about studying with Pärt and whose 1997 BBC interview with Pärt is revelatory, Keith Jarrett, who played on the 1984 ECM recording of *Fratres*, and Michael Stipe, whose quote "Arvo Pärt's music is a house on fire and an infinite calm..." has been used to endorse numerous Pärt recordings, all championed Pärt before it was fashionable to do so. As astute music journalists have begun to note, citing Pärt and his compositional techniques as influences are effective ways of establishing oneself in the milieux of post-rock, experimental hip-hop, post-minimalism, experimental, ambient and minimalist electronica, IDM (intelligent dance music), indie rock, and many others.[6] Pärt is well known in these milieux, and, by citing his influence, artists can stake claim to some of his prestige. In addition to Björk, Pärt is commonly associated with the music of Aphex Twin, Radiohead, and Sigur Rós (who sometimes play *Für Alina* before concerts) on music blogs and websites such as SoundCloud.[7] These associations reveal how Pärt is heard and valued across genres and within diverse soundscapes. This resonance is unsurprising to Pärt, as it corresponds to his understanding of musical truth: "I suppose we secretly love each other. Anonymously. That is a very beautiful thing."[8]

One finds similar things happening with Pärt in digital repurposings of his music, electroacoustic improvisation, and social media. In mixtapes and DJ mixsets, pieces such as *Da pacem Domine*, *Silouan's Song*, and *Nunc dimittis* are commonly used as an ambient outro at the end of 60 to 90 minutes of music. Artists such as Berlin-based DJ Hecq (Ben Lukas Boysen) or the Scottish collective of Joe Acheson and Hidden Orchestra use Pärt more integrally, however. In a 55-minute mixtape on the blog Headphone Commute, DJ Hecq moves from ambient vocal samples to the sounds of the Black Ox Orkestar, an experimental klezmer band from Montreal, and on to the surreal sounds of Reykjavik-based experimental musician Ben Frost's remixed Carpathian fiddling.[9] This transitions dramatically at 42:30 in the mixtape into Pärt's *Für Lennart in Memoriam*, which, after 4 minutes, bleeds extremely slowly into the next material.

In a 1:15 DJ mixset with live instrumentals on the Paris DJs website, Joe Acheson and Hidden Orchestra parade through their own work, post-rock, hip-hop, Pärt and Milhaud, Balkan brass bands, BBC radio dramas, and much more.[10] The set opens with ambient vocal samples and the rhymes of New York City underground MC Afu Ra layered over Radiohead's "All I Need." Forty-six minutes into the set, excerpts from a BBC Radio 3 drama called *Between Two Worlds* and samples of woodland sounds are superimposed over a passage from Ode II of Pärt's *Triodion*, which then gives way to another Radiohead track called "Reckoner."

Pärt is sampled in other ways as well. "Little Weapon," a track from Lupe Fiasco's 2007 album *The Cool*, speaks in blunt, critical terms about child soldiers and the cultures of violence that children encounter in video games and domestic gun ownership. The bassline of "Little Weapon" is a sample of the opening seconds of Paul Hillier's 1996 Harmonia Mundi recording of Pärt's *De Profundis* with some rhythmic alteration, increased tempo, and digital processing that largely obscures the text. Throughout the track, even smaller parts and more subtle manipulations of this sample are a key part of the beat. Beyond the connection of this sample to the broader digital presence of Pärt (this same bit of *De Profundis* is accessible on numerous ringtone download websites, for instance), Fiasco's use of *De Profundis* as the foundational sample in this track is interesting for other reasons. On the one hand, the text of Psalm 130 might not be entirely out of place in "Little Weapon," since it could be read in the common tradition of Abrahamic faiths as a counterpoint to the unrighteous violence in Fiasco's rhyme. On the other hand, *De Profundis* might fit into the hip-hop aesthetic and ethic of authenticity that privileges the unique, esoteric sample over the sample that is overused, borrowed, or 'bitten,' in hip-hop parlance.

Finally, there are the hosts of rearrangements, reworkings, and improvisations of Pärt's music in live performance, studio recordings, and online that do not employ sampling. These are part of a process of making arrangements and reworkings of pieces that begins with Pärt himself; in the case of *Für Alina*, the process uses his music as a basis for improvisation, specifically on the ECM *Alina* album. The Universal Edition website lists no fewer than sixteen arrangements of *Fratres*, twelve of *Spiegel im Spiegel*, eight of *Da pacem Domine*, seven of *Summa*, and five of *Pari intervallo*. This predilection for arrangement and reworking can be traced to the Neoplatonic processes of instrumental tintinnabuli music, whose mediation is decoupled from timbre, making timbre all the more important in this music. In contrast to sample-based engagements with Pärt, these rearrangements, reworkings, and improvisations stay closer to the integral form of his original work.

These kinds of rearrangements, reworkings, and improvisations include a 10-minute live recording of *Für Alina* by Seattle-based composer, multi-instrumentalist, and sound artist Rafael Anton Irisarri and Seattle-based pianist Kelly Wyse on SoundCloud.[11] Here, Wyse's extended performance of *Für Alina* is set against Irisarri's ambient samples, bowed electric guitar playing (à la Sigur Rós), and Phil Petrocelli's jazz ballad drumming, which Wyse subtly enfolds into the temporality of *Für Alina*.

In another example, the Austin-based instrumental post-rock band My Education has recorded an EP reworking of *Spiegel im Spiegel*, transposed down a fourth from Pärt's original, and lasting a little over six minutes. This rendering features slide guitar and a Hammondesque keyboard arpeggiation complemented by heavy bass, a slow rock beat, and ad lib guitar work. The additive melodic process of Pärt's *Spiegel im Spiegel*, which eventually spans a ninth on either side of the pitch center, is substantially attenuated here in favor of the new story that My Education tell through their incorporation of *Spiegel im Spiegel* into a post-rock instrumentation and temporality.

A final example is a minimalist bluegrass realization, on banjo and harmonica, of *Spiegel im Spiegel* on SoundCloud that is quite faithful to Pärt's original by Steve Wickham, a traditional and rock fiddler and multi-instrumentalist from Ireland.[12] Timbrally, his 'lonesome prairie' sound serves Pärt well, and vice versa. The social and cultural encoding of banjo and harmonica is transformed through this iconic tintinnabuli piece and, at the same time, hints of conventional bluegrass affective gestures evoke new genre-crossing resonances. Beyond the fantastic quality of Wickham's playing and the nuances possible in a solo performance of *Spiegel im Spiegel*, this track points to Pärt's place in cosmopolitan musical circulations and resonances – bluegrass and Irish traditional music, in this case.

Pärt is also established in mainstream twenty-first-century music histories such as those of Alex Ross and Richard Taruskin, as well as in other domains of music scholarship.[13] Through his enthusiastic participation in academic conferences devoted to his work and the mission of the International Arvo Pärt Centre, Pärt is invested in scholarship on his music, which has significant disciplinary implications for historical, ethnographic, and theoretical approaches to his music.

So how did we arrive at this moment in twenty-first-century musical life? And how did Pärt arrive here?

Emigration and tintinnabuli

Pärt's presence in these soundscapes is deeply connected to the transitions and transformations effected by his emigration from Soviet Estonia on January 18, 1980. The years surrounding his emigration, however, are easily cast in simplistic, black-and-white terms that fail to fully capture the personal, artistic, cultural, and political dynamics of dislocation and relocation. From perspectives both within and beyond 'the West' (and it is precisely this term that still dominates the historical discourse on Pärt), the experiences of Pärt and his family and his creative work in the late 1970s and early 1980s are represented and mythologized through a number of ready-made narratives. These include the embattled Soviet dissident, 'the West' as the site of spiritual and individual freedom, and the Cold War exile establishing himself through a cosmopolitan, peripatetic artistic life. Amid the ruptures and traumas of Pärt's emigration, however, were continuities that enabled Pärt and his family to cope and, indeed, thrive in Vienna, Berlin, the Estonian diaspora, and many other milieux. The more publicly perceptible of these continuities were tintinnabuli style, relationships with musicians such as Neeme Järvi, Gidon Kremer, and Alfred Schnittke, and the practices and texts of the Pärts' Christian faith.

The story of Pärt's emigration and ongoing musical transformation begins with the personal and compositional crisis, and harassment and persecution he and his family lived through before, during, and after the 1968 *Credo* controversy.[14] Beyond its political ramifications, *Credo* marked a critical artistic and existential moment in Pärt's life at a time when his physical and spiritual health were damaged. Pärt speaks to this in an often-cited excerpt from a 1968 interview with Ivalo Randalu on Estonian state radio:

> It's like we've been given some number to work with (1, for example), an equation that's extremely complex when divided up into fractions. Solving the equation takes a long time and requires much effort, but all the wisdom is in reduction. Now, if it's conceivable that many of these fractions (eras, lives) are united by a single solution (S), then that 1 is something more than the solution to only one fraction. It has always been the right solution to all fractions (eras, lives). So the limits of any one fraction are too narrow for it and it goes through all times ... It means that the most "contemporary" (and always the most contemporary!) is the work in which there is a sense of a clearer, greater right solution (1). Art must deal with eternal questions, not just with taking care of the issues of the day.[15]

The decisive, original statement of faith with which *Credo* opens ("Credo in Jesum Christum") reflects how Pärt began to address artistic and existential problems through what he understood to be the unity and eternal, universal truth of Christianity. By 1968, Pärt was already well along on the spiritual path towards converting to Orthodox Christianity, which happened in 1972 at the same time as he married his second wife Nora, also a convert. Deeply musical and articulate about Pärt's music, Nora Pärt has had a profound influence on his work and its reception since that time. There is much more in this interview quotation that bears on Pärt's music after his emigration as well – the importance of number, the value of purity and simplicity, a faith in human universals, and the notion that creativity addresses questions of the highest order.

Ideological, professional, and personal pressures continued to mount following the sensational debut of *Credo*, its subsequent silencing by Communist Party officials, and Pärt's increasing withdrawal and ostracization from official musical life in the Estonian Soviet Socialist Republic (ESSR). Subsequent controversies over Pärt's provocations of the Soviet regime led to a ban on the sale and distribution of his work (although not its performance) in 1972, intensifying the material hardships of his family's life in the 1970s and Pärt's embattled place in the Estonian Union of Composers.[16] Contrary to many popular references to and mythifications of Pärt's life in the early and mid-1970s, however, this was not a period of literal silence. Despite his increasing dissatisfaction with the materials and techniques of modernism, Pärt had written his Symphony No. 3 and a (later withdrawn) symphonic cantata called *Laul armastatule* (*Song to the Beloved*) by 1974.[17] To support his family, he continued to write film music as well. If this was a period of silence, it was an intensely musical silence:

> Before one says something, perhaps it is better to say nothing. My music has emerged only after I have been silent for quite some time, literally silent. For me, 'silent' means the 'nothing' from which God created the world. Ideally, a silent pause is something sacred… If someone approaches silence with love, then this might give birth to music. A composer must often wait a long time for his music. This kind of sublime anticipation is exactly the kind of pause that I value so greatly.[18]

The essential thing that occupied Pärt during the years between 1968 and 1976 was an intensive engagement with Gregorian chant (and medieval and renaissance polyphony) in order to understand for himself the secrets of monodic melody and its triadic implications:[19]

> I needed a single melodic line that would carry with it the kind of spirit that was present in ancient songs and in traditional singing: absolute monody, the naked voice, which is the basis of everything. I wanted to learn how to guide that melodic line, but I had no idea how to do it.[20]

To reach this understanding, Pärt devised a discipline for himself, filling thousands of pages of composition notebooks with melodic writing based on a sketch of a bird's wings, a photograph of a mountain landscape, or on the form and intonations of a psalm he had just read. This is what invests melody with the sense of objectivity that is so fundamental to Pärt's musical philosophy and what grounds the union of musical elements in tintinnabuli, which Pärt speaks of through the mystical arithmetic aphorism 1+1=1.[21] Although the exercises in Pärt's notebooks were not meant for any kind of performance, Andres Mustonen (the key figure in the Estonian early music scene since the early 1970s and a close collaborator with Pärt) and other members of his ensemble Hortus Musicus would occasionally read through Pärt's experiments to give him a sense of their live sound, especially as informed by period instruments and historically informed vocal techniques.

When Pärt's compositional impasse ended with an explosion of tintinnabuli works in 1976–77, it was Mustonen and his Hortus Musicus players who gave many of the first performances. Once tintinnabuli took form in pieces such as *Für Alina, In spe*, and *Fratres*, Pärt re-emerged as a major voice within the Soviet musical world and beyond. In a 1978 interview with Ivalo Randalu, Pärt described with characteristic simplicity what tintinnabuli was all about: "What are you trying to discover or find or achieve there [in tintinnabuli]? That fundamental tone and triad … what are you looking for there?" Randalu asked. "Eternity and purity" was Pärt's reply.[22] Later in the same interview, Nora Pärt reminisced about something Pärt once said: "I know a great secret, but I know it only through music and I can only express it through music. But how much I would like to possess it!"[23] It is essential to note that much of the iconic music that Pärt is most well known for in many different milieux was written in Estonia during these fecund years. This fact alone is enough to force the issue of continuity in terms of tintinnabuli and Pärt's emigration and to complicate facile Cold War distinctions between 'Communism' and 'the West.'

The originality and power recognized in Pärt's early tintinnabuli pieces was concretely related to the worsening professional and personal conditions that forced the family to make the difficult decision to emigrate. Beginning in 1978, there was a growing demand for Pärt's early tintinnabuli pieces at nonconformist performances and festivals in Estonia and outside the Soviet Union, including important performances of *Tabula rasa, Arbos, Fratres*, and *Missa syllabica* in Cologne, and *Cantus* in London. At the 1978 Festival of Early and Contemporary Music in Tallinn run by Mustonen, Pärt met Alfred Schlee, director of Universal Edition, the publisher that was to play a vital role in his emigration and career. As was the case with composers such as Edison Denisov, Sofia Gubaidulina, Alfred Schnittke, Valentin Silvestrov, and Andrei Volkonsky, these contacts and successes outside the Soviet Union made life in Estonia increasingly difficult for Pärt and his family. While the ideological climate in Tallinn was more temperate in comparison with Moscow (which shaped the Communist Party's response to Pärt's earlier nonconformist work), the scale and cumulative effects of Pärt's success abroad and controversies at home forced the issue with Communist Party officials. With increasing frequency, Pärt was banned from traveling to performances abroad. This prompted him in 1979 to deliver a caustic speech to the Estonian Union of Composers about his suppression while mockingly wearing a long-haired wig.

These pressures escalated in 1979 until a member of the Communist Party Central Committee made the direct suggestion to Pärt that he emigrate, using Nora's official Jewish ethnicity as the purported reason. This would allow the Soviet regime to appear neutral with respect to Pärt, although the intensifying hardship his family would face if he did not emigrate was clear. He was soon asked to step down from the Estonian Union of Composers, effectively denying him the opportunity to participate in official musical life and earn a living. Owing to their experiences during previous travels in Western Europe, emigration was at least imaginable for Pärt and his family.[24] Given the unsustainable pressure from Communist Party officials, the decision was made to leave Estonia, officially bound for Israel (like all Jewish émigrés from the Soviet Union at that time) by way of Vienna. Leaving was frantic and difficult – a "trip into the unknown," in Pärt's words.[25] At the Brest-Litovsk train station on the Soviet border, Pärt was able to cross with his scores and notebooks, despite the fact that they were notarized by the ESSR Ministry of Culture and were technically state property. This was on January 19, 1980, the day before the Soviet invasion of Afghanistan escalated, the border was closed, and emigration was forbidden.[26]

Upon their arrival in Vienna, a representative from Universal Edition, probably tipped off by Alfred Schnittke, located Pärt and his family and offered them assistance with obtaining Austrian citizenship in exchange for working with Universal Edition (a relationship that has lasted into the present). Later, Alfred Schlee made arrangements for Pärt to apply for a DAAD fellowship to Berlin, where the family settled. In Estonia, a complete ban on performances of Pärt and any public mention of him and his work went into effect in 1980. It was only to fully end with the transformations brought about by perestroika and the Singing Revolution (1987–1991) in the late 1980s.

Works, collaborators, and mediators in the 1980s, 1990s, and 2000s

After emigration, the story of tintinnabuli and Pärt's place in the sound-scapes of twentieth- and twenty-first-century musical life is deeply entwined in his relationships with collaborators and mediators. While some of these relationships were forged in Estonia prior to his emigration, many more were the product of the expanded sonic and technological horizons and material stability he enjoyed in Berlin. They were also part of the self-reinforcing buzz that Pärt's tintinnabuli engendered at a particular Cold War, 'postmodern' cultural moment in the 1980s and 1990s. I focus here on Pärt's most established and enduring collaborators and mediators. Along with the specific contexts for Pärt's endless flow of commissions (*Te Deum* by Westdeutscher Rundfunk Radio or *Lamentate* by the Tate Modern gallery in London, to name just two) and the form and qualities of the texts he works with, these musicians and institutions profoundly shape the sonic and technical possibilities Pärt has at his disposal. These collaborators and mediators are central to Pärt's musical imagination.

Consider *Passio*, for instance. Pärt had a clear conception of this tintinnabuli masterpiece before emigrating, and brought sketches of *Passio* with him in 1980. After Pärt was settled in Berlin, Alfred Schlee arranged for a commission from Bavarian Broadcasting and Pärt quickly finished the monumental work, which was premiered in Munich in 1982. Something both sonic and spiritual was missing in this performance, however, and it wasn't until performances by the Hilliard Ensemble that Pärt's conception was fully realized. In conversation with Enzo Restagno, Nora Pärt recollects: "Arvo wasn't certain of the work's quality for many years, and his opinion changed only when he heard the Hilliard Ensemble's performance years later."[27] Pärt himself continues: "The Hilliard Ensemble brought their exemplary intonation [to *Passio*], and this work requires really perfect intonation. The same thing also happened with *De profundis*, *Cantate domino*, and *An den Wassern zu Babel*. Only after their performance was it clear to me that I had made the right decisions and that this music was justified in its existence."[28] And again Nora Pärt: "Everything was ideal – the intonation, phrasing, and everything was sung with the right expression. I remember what Arvo said after hearing them for the first time: 'There is nothing one can add to that. Everything is ideal.' We were almost moved to tears and so extremely happy that we had found the people who suited that music in every possible way."[29]

Similarly, with *Miserere*, Pärt has stated concisely that "without the Hilliard Ensemble, there would be no *Miserere*."[30] Following on the land-mark ECM recording of *Passio* in 1988 with the Hilliard Ensemble, the sound and capacities of these musicians were an intimate, basic part of the conception of *Miserere*. Pärt's works, in other words, are fundamentally related to his collaborators and mediators; the imagination of specific voices and recording conditions are a constitutive part of many, if not most, of Pärt's works (Pärt is, after all, an expert sound engineer). The remarkable logogenic qualities of *Passio* and *Miserere* that seem to make tintinnabuli emerge organically from the intonations and structure of a text (thereby effacing Pärt's subjective role in the production of musical affect) are coupled to the grain of specific voices (the Hilliard Ensemble) and the sensibilities of specific collaborators (Paul Hillier).

The Hilliard Ensemble has an extensive ECM catalog apart from their Pärt recordings, placing them in the pioneering group of musicians brought together by ECM founder and producer Manfred Eicher. Pärt, Eicher, and ECM have had a productive, symbiotic relationship since the 1984 release of *Tabula rasa*, which was the inaugural project in the label's branching out from jazz through the ECM New Series. The 1984 *Tabula rasa* recording put Pärt on the map of twentieth-century musical life, establishing a sound, production style, and mode of visual representation that have become iconic of Pärt's persona and the ECM label.[31] At present, there have been nineteen ECM releases featuring Pärt's music, totaling forty-four different works. Pärt, ECM, and Universal Edition have come to be identified with one another in many ways, not least through their echoing of minimalist design elements and images of Pärt as an ascetic mystic, all emblematized in the 2010 collaborative re-issue of *Tabula rasa*. The incredible success of this integration registers the extent to which Pärt's relationship with his mediators and collaborators is fundamental to his creative work. Pärt himself recognizes this in his relationship with Manfred Eicher:

> My contact with ECM is beyond categorization: it is a natural supplement to my composing. Manfred Eicher's record producing is an art in itself. Of what kind? I don't know how to describe it. He is a performer, and his instrument is sound, acoustics, the sounding space which can be heard only by him. It is said that the talent of a sculptor lies not in the hands but in the eyes, in a special way of looking. Similarly, Manfred Eicher hears in a special way and his records are a result of this hearing. What I call a piece of art made by Manfred is actually a rich and sensitive complex of hearing, thinking, feeling, taste and artistic skill: a whole philosophy. It is also something very lively and in continuous formation. Our work together making new records is always a celebration, and has been for more than twenty years now. I count Manfred Eicher and his team among my co-authors, my blessings.[32]

Here Pärt outlines the interpenetrating levels at which his collaboration and mediation work. Eicher's ear and musical sensibilities are attuned to Pärt's music in ways that both reveal important aspects of a work apart from its mediation and, through the recording and production process, shape what a Pärt work is. Eicher's attunement to Pärt's music and the central place Pärt has assumed in the ECM catalogue have their own mythology as well. Listening to the radio while driving, Eicher had his 'road-to-Damascus' moment during a broadcast of the 1977 Westdeutsche Rundfunk recording of *Tabula rasa* with Gidon Kremer, Tatjana Grindenko, Alfred Schnittke, and Saulius Sondeckis.[33] Eicher stopped driving, listened to all of *Tabula rasa*, and immediately started working to find out more about Pärt and his music. That recording of *Tabula rasa* was the centerpiece of Pärt's 1984 debut with ECM. Eicher tells another anecdote about his attunement and the production of landmark Pärt recordings:

> I remember an event with Arvo Pärt when we recorded the *Passio* in London and the wind was blowing very intensely around St Jude-on-the-Hill. We had to decide either to stop the recording because of the wind, or to use the wind. This was one of the best decisions we ever made, as the wind was blowing in the right key.[34]

From Pärt's perspective, collaborating with Eicher and ECM means participating in a business model and artistic ethic that resonates with him. The ECM back catalog remains, by and large, in print and accessible, ensuring that Pärt's collaborations and mediations have a lasting presence. In terms of ECM's artistic ethic, Arvo and Nora Pärt cite the examples of the *Passio* project, which was recorded only after twenty to thirty performances with the Hilliard Ensemble, and the *Miserere* project, in which an entire two days were spent experimenting with microphone placement to record a particular passage.[35]

The other Pärt collaborators intimately associated with ECM are Tõnu Kaljuste and the Estonian Philharmonic Chamber Choir (EPCC). Since their 1993 *Te Deum* recording, Kaljuste and the EPCC have joined the ranks of the Hilliard Ensemble as the iconic voices of Pärt, providing him with a fuller sonic palette to complement the transparent purity of the Hilliard Ensemble.[36] Like the Hilliard Ensemble/Hillier recording of *Passio*, the EPCC/Kaljuste recording of *Te Deum* was the first time Pärt heard a performance that fully realized his conception of the piece.[37] This collaboration has flourished through the 1990s and 2000s, installing Pärt, Kaljuste, and the EPCC in their position of global fame through the mediation of ECM (along with the celebrated collaborations of Hillier and the EPCC on the Harmonia Mundi label).

The collaboration is also, of course, about Estonia. The *Te Deum* project took shape in the early 1990s just as the Estonian Philharmonic Chamber Choir (EPCC), which Kaljuste founded in 1981, was establishing itself as one of the premier choral ensembles in the world at a moment of national elation, material hardship, and tangible transition in Estonia. Through the dissolution of the Soviet Union, Estonia again became an independent state in 1991 and re-introduced its own currency in 1992, but Soviet troops remained in Estonia until 1994, social changes were traumatic for many, and the pigeonhole of the 'post-Soviet' with its fraught dynamics of retrospection dominated cultural discourse. It is not difficult to imagine the appeal of this collaboration for Pärt, Kaljuste, and the EPCC, first and foremost on artistic grounds, but also as a means of reconstituting Pärt's connection to Estonian musical life in substantive ways and establishing his Estonianness as his international renown continued to grow. Through this collaboration, the 'around-the-world trip' of Pärt's emigration was returning to Estonia in ways that echoed other 'post-Soviet' Estonian narratives of return and restoration.[38] Tintinnabuli was returning to its origins quite concretely through the EPCC/Kaljuste recordings made in the Niguliste Church in Tallinn and visually documented by Tõnu Tormis (a member of the EPCC and son of the composer Veljo Tormis, Pärt's one-time composition and theory teacher) on ECM albums such as *Litany*, *Kanon Pokajanen*, and *In principio*.[39]

As the possibilities of uniting tintinnabuli to words and texts led Pärt to write in a choral idiom of considerable difficulty (and to think in terms of texts in his instrumental music – *Silouan's Song*, *Lamentate*, *Für Lennart in Memoriam*, and the Symphony No. 4, for instance), it is natural that he would find a choir with the technical and artistic ability to realize his music in Estonia. The EPCC emerges from the vital grassroots choral tradition in Estonia, emblematized by the UNESCO-recognized Estonian National Song Celebration (*üldlaulupidu*), which produces world-class musicians such as Kaljuste and members of the EPCC. Pärt's connection to the Estonian choral tradition, like his connection to conventional Estonian cultural narratives and identities, is not straightforward, however. In terms of style, difficulty, and expression, Pärt's tintinnabuli music does not integrate into the popular, mainstream Estonian choral repertoire, although pieces such as his *Magnificat* are staples for many Estonian choirs in international competitions. The Pärt/Kaljuste/EPCC collaboration, then, is grounded not in the conventional style and cultural significance of the national choral tradition, but in the highest level of professionalism that the EPCC has achieved, the choral sound and technique that Kaljuste and Hillier have molded, and the practicalities of working together in Estonia and for extended periods of time prior to a recording project.

Pärt's close relationship with Kaljuste and the EPCC is enshrined in one of his most important works, *Kanon Pokajanen*, which is dedicated to them. Like *Passio*, *Kanon Pokajanen* is thoroughly logogenic, as Pärt explains: "I wanted the word to be able to find its own sound, to draw its own melodic line ... [T]he entire structure of the musical composition is subject to the text and its laws: one lets the language 'create the music.'"[40] This ancient text composed by St Andrew of Crete in the eighth century is the prototype that Pärt renders in sound through tintinnabuli proc-esses that are intimately attuned to the intonations of Church Slavonic, the structure of the verses, and the formal arrangement of the Odes[41] (each consisting of an introductory *eirmos* based on a biblical canticle and four *troparia* verses expanding upon the theme of the *eirmos*, interspersed with short penitential litanies and doxologies) and other hymns that make up the Canon (*Sedalen, Theotokion, Kontakion, Ikos*, and the Prayer After the Canon). The generative force of prayerful language is plainly audible in *Kanon Pokajanen*: stressed syllables always fall on downbeats, the number of syllables in a word determines the melodic contour, and punctuation determines the values of notes and rests, for instance. These formulaic aspects of tintinnabuli are what Pärt describes elsewhere as the "object-ivity" of logogenic melody.[42] This is quite in keeping with theologies of language and sound in Orthodox Christianity, where semantic content is not distinguished from the aesthetics of recitation and melodic perform-ance, and where truth and beauty are mutually constitutive. An analogy can be made here to the Orthodox theology of the icon with its significant Neoplatonic vein as well. The tintinnabuli process and formula derived from a sacred text are the prototype that Pärt renders in sound, attenuating or effacing his own subjectivity to make manifest the beauty and truth of the prototype, similar to the prayerful ascetic discipline of creating an icon according to a sacred prototype.

But *Kanon Pokajanen* is profoundly human as well, most notably in the nuances of texture, tintinnabuli processes, rhythmic hocketing, octave dis-placements, and voicing that accentuate the poetics of the hymns and the different prayerful registers at which they operate. Across the Odes, it is possible to hear where one is in the text based on the qualities of Pärt's setting, which reveals in an embodied, affective way a host of symmetries and correspondences throughout the Canon. The subtlety and sophisti-cation of Pärt's engagement with the possibilities of tintinnabuli in *Kanon Pokajanen* is on a par with *Passio* (a work that has received much more analytical attention), although the qualities of Church Slavonic and a more liberal use of tintinnabuli procedures distinguish *Kanon Pokajanen* from *Passio*. When experiencing the "Prayer After the Canon," one of the most beautiful moments in Pärt's oeuvre, it is worth remembering that the rationality of tintinnabuli procedures is a means to an end. Nora Pärt puts it concisely: "I believe that Arvo's music is meant more for the ears than for the intellect."[43]

Kanon Pokajanen did not come easily for Pärt – he worked at it for two years, incorporating earlier engagements with the same text (*Nun eile ich zu euch* and *Memento*) into the finished score. Given Pärt's dedication of *Kanon Pokajanen* to Kaljuste and the EPCC, it is not a stretch to say that their collaboration is what enabled Pärt to conceive of the piece on the scale it assumed, requiring, in Pärt's words, "90 minutes of perfect intonation," and considerable musical and linguistic ability to perform a score with almost no expressive directions.[44] The collaboration of Pärt, Kaljuste, and the EPCC in the *Kanon Pokajanen* project and its mediation through ECM (it was recorded in Tallinn at the Niguliste Church prior to its premiere at the 750th anniversary of Cologne Cathedral in 1998) illustrate how Estonianness as a quality of sound and performance, relationships forged through shared language and experiences, and an acoustic place relate to the universality that Pärt seeks in his work.

Back in Estonia

Pärt could not return to Estonia until 1989, and then for a visit known only to family and close friends. His public return to the newly independent Estonia was in 1992 and marked the beginning of a long process of overcoming the estrangement and complexities of being a Soviet émigré, rehabilitating his music and status after Soviet malignment, and reforging artistic and spiritual relationships in Estonia. The official ban on performances of Pärt's music and public discussion of his work was perforce lifted with the political, social, and cultural changes of perestroika and the Singing Revolution in the late 1980s. In fact, one can interpret the re-emergence of Pärt in Estonian musical life as a tangible index of the dramatic changes in Estonia (and throughout the Soviet sphere of domination) in the late 1980s and early 1990s. By 1987, Mustonen and Hortus Musicus were performing the early tintinnabuli works on Estonian radio, and the Hilliard Ensemble performed Pärt at their Estonian debut in 1987.

In 1988, three important pieces on Pärt appeared in *Teater. Muusika. Kino*, a leading Estonian popular scholarly monthly.[45] Leo Normet's "The Beginning is Silence" radically reoriented the discourse on Pärt away from Soviet aesthetic ideologies and his political entanglement. The tone and language in which Normet writes immediately indicate the transformations under way in 1988, placing Pärt's work from the 1960s within the mainstream of European experimentalism without any reference to the controversies that culminated in the *Credo* scandal. Normet goes on to engage with Pärt's early tintinnabuli work (including examples from *Missa syllabica* and *De profundis* with religious texts) in sensitive, sympathetic, sophisticated ways that would have been unthinkable earlier in the 1980s and have aged well.

Merike Vaitmaa's "Tintinnabuli – eluhoiak, stiil ja tehnika" (Tintinnabuli – way of life, style, and technique) has aged just as well, both echoing and establishing the discourse on Pärt beyond Estonia. Here, Vaitmaa is able to place Pärt's early tintinnabuli work in the context of his collaboration with Mustonen and Hortus Musicus and his work after emigration, approaching tintinnabuli on its own terms and through its own values as an encompassing musical philosophy. In linking Pärt's re-emergence on the Estonian musical scene to the social and political transformations of the late 1980s, she plainly criticizes Pärt's silencing in Estonia after his emigration, particularly the recordings and films that were kept from the public. Finally, Vaitmaa's sense that Pärt's work from the 1970s can be linked to the minimalism of Steve Reich and Estonian composers Lepo Sumera and Erkki-Sven Tüür is emblematic of the different and, at times, contested ways tintinnabuli is situated as style and technique within broader soundscapes.

Ivalo Randalu's "Arvo Pärt novembris 1978" (Arvo Pärt in November 1978) is a transcript of an extensive interview with Arvo and Nora Pärt for a documentary film by Andres Sööt of the same name. *Arvo Pärt novembris 1978* and another Sööt film about Pärt called *Fantaasia C-duur* (*C-Major Fantasy*) had still not been shown on Estonian television in 1988, and Randalu's piece was an effort to bring the interview to light. The interview itself is invaluable for the impression it gives of Pärt at this fruitful, turbulent moment in his life, the extent to which he speaks about his creative process and worldview, and for the quintessentially Pärtian aphorisms he offers. On his hard-won turn from modernist experimentation towards tintinnabuli, for instance, he remarked: "When you feel like you're dirty, then you go to the sauna."[46]

Estonian scholarship on Pärt and media coverage of his life and performances slowly mounted through the late 1980s and into the 1990s.[47] In 1989, the Estonian filmmaker Dorian Supin, Pärt's brother-in-law, made the first of several documentary films on the composer, called *Siis sai õhtu ja sai hommik* (*Then Came The Evening And Then The Morning*), which aired on Estonian television. Supin has since made several more Pärt documentaries: *Cecilia* (2002), *Orient Occident* (2002), *Sinu nimi* (*Your Name*, 2002), and *24 prelüüdi ühele fuugale* (*24 Preludes for a Fugue*, 2002). Pärt's presence in Estonian musical life gradually intensified as well (the family took an apartment in Tallinn in the early 1990s), particularly through his flourishing relationship with Kaljuste and the EPCC. That said, Pärt did not fit conveniently into the cultural and political narratives of the 1990s the way Veljo Tormis did, for instance. Pärt's music was not suited for mass amateur performance at Estonian song festivals, he did not write in Estonian, his religious texts were alien to many, scores and recordings of his music were prohibitively expensive, and he was perceived by some as more cosmopolitan than Estonian: successfully established in Berlin and not firmly rooted in Estonia. Over the course of the 1990s and into the 2000s, this has changed substantially through the reorientation of Estonian cultural discourse away from the 'post-Soviet' in ways that can more naturally accommodate Pärt and his music, and through the frequency and eventfulness of Pärt performances in Estonia, particularly with Kaljuste and the EPCC. For his seventieth birthday in 2005, Pärt was the featured composer at the Estonian Union of Composers annual festival, and his membership in the Estonian Union of Composers was renewed that same year, bringing his professional connection to Estonia full circle. Pärt was commissioned by Lennart Meri, President of Estonia from 1992 to 2001, to write *Für Lennart in Memoriam* for Meri's funeral, which took place in 2006.

Pärt at 75

In the 2000s, Pärt's work remained rooted in the choral tintinnabuli sound that is his trademark – *Nunc dimittis* and *Da pacem Domine* stand out in this regard. Thanks in part to the particulars of recent commissions, his work has also ventured back into traditional concert idioms with works such as Symphony No. 4, *Lamentate* (piano and orchestra), and *Adam's Lament* (choir and orchestra). Beyond revealing the new possibilities of tintinnabuli and his evolving relationship with his compositional process, Pärt's recent work reveals that tintinnabuli is not only about the sonic play of rationality and sensuality, but can also be framed to address urgent moral issues. In response to the murder of journalist Anna Politkovskaya and his deep concern for the human rights situation in Russia, Pärt stipulated that all performances of his works in 2006–07 be dedicated to her memory and asked that performers communicate his wishes to their audiences.[48] Similarly, Pärt dedicated his Symphony No. 4 to the courage and moral clarity of imprisoned anti-Kremlin businessman Mikhail Khordorkovsky, whom he took pains to mention while accepting the Composer of the Year prize at the 2011 Classic BRIT Awards. Given Pärt's experience of Soviet suppression, it is not hard to imagine why he feels compelled to explicitly address the situation in Russia in this way.

Adam's Lament, written to symbolically unite the European Cultural Capitals of Istanbul (2010) and Tallinn (2011), uses a poem by the Russian

St Silouan of Athos to emphasize the common heritage of Islam and Christianity in the person of Adam. Pärt comments:

> For me, the name Adam is a collective term not merely for the whole of humanity, but for each individual, regardless of time, era, social class or religious affiliation. And this collective Adam has suffered and lamented on this earth for millennia. Our ancestor Adam foresaw the human tragedy that was to come and experienced it as his own guilty responsibility, the result of his sinful act. He suffered all the cataclysms of humanity into the depths of desperation, inconsolable in his agony.

Another rigorously logogenic work, *Adam's Lament* reflects Pärt's belief in the capacity of tintinnabuli to address the potent historical meanings of Turkey and Estonia representing European culture, and Adam as a figure who both unites and transcends Islam and Christianity through the recognition of suffering and violence. It also reflects how composition is at once an ethical and technical act for Pärt.

In 2010, Pärt turned 75 and was fêted around the world. In Estonia, Pärt's jubilee was marked by a month of performances that secured and celebrated his Estonianness. The programming of the month-long festival purposively recontextualized Pärt's pre-tintinnabuli, pre-emigration work in current Estonian musical life. Sharing space in venues across Estonia with a staged version of *In principio*, Estonian premieres of *Adam's Lament*, new arrangements of earlier works, and a complete performance of *Kanon Pokajanen* were the sounds of Pärt's work in Estonia during the 1960s and 1970s. These included the Symphonies Nos. 2 and 3, the cantata *Meie Aed* (*Our Garden*), the *Collage über B–A–C–H*, a festival of films with his original scores, a concert pairing dances from Pärt's music for children's theater with works by his teacher Heino Eller, and a restaging of the 1977 premiere of *Tabula rasa* with Kremer and Grindenko. The unambiguous purpose of this programming, and its naturalness in an Estonian context, was to reorient the commonplace, cosmopolitan association of Pärt and tintinnabuli relative to his work in Estonia, for Estonian media, and in the Estonian language, thereby renewing his connection to the history, identity, and soundscape of the nation.

For Pärt's birthday on September 11, the celebrations were centered in Rakvere, the town where Pärt spent most of his childhood. For that day, Pärt created *Kyrie* for the five new bells of the Lutheran Church of the Trinity in Rakvere. Beyond the self-evident connection to tintinnabuli, this piece, written at the request of the Estonian Evangelical Lutheran Church and the Rakvere municipality, made tangible a deep connection between Pärt and place; it emplaced Pärt anew in Rakvere by incorporating his work into the public and religious soundscape of the town. With typical Pärtian good humor, *Kyrie*, which now chimes each day at noon in Rakvere, ends with a fleeting reference to the Estonian children's song "Juba linnukesed" ("Outside, the Birds Are Already Singing"), recalling both Pärt's childhood and the constant promise of spring.

Directly after the performance of *Kyrie*, there was another emphatic placing of Pärt in Rakvere and in an Estonian national consciousness. Taking as a point of departure the well-known story, related in Supin's documentary *24 Preludes for a Fugue*, of the young Pärt circling a loudspeaker for hours in the Rakvere market square on a bicycle, listening to symphony broadcasts and dreaming of becoming a composer somehow different from those he was hearing, the Estonian artist Aivar Simson created *Noormees jalgrattal muusikat kuulamas* (*Boy on a Bicycle Listening to Music*), a sculpture now part of an installation in Rakvere. The video production of the opening performance in Rakvere on September 11 ends with the voice of Pärt relating the story of himself as that boy on a bicycle listening to music.[49] What is particularly noteworthy about this production is its natural emphasis on Pärt's music for children, since he is himself a child in the sculpture. Drawn from Soviet Estonian animated films including *Väike motoroller* (*The Little Motor Scooter*), *Ukuaru*, and one of the "Operaator Kõps" ("Cameraman Kõps") animated films, these are some of Pärt's most unproblematically Estonian sounds – they are local, vernacular, and popular in a way tintinnabuli is not, and are, therefore, most apt for recontextualizing Pärt's Estonianness.

In the future, the International Arvo Pärt Centre outside Tallinn in Laulasmaa will be a museum, a place for research and performance, and will make many of Pärt's materials digitally accessible – a prescient initiative by Pärt and his family to help the story of his music continue to be told. A small example of things to come: as part of Pärt's public engagement through the center, he worked in June 2011 with a group of schoolchildren to put on a concert of eighteen of his works at the Swedish Church of St Michael in Tallinn. The music ranged from early works such as *Diagrams* for solo piano and children's songs such as "Mina olen juba suur" ("I Am Already Big") to *Da pacem Domine* arranged for recorders, *Veni Creator* for boys' choir, and *Peace Be Upon You, Jerusalem* for girls' choir. In a gesture that typifies Pärt's enthusiastic outreach, he joined a boy soprano at the piano for his *Vater Unser*, a short non-tintinnabuli piece given to Pope Benedict for the sixtieth anniversary of his ordination in July 2011.

Further reading

Maria Cizmic. "Of Bodies and Narratives: Musical Representations of Pain and Illness in HBO's *Wit*." In Neil Lerner and Joseph N. Straus, eds., *Sounding Off: Theorizing Disability in Music*, New York: Routledge, 2006.

"Transcending the Icon: Spirituality and Postmodernism in Arvo Pärt's *Tabula Rasa* and *Spiegel im Spiegel*," *Twentieth-Century Music* 5(1) (2008): 45–78.

Jeffers Engelhardt. Review of Arvo Pärt, "'Solfeggio per coro'; 'Cantate Domino canticum novum'; 'Missa syllabica'; 'Sarah Was Ninety Years Old'; and Others," *Notes* 57 (4) (2001): 987–93.

Arvo Pärt. "Tintinnabuli: Flucht in die freiwillige Armut." In Hermann Danuser, Hannelore Gerlach and Jürgen Köchel, eds., *Sowjetische Musik im Licht der Perestroika: Interpretationen, Quellentexte, Komponistenmonographien*, Laaber Verlag, 1990: 269–70.

Enzo Restagno. *Arvo Pärt allo specchio: Conversazioni, saggi e testimonianze.* Milan: Il Saggiatore, 2004.

Enzo Restagno, Leopold Brauneiss, Saale Kareda, and Arvo Pärt. *Arvo Pärt im Gespräch.* Vienna: Universal Edition, 2010.

4 Musical archetypes: the basic elements of the tintinnabuli style

LEOPOLD BRAUNEISS

I Archetypes

It could be said that, like the music of Haydn, Pärt's music is appreciated all over the world. One reason for this rather rare phenomenon for a contemporary composer is that he found ways of (re)building the music out of very simple basic elements or patterns such as scales, which are commonly recognized. I suggest characterizing these elements or patterns as 'archetypes': this multilayered Greek term can literally be translated as 'original or primal image' (*arche* = beginning, source). In the twentieth century, it has been known primarily through its use in Carl Jung's analytical psychology, where it is linked with the equally important concept of the collective unconscious. For Jung, this means a deep layer of the unconscious mind, which can be called collective inasmuch as it is "not a personal acquisition but is inborn" and thus "not individual but universal."[1] Jung calls the contents of this collective unconscious 'archetypes.' These "contents and modes of behavior that are more or less the same everywhere and in all individuals"[2] are by no means to be perceived as concrete images or ideas: in Jung's understanding, the archetypes are rather "definite forms in the psyche which seem to be present always and everywhere."[3] Elsewhere, Jung also strongly emphasizes that:

> archetypes are not determined as regards their content, but only as regards their form and then only to a very limited degree. A primordial image is determined as to its content only when it has become conscious and is therefore filled out with the material of conscious experience. Its form, however, as I have explained elsewhere, might perhaps be compared to the axial system of a crystal, which, as it were, performs the crystalline structure in the mother liquid, although it has no material existence of its own … The archetype in itself is empty and purely formal, nothing but a *facultas performandi*, a possibility of representation which is given a priori. The representations themselves are not inherited, only the forms, and in that respect they correspond in every way to the instincts, which are also determined in form only.[4]

The idea of the human soul possessing a "net-like basic pattern," which Arvo Pärt put forward in his acceptance speech for the Internationaler Brückepreis der Europastadt Görlitz (International Bridge Prize of the European City of Görlitz), is not too far removed from Jung's image of a crystalline system of coordinates.[5] Pärt's point of origin is the empirical fact that diverse items and substances have very similar basic patterns when examined through a powerful microscope. If one were to imagine that the human soul could also be examined through a microscope lens, it could be expected that – at a certain degree of magnification – a comparable "net-like basic pattern" would be detected. In his Görlitz speech Pärt notes:

> Perhaps one might call it 'human geometry', neatly sorted, quietly formed – but, most of all, beautiful. In this depth, we are all so similar that we could recognize ourselves in any other person … I am very much tempted to see this beautiful and neat Ur-substance, this precious island in the inner seclusion of our soul, as the 'place' where, over 2000 years ago, we were told that the Kingdom of God would be – inside us. No matter if we are old or young, rich or poor, woman or man, colored or white, talented or less talented. And so, I keep trying to stay on the path that searches for this passionately longed-for 'magic island', where all people (and for me, all sounds) can live together in love.[6]

Just as we strive to treat our fellow people with love and care in daily life, the composer aims at creating a world in which all sounds, despite their superficial differences, are connected with love. The parenthesis in the last sentence "and for me, all sounds" shows how we are to picture the connection between life and art in the tintinnabuli style: the same ideals apply to the composer's handling of sounds and musical figures and in our relationships with the living environment. Hence, the goal in music is to advance to the deeper layers of primal pictures and substances which could be identified as musical archetypes. Like the mental archetypes in Jung's analytical psychology, they have to be general, supra-individual, and preexistent. The quest for the 'magic island' in universal human existence, which is also the place of encounter with the divine, corresponds, in music, to the quest for the universally musical: in both, the common and connective elements do not arise from a complex variety of interwoven heterogeneous elements but through the fact that outward individual differences can be reduced to homogeneous and simple basic patterns which thus can be more readily overcome.

As with Jung's psychic archetypes, musical archetypes are fundamentally empty forms with no contents. They only appear and become analytically graspable when musical material 'crystallizes'. In the tintinnabuli style, the regular crystalline structure corresponds to basic formal relationships such as mirroring, parallel motion, additions, and multiplications, all of which determine the musical processes on small and large levels. On the one hand, it is possible to explain these processes in numbers; on the other hand, they can also be illustrated graphically. The general archetypical element not only connects all tones in music; it also joins music as a whole with both the numerical world of mathematics and physical processes, as well as with the visible world of geometry and visual representation in general.

In fact, the parallelism of image and musical process plays an important role in tintinnabulation, as the pictorial titles of some works show. For example, in the short piece *Arbos* (*Tree*), a tree's branching is translated into musical structure. Similarly, in *Silhouette* (subtitled *Hommage à Gustav Eiffel*), the contour of the Eiffel Tower in Paris, a structure in which the openly visible construction determines the building's character and architectonic statement, becomes the basis for the piece. In Pärt's introductory remarks to *Silhouette*, he not only writes about how he was fascinated by the Eiffel Tower's building plans during the composition process, he also cites the details, in which the architectural and musical structures follow the same principles: "From a composer's perspective, one would be able to find a lot in Eiffel's tower which could be compared with musical structure – the building segments and their arrangement, the transparency of the construction, and many others. Also, statics, a very significant aspect in architecture, is an important subject for the formal structure of a musical composition."[7]

With the title of the organ piece *Mein Weg hat Gipfel und Wellentäler* (taken from a poem by Edmond Jabès, translated by Henriette Besser), we return, in a certain way, to the beginning of our considerations: the highs and lows of a winding road – a visual phenomenon – can be found again in the wave-like progressions of melodic lines in the music. However, while the poem speaks about the turns and twists on the path of life – with its different mental states, exaltations, and deep desperations – the music, via the image of the road, refers back to the imaginary landscape of the soul, as outlined in the beginning of this article. In the idea of an archetype, an Ur-picture, the audible texture of the music is connected on a deep structural level with visible forms, shapes, and events – natural ones (a tree, a mountain range, or a bird's flight) or man-made ones (the Eiffel Tower or the Shroud of Turin [*La Sindone*]) – as well as with imagined structures of the human soul. This essential connection also means that these superficially different areas can influence each other, for instance when, as mentioned before, visual images and ideas prove inspiring during the genesis of a composition. Most of all, however, the idea of a musical structure that is parallel to human constitution makes it possible to again seize the ultimately classical idea that music which is, in some way or another, well organized and rightly proportioned is able to gear into the human soul in a quasi-regulative fashion.

The aesthetic of the archetypical is, most of all, the aesthetic of the universal. In addition, the beautiful and the inner in the passage from Pärt's acceptance speech are, without a doubt, keywords. Even if the basic pattern (of the soul as well as of music) is, in Pärt's words, "most of all, beautiful," this beauty is, despite its paramount importance, not an end in itself; its function and reason are to promote this affectionate conjunction of sounds, which can serve as an aesthetic model for the affectionate coexistence of humans. As we will see, the core of the "beautiful structures" is the linking together of two opposed poles in music: the steps of a melodic movement and the jumps in a static sound. The "beautiful structures" do not deny the conflict but integrate it: compositionally, they are expressed in diatonic dissonances between melodic movement and static sound. In the sense of the aforementioned parallelism of art and life these dissonances stand for individual inadequacy and personal errors; at the same time, they are being corrected – theologically: they find forgiveness – by being integrated in superior structures.

The archetypical in Pärt also shares with Jung's analytical psychology that the path that goes inside, if it is taken consistently all the way to the end, does not lead to an overly individualized ego and a vast loss of the outer world but to a common state in which bridges are built – to the lives of others and to God, and, in music, to notes and sounds. On the one hand, the aesthetic of the universal corrects the lopsidedness of an aesthetic of the beautiful which, in the twentieth century, has increasingly been perceived as precarious and which, in the tintinnabuli style, precisely does not deny conflicts and tensions. On the other hand, it also corrects the dangers of an aesthetic of the inward, which, in tintinnabulation, can precisely not be equated with escapism.

By comprehending the tintinnabulation as a quest for the universal in the archetypical, common labelings such as New Simplicity or Holy Minimalism, which are often not free of negative connotations, can be corrected: there is no doubt that the tintinnabuli music is affected by a voluntary self-restraint in choosing musical means. The concept of reduction grasps the meaning of this process much better than the concepts of simplification or minimalism; after all, the appropriate sense of the word reduction (from the Latin 'reducere' meaning 'to lead back') means returning external variety to the common basis of archetypes. Turning to the archetypical means a humble overcoming of the personal ego, which partly dies with the first step, to be born again in various contexts and relationships to fellow human beings and to God. The negative term minimalism only cuts the significant second step from the reduction, which deprives it of its actual purpose, the maximal opening of the self to multifaceted relations, as facilitated by the reduction.

Before I discuss the musical-analytical techniques, one last thought: the archetypical is the primal element; hence, it transcends not only the limitations of the individual ego but the temporal limits of here and now as well. The idea of timeliness thus gains another meaning: it is not about artistic expression in the present point in time any more but about the always current, the archetypical basics of life and art, about never-changing basic questions and their possible answers. In an interview from 1968, almost a decade before the first tintinnabuli compositions, Pärt cites Bach, whose works he had quoted repeatedly in his collage works from the 1960s, as the example of such archetypical timeliness: "I think that the so-called 'timeliness' of Bach's music will not disappear in the next 200 years, ... The secret of this 'timelessness' is not how extensively its author perceived his own present but all of existence with its joys, worries, and secrets ... Art should concern itself with the eternal and not just the current."[8]

The fact that some details of the tintinnabuli style might be reminiscent of different forms of early music (before 1600), just like the return to tonality, means neither an atavistic turning back of the wheel of history (which, after all, can be neither stopped nor turned back), nor an escape from the present and its problems; rather, it emerges from the quest for the archetypical, supra-temporal basis of life and art. The similarities with some details of early music are in a manner newly born out of the structural patterns. Here, as well as with the return to tonality, one can speak about a renaissance, which interprets the archetypical tonal elements of triad and scale for today.

In his Görlitz acceptance speech, Pärt says that, in a fictive examination of the human soul under a microscope, "the outer characteristics of a human being, with all his weaknesses and peculiarities, more and more disappear from the picture."[9] In a musical-analytical systemization of the archetypical basic elements we will follow the compositional process and proceed backwards from the highest degree of magnification, thus arriving at the evidence of a work's individual surface last. Figure 4.1 experimentally shows the different musical layers of depth and thus also offers a plan for this introduction into the depth of the tintinnabuli style. However, inasmuch as formal dispositions are only comprehensible analytically when they appear with individually selected musical material, the individual levels of Figure 4.1 cannot always be discussed separately.

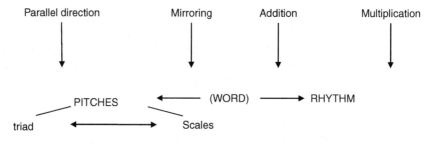

Figure 4.1 Different layers of the tintinnabuli style

II Scales and triads

Scales (the melodic line)

Scales have all the aforementioned attributes of a musical archetype: they are a globally prevalent, pre-existing and supra-individual musical resource. A scale is a formal arrangement of the basic tonal material in the tightest possible space, which makes the distances between the individual pitches of the resulting scale immediately comprehensible. Most of the time, as in Pärt's music, these distances are not equally big, whereas these quantitative differences are connected with significant qualitative ones: that is to say, not all notes are equal; the tonal center (the so-called root) is of superior importance. In order to set the root, the different distances in a scale are not enough. For instance, in the seven diatonic basic notes – the white keys on a piano – two notes can be the root (of a major scale and the so-called relative minor scale). In the older modal system, there are six notes that can be the root. In a piece in just one part, the root usually manifests itself by being the last note. Ultimately, melodies come to a resting point by arriving at the tonal center of gravity. Historically, as music developed, the notes a fifth and an octave above are played above this final tonal root; these pitches are mathematically related to the root in terms of the frequency of the pitch: for an octave the relationship 1:2, for a pure fifth 2:3. In due course, historically, a third completes the chord to form a major or minor chord.

This long description of scale formation is necessary in order to figure out the ways in which scales have regained their quasi-archetypical power and thus their symbolic value in the tintinnabuli style. In traditional tonal music, scales are foundational to the compositional process and are generally used to demonstrate instrumental virtuosity, or are found in transitions that connect individually molded themes. An essential feature of the scale as an archetype is that the movement going in a certain direction – simple and conclusive as it is – can be continued indefinitely. In geometry, a line drawn on a piece of paper can be defined as visually realizable excerpts of an endlessly continuable row of dots; in the same way, a sounding scale is an audible excerpt of what is, in principle, an endless row of tones: in this way, the limited material of a composition and the inconceivable limitlessness are thus connected in a simple as well as graphic way.

Furthermore, the qualities of tones in a scale return after a certain number of notes in a different octave: the linear progression thus contains a cyclical repetition on other levels. In scale practice, this return also supplies the turning point. If a pianist plays the white keys on a piano upwards and downwards starting on C, they use this same pitch as the pivot note and finish on it, thus labeling it as the root. With the much more sophisticated use of scales in musical works, the designation of the root and the turning points are not necessarily in such simple interplay anymore. Formulaic melodic (in traditional one-voiced tonal music) and harmonic (in multivoiced music; called chord progressions or cadences) models determine which note is counted as the root. In Pärt's tintinnabulation, there are melodic central notes, which are, as in the playing of scales, the simple result of whichever note begins or ends the scales. The root note is mostly defined by a given omnipresent triad.

Triads (the 'sounding bells')
Instead of the standardized chord progressions found in Western harmony, tintinnabulation usually uses a specific combination of the melodic archetype of the scale with the harmonic archetype of the triad. The latter can be counted as an archetype, inasmuch as it has found use in the specific European form of common practice harmony through many centuries and across many differences of epochal or personal styles. The major triad is also preexistent, discovered, and thus is also not individual material because it is pre-formed in the 'natural' physical phenomenon of the harmonic series.[10] The most important formal-archetypical element of the tintinnabuli triad is the merging of three single notes to one 'pure' harmony that is perceived as a unit and is self-contained. In Pärt's words: "I'm intrigued by the triad's natural purity, its laconism and euphony."[11]

Tintinnabulation: the joining of scale and triad
In tintinnabulation, every single note of a melody voice formed by scales (which Hillier calls the M-voice) ideally gets assigned a note of a triad at a certain distance to this M-voice. In the so-called first position above (+1) or below (-1) the M-voice, this produces diatonic dissonances of minor and major seconds and also thirds and fourths; in second position (+2, -2) we get fourths, fifths, and sixths (Examples 4.1a and 4.1b).

Example 4.1 Tintinnabuli voice positions

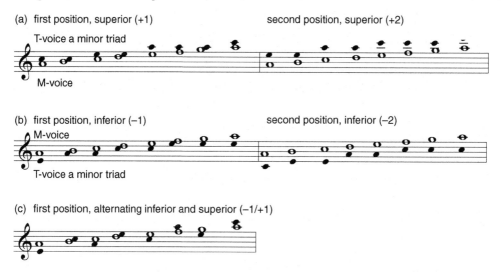

(a) first position, superior (+1)   second position, superior (+2)

(b) first position, inferior (−1)   second position, inferior (−2)

(c) first position, alternating inferior and superior (−1/+1)

By this method, a second voice develops consisting exclusively of triad notes which sounds throughout the whole composition like the peal of bells. From this we get the terms tintinnabuli-voice (T-voice), and tintinnabuli triad (T-triad), which itself consists of three tintinnabuli-notes (T-notes).[12] Pärt's wife Nora summarizes the effect of these two voices, noting that: "The natural feeling for euphony as well as for balance, harmony, and purity is emphasized by the title 'little bells' ('tintinnabuli'). The beauty of the 'little bells' natural sound is, in the composer's understanding, associated with euphony, or more concretely: the triad."[13]

An alternation between the first position above and below is a frequent device used by Pärt (Example 4.1c). In this process, voice crossings, which are often found in early music (for example between the lower voices of an early motet, called tenor and contratenor), can become a consequently employed rule of composition for a specific piece. This effect of constant alternation, where the M-voice and the T-voice are alternately on top or on bottom, produces the sensation of additional pitches, which is often a feature in American-style minimal music. So Pärt's systematic use of all possible interrelations between M- and T-voice bears relation to early as well as contemporary music.

The triad notes determine which scale note becomes the tonal center of gravity. Because the T-voice follows the M-voice in a kind of reflex it is thus not formed by the composer in detail and, in one sense, it can therefore be perceived as a ubiquitous, objective fact. In this quasi-objective way, the notes of the scale that don't accord with it can be seen as variances or aberrances. At the same time, by fitting them into the greater unit of M- and T-voice, tintinnabulation correctively directs them towards the focus of the triad. In contrast to the objective (determined) nature of the triad, the melody, which in some way must be deduced from the scale, can be seen as subjective (composed). It is by interpreting this aberrance and integration of the M- and T-voices theologically that one comes to the terms sin and forgiveness. Pärt has repeatedly mentioned this analogy. In a conversation with Enzo Restagno in 2003 he said: "Maybe I could say that the melody represents my sins and my imperfect being, whereas the second voice is the forgiveness that is granted to me. In this case, my subjective errors are being corrected."[14] In a 2010 interview, he stated it even more personally: "One line [the M-voice] is who we are, and the other line [the T-voice] is who is holding and takes care of us."[15]

Scales and triads employed by Pärt

What kind of scales and triads does Pärt use to make this constellation of archetypes audible? In the early tintinnabuli compositions, the so-called natural minor (called the Aeolian mode in the twelve-mode system of early music), prevails. Pärt uses it in *Cantus in Memory of Benjamin Britten* (1977/1980) as well as the main part of the first movement "Ludus" ("Game") of *Tabula rasa* (1977), in its pure form with exclusively diatonic scale notes and the root A. In both cases he combines it with an A-minor T-triad and the melodic central note A (Example 4.2a).

There are commonly two versions of the minor scale, 'melodic' and 'harmonic'. In the 'harmonic minor', the seventh scale degree is raised a half-step in order to make the step to the root smaller and thus more compelling in final cadences; this leads to an accordingly bigger distance between the sixth and seventh degree (an augmented second) and it is this which gives this variant of the scale a special character (Example 4.2b). Pärt frequently uses this 'harmonic minor' scale, and often the fifth degree of the harmonic minor (for example, the pitch E in A minor) functions as a central note. In *Psalom*, for instance (a work without tintinnabuli voices), the tonal center thus remains characteristically suspended. This work crosses two patterns which together form the seven notes of the scale: first, an oscillating movement between E and F; and, second, a chain of thirds arranged in an arch in which the note E acts as a root as it is the lowest. Added together, this produces the triads on E and A, which, according to the system of a traditional cadence, effectively makes the middle A-minor triad the tonal centre (tonic, labeled T in Example 4.2c), to which, in the matter of a so-called dominant (labeled D), the sounds on E, whose root is a fifth higher, lead up to (Example 4.2c). It depends on the way of hearing if E or A acts as a root. *Psalom* is tonally ambiguous because of the specific way in which it arranges tonal elements. Thereby it does not come to a traditional close

Example 4.2 Pärt's use of scales: (a) and (b) *Cantus*, "Ludus"; (c) *Psalom*; (d) *Mein Weg hat Gipfel und Wellentäler*; (e) *O Morgenstern*

but finishes open-ended and makes the piece seem like a sounding excerpt from a continuum which could keep sounding infinitely.

Most other pieces that use this scale are also centered on the note E through an E-minor or E-major tintinnabuli chord. This produces a scale with a characteristic half-step above the root, followed by an augmented second from the second to the raised third degree. This scale is used in Jewish music as well as in Spanish flamenco music and can thus lend an oriental or Spanish flair, as can be heard in *La Sindone* and *Como cierva sedienta* respectively. As in flamenco music, the third scale degree can be found raised as well as natural. In Pärt's *Mein Weg hat Gipfel und Wellentäler* both of these third scale degrees are heard together: the G♯ in the melody is heard alongside the G♮ of the E-minor T-triad (Example 4.2d). *Fratres* shows similar relationships, differently transposed depending on the version, and in the fifth *Magnificat-Antiphonen* (*O Morgenstern*), the reverse of *Mein Weg* can be heard: the G♮ in the melody is combined with the G♯ of the E-major T-triad (Example 4.2e).

Example 4.3 Raised scale degrees in three works: (a) *And One of the Pharisees*; (b) *Orient & Occident*; (c) *Adam's Lament*

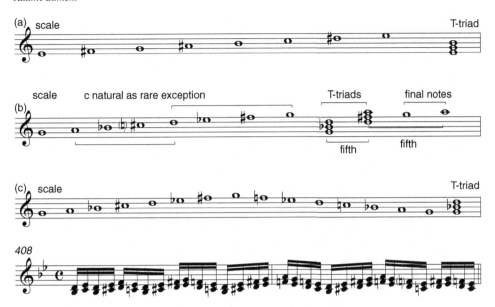

In some compositions, such as *And One of the Pharisees* or *Most Holy Mother of God*, not only the seventh but also the fourth scale degree is raised, which provides for another half-step and another augmented second in the scale Pärt employs (Example 4.3a). This scale also imparts an oriental character. Accordingly, it is the base for the melodic voices of *Orient & Occident*, a dualistic work with a small-sectioned interplay of oriental monophony and European polyphony. Yet this dualism can also be found in the polyphonic passages; in sections, a (dominant) D-major T-triad alternates with a (tonic) G-minor T-triad (Example 4.3b). This in turn corresponds to the scale, in which two equally formed groups of four notes can be discerned, which, because of the raised pitches, lead to D and G respectively. Because of other rules, which cannot be explained here, the piece does not end with any of these two notes but with the note progression G–A, played on the string instruments' open strings, whereby the upper note, A, is a fifth above the D. In the dualism between orient and occident, none of the two antagonists gets the upper hand through the heightened musical significance of being given the last word.

Occasionally, as for instance in Example 4.3c, an excerpt from *Adam's Lament* (mm. 408–409), the fourth and seventh degree of the natural minor scale are only raised when they move upwards from the lower note. Also, it is always possible that pitches are raised only at certain moments in the course of a piece in minor.

Example 4.4 Symphony No. 4, major/minor tonalities in mm. 109–120

Works in which a major scale is connected with a tonic T-triad are comparatively rare in the tintinnabuli style. Examples are the well-known *Spiegel im Spiegel* (F major in the version for violin and piano) and *Cantate Domino canticum novum*, a setting of the 95th psalm for choir or soloists (SATB) and organ (B♭ major). In the *Te Deum*, the initial D minor repeatedly brightens to D major (both the scale and the T-triads), until the work ultimately ends in D major.

In the last part of the last movement of Symphony No. 4 ("Los Angeles"), A major and A minor don't sound consecutively but concurrently in stacked belts of sound. Example 4.4 shows the melodic basic structure of measures 109–120. Here the upwards scale is interrupted with a rather basic pattern: after three notes, the movement jumps backward to the previous note. This pattern is multiplied by parallel moving tenths (a third plus an octave, the two highest layers at the end in thirds); the second and fourth layer from the top (including their attached T-triad on A) sound in major, the other three layers in minor. The superimposition of major and minor blurs the tonal contours and thus creates a scintillating, ethereal web of sounds.

In a few works, Pärt uses the so-called 'chromatic scale' with all available twelve notes in one octave. In the tuning system used today, the distances between these notes (half-steps) are equal, a neutral uniformity without any relation to a tonic. However, the centripetal power of the T-voice or of a pedal point often proves strong enough to provide tonal footing and center it on a tonic. In the piano trio, aptly named *Scala cromatica*, melodic movements are reduced to a single downwards moving chromatic line; by contrast, in *Wallfahrtslied*, two chromatic lines moving in opposite directions diverge, cone-like. Finally, in the *Passacaglia*, a downward whole-tone scale (with steps that are twice as big as in a chromatic scale), counterbalances chromatically rising thirds in the upper voices. The pedal point A–E in central middle range allows for the tonal centering on A (Example 4.5).

Despite the enormous variety of different scales out of which subjective M-voices are composed, the objective character of the T-voice only

Example 4.5 *Passacaglia*, scale patterns

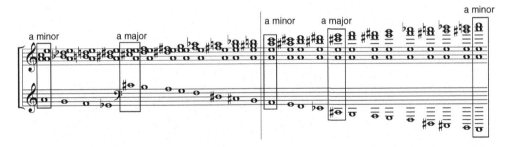

allows for the choice between major and minor triad. Still, in a few cases, Pärt uses a four-note chord rather than a T-triad. In a diminished seventh chord, the tonally stable 'natural' pure fifth of the triad and its division into a major and a minor third are replaced by an 'artificially' diminished (that is to say, a half-step smaller) fifth. It divides the octave into two equal halves and, in the diminished seventh chord, each is subdivided into two equal intervals (minor thirds). It is these equal distances that make this chord exemplary for a tonally ambiguous sound that is not rooted in a specific key. In the same way as the diminished fifth results from the distortion of the pure fifth, the whole chord can be understood as a distorted picture of the triad. In *Von Angesicht zu Angesicht*, a setting of part of 1 Corinthians, it is not only a general symbol for negative conditions of whatever kind but also provides the tintinnabuli sound in the passages that speak about our present, unclear and fragmented perception ("For now we see through a glass, darkly ... now I know in part"). In contrast, the complete gnosis (*von Angesicht zu Angesicht* means 'face to face') promised for after death is characterized by the exclusive use of triads.

In parts of the second and third movements of the Symphony No. 4, a T-triad in the major key is complemented with a minor seventh. This sound, which in traditional harmony is called a dominant seventh, does not sound finished but seeks resolution, typically to a tonic triad whose root is a fifth lower. For instance, in measures 21–26 of the third movement, the surging upward movement (marked "Insistamente") consists of three melodic voices in parallel sixths in the harmonic version of A minor, with a T-triad on E major plus the pitch D (see Example 4.6). This resolves to an A-minor triad (marked "Con intimo sentimento" in m. 26).

III Mirrorings: four melodic modes

In Pärt's tintinnabulation, mirrorings, parallel movements, additions, and multiplications are connected with each other in many ways, so it makes

Example 4.6 Symphony No. 4, third movement, mm. 21–26

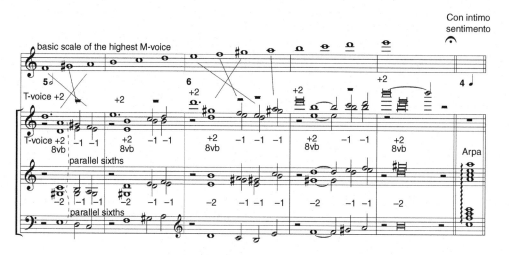

Example 4.7 Tintinnabuli mirroring

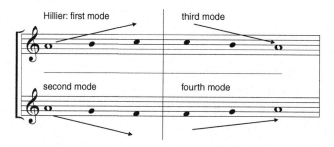

sense to show them in context. Fundamental to all tintinnabuli mirrorings is the system to assign ascending and descending scales a melodic central note: as these central notes can be either at the beginning or the end of the scales, there are four possibilities in total, which are symmetrical to each other on a vertical and a horizontal axis (Example 4.7 shows this for a group of three notes). Hillier called them "modes."[16] All four are equal, so that only the contexts in the individual works can decide which one is set as a basic row from which the other variants of retrograde, inversion, and retrograde inversion are taken.

Spiegel im Spiegel (*Mirror in Mirror*) is an excellent example of mirroring in the melodic voice. It is also a graphic picture for the formal-archetypical aesthetic of the tintinnabuli style in general: if one holds two mirrors against each other, the two-way reflections show a picture whose representations trail off endlessly, like an optical cone into infinity, formed by a rational, technical arrangement. In that sense, one can call the tintinnabuli style an acoustic cone into infinity: proceeding from one note, the

Example 4.8 *Spiegel im Spiegel*

array and mirroring of the step to the neighboring note triggers rationally calculated formal processes, which can be continued indefinitely. In *Spiegel im Spiegel* (version for violin and piano) the melodic central pitch A′ is the third of the tintinnabuli triad F major. As opposed to the system in Example 4.7, it is always at the end of the scale (see Example 4.8).

The variations mirrored around the central pitch A′ sound consecutively and form pairs, which are symmetrical about an horizontal axis. Two consecutive pairs are symmetrical on a vertical axis (except for the central pitch), and for each repetition a scale note both from above and below is also added to every pair (+1). This principle of addition is often connected with the mirroring technique and expands the melodic range in cone shape. These simple as well as continual processes could be continued ad infinitum, but, as only a limited amount of time is available in a work of art, they must be abandoned at some point. *Spiegel im Spiegel* ends when the steps to the neighbor notes of the central pitch, which begin the process, have reached the octave (B♭″ to A′, then G to A′): this suffices to be able to perceive the finite time of a work of art as an excerpt of an endless continuum. The key (F major) is chosen so that the lowest note of the

Example 4.9 "Ode 1" from *Triodion*, mm. 16–23

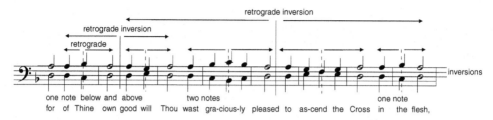

expansion process is also the lowest note that can be played on the solo instrument, the violin.

This basic line multiplies according to simple rules to a many-voiced texture: the first and third note of the three-note accompaniment figure are always a third or an octave, respectively, above the notes of the melody; thus, put together, they form two melodic voices parallel to the melody in the solo instrument by a third or an octave, respectively. In between, there is a tintinnabuli note (the T-triad is F major) in first position below the third note. When the three-note group is repeated, tintinnabuli notes appear alternately in higher range (second position above the third note of the accompaniment figure, first position one and two octaves higher for the central pitch) and lower range (second position below the first note, first position one and two octaves lower for the central pitch). With steady quarter-note movement, this forms a $\frac{6}{4}$ bar for every melody note, except for the central pitch, which is emphasized by an extension over three bars (×3: multiplication principle). The analysis of this simply constructed work shows a general characteristic of the tintinnabuli style: the individual shape of a work results from the way melodic and tintinnabuli voices and mirrorings, parallel movements, additions, and multiplications intertwine.

Mirrorings can sound not only consecutively in one voice but also simultaneously in two voices. In Example 4.9, from "Ode I" from *Triodion* (mm. 16–23), both are the case. It is not difficult to identify an addition process which is here followed and balanced by a subtraction process (1 step up and down, 2 steps up and down, 1 step only up). As a result, the simple structure is woven through by a net of higher and lower axes of symmetry (Example 4.9).

Parallel movements

Because mirrorings can be executed around differently set axes, an abundance of connections appear, especially with simpler material, if they are examined from different perspectives. In contrast, use of parallel movement is a much simpler system with which to create a multi-voiced texture from one melodic voice. The determining factor is always use of the

Example 4.10 *Pari intervallo*, end

Example 4.11 *Fratres*, m. 9

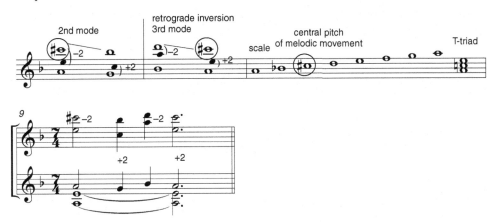

same interval between the melodic voices (one might call this technique 'pari intervallo', which is actually the title of an early tintinnabuli composition). In the tintinnabuli style, it is preferentially sixths and thirds, the latter often stretched over one or more octaves. As Example 4.4 shows, it can also be more than two voices, with one third plus an octave distance each. In the piece *Pari intervallo*, we also find a third-and-two-octaves distance between the two melodic voices, which is ultimately narrowed to a double octave. Here, the two T-voices (second position above and below the topmost melodic voice) enter staggered and are accordingly held over to the next note of the melody (Example 4.10).

In *Fratres (Brothers)*, the distance between the two melodic voices is a third and an octave throughout. They include a T-voice, which is positioned alternately in second position below the upper voice and above the lower voice (Example 4.11). The title of the piece, rich in associations, may also point to the brotherly harmony and cadence of these melodic voices.

The euphonic closeness of two voices in thirds has been a sounding symbol of intimate togetherness and consoling security for centuries, and it has retained this meaning in the tintinnabuli style. For example, the

Example 4.12 *Lamentate*, section L, m. 455

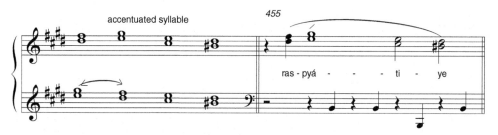

Example 4.13 *Weihnachtliches Wiegenlied*, beginning

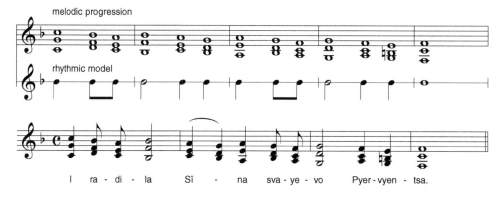

thirds in section L of *Lamentate*, marked "Conciliante," on the pedal point
G♯, sound conciliatory (Example 4.12).

In the sections of *Kanon Pokajanen* sung by male voices, we also find
parallel fourths. Combined with below-set parallel thirds, which switch
to the lower fifth with every third chord, they also mark the beginning of
Weihnachtliches Wiegenlied (Example 4.13).

This basic form of a three-part composition was significant particularly
in the fifteenth century and is known as fauxbourdon. However, this system
is not just copied by Pärt, but is reconfigured by the structural contexts of
the tintinnabuli style. The descending sequences of the three-note groups
are a simple fracturing of the scale, as we have already encountered it in
an ascending form in Example 4.4. The rhythm of these three-note groups
appears every second time with double note values. It is this fusion of old,
familiar material and its structural permeation that characterizes tintinnabulation: the familiar keeps the rational structures from being merely
self-sufficient, demure mechanics.

While all parallel movements so far have not exceeded the pool of notes
provided by the scale, in more recent works (from *Como cierva sedienta*
(1998/2002) onwards), we also encounter parallel moving diminished
fifths/augmented fourths, a part of the aforementioned diminished seventh

Example 4.14 Symphony No. 4, the word 'disobedience', mm. 117–119

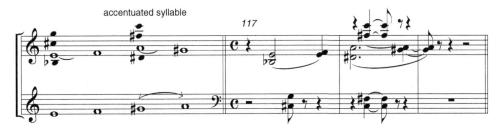

chord. With this interval, reference to a tonic gets lost to a large extent, especially when there are no tintinnabuli voices and no melodic central pitch, as in the excerpt from the Symphony No. 4 shown in Example 4.14 (second movement, mm. 117–119). In the text this passage is based on, human, God-rejecting errors such as lying or pride are listed. In Example 4.14, the subject is the four-syllable Church Slavonic word for disobedience (непокорством).

Here the notes of the A-minor scale with raised fourth and seventh degree are reorganized so that the accentuated third syllable gets the highest note. To this, either an augmented fourth/diminished fifth lower is added to the notes of the A-minor scale (in Example 4.14, non-scale notes B♭ and D♯) or the preceding melody note is held over. This occurs in permanent alternation, and the accompanying voices add the notes missing for a diminished seventh chord. The result is tonal disorientation as musical/structural expression of estrangement from God.

Addition and subtraction

Like mirroring, the principle of addition can also be effective in two dimensions: in the succession of the number of notes as well as in the superimposing of the active voices. The Kyrie of *Berliner Messe* (Example 4.15) shows both in connection with an important basic principle: the number of syllables of every single word determines how many scale notes are added to or subtracted from the centre pitch (G′ in the alto, B♭ in the bass).[17] The accented syllable gets two notes, of which the second is extended by three beats, the others get one note.

As already mentioned when discussing Example 4.14, the position of the accented syllable in the word can also influence the course of pitches: in Example 4.12 as well as in Example 4.14, the notes of the scales that descend to the center pitches G♯ and B♯ (four notes for the four syllables of the word) get rearranged so that the accent syllables occur on the respective highest note. Thus, the parameters of the text connect the principle of addition (which regulates the pitches), and the principle of multiplication (which determines the durations).

Example 4.15 *Berliner Messe*, Kyrie, mm. 2–3 and 5–6

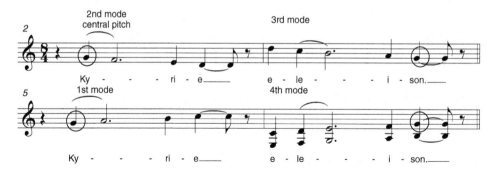

Table 4.1 Berliner Messe, *melodic modes in Kyrie*

	K	e	K	e	C	e	C	e	K	e	K	e
Soprano		T	T	T	T	T	T	T	T	T	T	T
Alto	M	M	M	M	M	M	M			M	M	M
Tenor		T	T	T	T					T	T	
Bass			M	M								M

K = Kyrie C = Christe e = eleison

In the Kyrie, the four modes of the melodic movement are tied together as pairs in such a way that the second pair is a mirroring of the preceding one on a horizontal axis (Example 4.15). Table 4.1 shows how a new voice appears with every word (Kyrie eleison twice), then symmetrically disappears (Christe eleison twice) and ultimately reappears (Kyrie eleison twice). The roles of the voices are determined exactly: alto and bass are M-voices (M, in parallel sixths), soprano and tenor are T-voices (T, with changing positions).

In an understandable variation from the scheme, the M-voice alto begins instead of the T-voice soprano. Later on, at the end of the Christe section and beginning of the second Kyrie section, the soprano follows the simple scheme and sings tintinnabuli notes to a melodic voice, which does not sound in the alto but can easily be deduced from the rules outlined above (Table 4.1).

Multiplication
While additions and subtractions regulate the number of notes in melody or harmony, multiplications exclusively affect rhythm. The (historic) model of composition in which the multiplication of note values (and thus simple proportions) determines the relation of the voices to each other is called the 'proportional canon.' Contrary to the traditional canon,

Example 4.16 Proportional canon

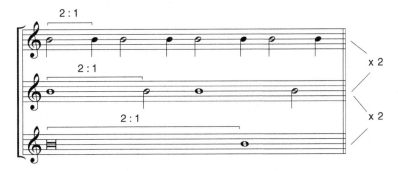

in which the voices enter in the same rhythm consecutively, in the proportional canon the note values of the original voice are lengthened or shortened in a certain ratio. Pärt reduces this compositional model to its archetypical simplest form, which is fundamental to all his proportion canons: the simplest form of multiplication, duplication, determines the ostinato three-beat rhythm of every single voice (2:1 long-short) as well as the relation between the voices (1:2 (2=2x1), 2:4 (4=2x2), 4:8 (8=2x4) and so on).[18] Most of the time, the distance between the voices is one octave, and, as in a traditional canon, they can enter consecutively or simultaneously (Example 4.16).

The very titles of Pärt's works give strong hints for their interpretation. The title *Arbos* (*Tree*) translates the archetypical formal disposition of the tree into the visible realm: in a canon of proportions, the same melodic line is audible two, three, four times, and so on; in a tree, the trunk divides into two branches and these split up into two smaller branches, and so on. The proverbial title *Festina lente* (*Make haste slowly*), on the other hand, points towards the paradoxical time structure of the canon of proportions: as the melody proceeds fast and slow at the same time, the fastest voice always sounds at the same time as its own stretched past. In such a way, the linear perception of time, which proceeds from the past into the future, is being split, and perception changes to the sense of a static surface with inner movement.

IV Melodic motion

There is a set of possibilities for how Pärt utilizes the four modes of melodic motion to design musical lines in connection with the principle of addition. Two groups of possibilities determine a large number of works and can thus be viewed as archetypes that are more concrete than the aforementioned ones but that are still general enough to permit various individual characteristics with different symbolic value: first, descending or ascending scales (i.e. melodic lines formed out of one of the four modes); second, wave movements that combine all four modes.

Falling and rising scales

The concept of falling is connected to the concept of gravity: accordingly, falling scales follow a kind of melodic gravity which has its center in the tonic. For rising scales, in another translation of known physical laws into musical terms, force is needed to overcome this gravity. This force might be seen as not intrinsic in the musical material like the melodic gravity, so it can also be understood as a lifting up from the depths which is produced by an outside force; this depth has for centuries been a symbol for darkness, underworld, death, damnation, desperation (*De profundis clamavi*), or degradation. A falling scale, however, does not only lead into this depth but, viewed from a different perspective, it also leads downward from above. Therefore, it depends on the situation and the concrete context which symbolic form is taken on by this archetypical constellation of the descending scale.

In tintinnabuli pieces, the ascent and the descent often are in accordance with one another. For instance, a descending scale over the setting of the opening ("Exordium") text, "Passio Domini nostri Jesu Christi secundum Joannem," of *Passio* introduces the basic tonal material of the Evangelist's part (A-minor scale for the M-voice and A-minor T-triad). In contrast, the piece ends with a simultaneously ascending and descending D-major scale, set to the added words "Qui passus es pro nobis, miserere nobis. Amen." The A minor of the Evangelist's text, which throughout the whole *Passio* was perceived as the tonic, ultimately turns out to be a dominant preparation for the 'actual' tonic D, a fifth lower. The strong effect of this D-major closing ("Conclusio") is based on the interplay of the surprising reinterpretation of A minor from tonic to dominant, the brightening into major, and the scales moving in opposite directions with the ascending line now in the upper voice. In religious interpretation, this becomes a sounding symbol of the anticipated or rather promised resurrection as well as the hearing of the uttered plea.[19]

La Sindone is also framed by ascending and descending scales. In a dramatic gesture, this work starts with a loud dissonant sound: as in Example 4.14, parallel tritones and held notes, which further sharpen the sonic picture, dominate (Example 4.17).

The ascending movement at the end of the piece moves from the diatonic world of A minor in the tritone-rich, tonally vague sound world of the beginning; however, this time it is rooted by the sustained tonic E', into which all string instruments (which have been ascending to the highest registers), fall little by little. As careful as one might want to be

Example 4.17 *La Sindone*, opening

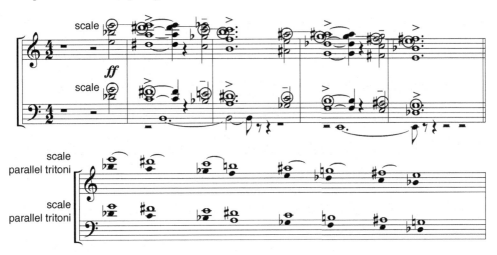

Example 4.18 *Litany*, opening

with interpretation in regard to contents, in context with the 'theme' of the composition offered in the title (*La Sindone* refers to the Shroud of Turin), the association of burial appears at the beginning at the piece, whereas the end might suggest resurrection. Nevertheless, the work does not close with a quasi-triumphal consonance but with a soft four-note chord on E, with both major and minor third. We don't yet see face to face.

While *La Sindone* ascends to the highest range at the end, the beginning of *Litany* descends from there to the earthly, human middle range of a sung prayer (Example 4.18). Here, polyphony is created by sustaining paired scale notes in different octaves. There are no T-voices at all. The symbolic message here can be seen as God's turning to man, which precedes the prayers set in *Litany*. In conversation with Restagno, Pärt describes the beginning of *Litany* as such: "In the beginning, there is a voice singing a beautiful prayer, and in the same instance the answer comes from heaven … Before man can ask God for help, He is already with him. The time in which these actions take place does not belong to us."[20]

Example 4.19 *Cantus*, opening

Cantus in Memory of Benjamin Britten (the Latin word *cantus* means chant) from 1977 is the earliest and best-known example of a descending scale, which, beginning with a single note, expands by one note every time it repeats. The principle of addition is connected with the multiplication of note durations in the rhythmical mode of the individual voices (long-short, 2:1) as well as in a canon of proportions with five time layers in total (Example 4.19).

With its title, this work looks back on an important tradition, predominantly in the fifteenth century, in which, in a special kind of dedicated composition (called a deploration), the death of admired composers is lamented and their compositional style is recognized. Therefore, the symbol of this 'chant' on the descending scale is the 'lament', an affect which is traditionally illustrated by a descending motion. But *Cantus* is more than that, and in the context of the general meaning of archetypes, it is also more than a posthumous homage to an individual composer: one could call it a musical verbalization of the human consciousness of life's finite nature. It is obvious with the first appearance of notes in the sound-world of this piece that the continued process of addition has to get to the limit of music playable in the low range of the instruments. Very close to this limit, all the voices gather to form the A-minor T-triad, the constant movement stops, and the diatonic dissonances in the moving surface are resolved. This over-long held sound, however, is not the end of the piece; instead, it is the transition to the silence of the final rest, in which the reverberation of the bells leads to sounding silence.

Waves

Ascending and descending scales have a directional tendency, which, as in *Cantus*, can be made relative by making all scales return to their initial point of departure. In contrast, musical curves, which can be called wave-shaped, are characterized by symmetry and balance. In the simplest wave form, a movement away from a central pitch is balanced by a movement back to it. The resulting 'half circle', composed of two scale modes, is then mirrored around the center pitch. Only the principle of addition or subtraction allows for a cone-like sound area to develop. In *Most Holy Mother of God* the wave motion and the subtraction process are clearly

Example 4.20 *Most Holy Mother of God,* M-voice mm. 1–23, wave motion

Example 4.21 *Tabula rasa,* "Silentium," opening

identifiable but they are modified by the structure of the text: each one of the four calls begins alternately with the highest and the lowest note of the tightening wave and stays in the framework given by the subtraction process (Example 4.20).

A widening wave proceeding from the center pitch regulates every detail as well as the progression of "Silentium," the second movement of *Tabula rasa,* another canon of proportions. At the end of this movement, in the low range, every pair of voices also crosses the border from played music into sounding silence (Example 4.21).

The main section of *La Sindone* is also based on an expanding wave motion, which multiplies to a multi-voiced web of sound in a canon of proportions. Here, however, the T-notes (alternating barwise -1 +1/ +1 –1) join with the repeated notes of the wave, creating voices with strong melodic characteristics. In addition, the wave does not sound completely

Example 4.22 *La Sindone*, mm. 25–26, 28–30, 33–40

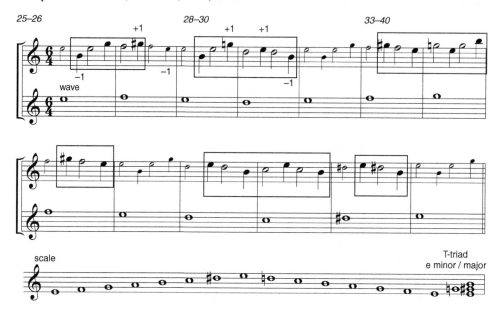

but only the section around the highest and the lowest notes (in Example 4.22 the notes in the marked areas); later we also hear the notes around the axis note E and, increasingly, all notes. The lines of the musical portrait get lost just like the facial features on the shroud or like the fragmentary way we can grasp the origin and story of this shroud: the net of musical voices becomes the image of the texture of the shroud and its historic entanglement.

V *Arbos*: the tree

In the context of this introduction to the basic elements of the tintinnabuli style it is neither possible nor reasonable to describe all its ramifications. To stay with the image of a tree: as a basic rule, one can determine that whichever way tintinnabuli works grow most develop from the two main branches of triad and scale or, viewed reversely, compositionally join together to the unity of the trunk. The schematic image of a tree is also found in family trees which document lineage. In *Which Was the Son of…*, a choral work, Pärt set Jesus' family tree to music. He finishes with the lines "which was the son of Adam, which was the son of God." Inasmuch as this is true for all of us, the musical tree of a composition ultimately becomes a mirror of our lineage and thus our status as God's children.

Further reading

Leopold Brauneiss, "Arvo Pärt's Tintinnabuli – Style: Contemporary Music Toward a New Middle Ages?" In *Studies in Medievalism,* vol. 13, *Postmodern Medievalism*; (Woodbridge: Boydell & Brewer, 2005), pp. 27–34.

Hermann Conen (ed.), *Arvo Pärt: Die Musik des Tintinnabuli-Stils* (Cologne: Verlag Dohr, 2006).

Paul Hillier and Tõnu Tormis, *On Pärt* (Copenhagen: Theatre of Voices Edition: 2005).

Peter Sloterdijk, *Kopernikanische Mobilmachung und ptolemäische Abrüstung* (Berlin: Suhrkamp, 1987).

5 Analyzing Pärt

THOMAS ROBINSON

Introduction

The music of Arvo Pärt is challenging. It exhibits such simplicity on the surface that just beginning an analysis can be demanding. Consequently, in the music-theoretical literature, few scholars have attempted full-scale analyses. Nevertheless, Pärt and his music make regular appearances in both the scholarly and the popular presses. Both venues offer biographic profiles, reviews of recordings and performances, and reflections upon his cultural milieu or his representation in the media. This valuable commentary would only be strengthened by a complementary assortment of analyses that engage a number of existing theories and develop new methods.

What can explain the paucity of music-theoretical scholarship on Pärt's music? First, he is a living composer. Not only have his predecessors from bygone centuries had more time to become objects of interest, but also their temporal distance equates, for many, to the critical distance necessary for informed analysis to occur. The second problem facing Pärt's music is its inescapable label: 'minimalist.' As labels go, this one is not problematic, and its accepted definition applies reasonably to his music, but it is a deterrent to theorists and analysts who find minimalist music of little value, regardless of composer, regardless of technique. Finally, Pärt's enormous success and popularity, coupled with an austere and reclusive persona, arouses suspicion in some casual observers. Despite these impediments it is not axiomatic that music composed by a living, minimalist, unusually popular composer cannot reward rigorous analysis, but it remains to be seen what kind of analysis is the most rewarding in Pärt's case.

One engaging recent analysis of Pärt's music simply couldn't have been done in the same way just twenty years ago. John Roeder's analysis of *The Beatitudes* employs relatively new ideas about triadic transformation, and it unfolds in real time through computer animation.[1] Ideal for those who prize being 'present' in the music (a disposition that for some precludes any analysis at all), Roeder's analysis does not break the meditative focus; it enhances it. The triadic transformations are displayed and mapped as the music progresses in real time. Of course, one can simulate this by simply reading any printed analysis while listening to a recording of the piece in question. Roeder's analysis, however, does this for the reader, which is significant. It doesn't just bridge the gap between the music and the analysis; it merges the two.[2] What is more, the analytical apparatus itself stands as a beautiful and moving complement to both music and text.

Describing the nature of musical analysis, theorist Ian Bent maintains that analysis "is the means of answering directly the question 'How does it work?'"[3] To analyze Pärt's music, then, is to determine how it works, and even people with only a passing familiarity know that Pärt has developed his own specific, idiosyncratic technique called tintinnabuli. While it is at one level merely a 'procedure' that allows its user to generate music *from* music, the tintinnabuli technique no more explains how Pärt's music works than the twelve-tone technique explains how Arnold Schoenberg's works. Because the tintinnabuli technique is so crystal clear, critics of Pärt's music might conclude that the 'how' is already answered and is presented forthrightly on the surface of the piece, leaving the analyst with nothing to do.

There is more to do, of course. Bent continues on the nature of analysis: "Its central activity is comparison. By comparison it determines the structural elements and discovers the functions of those elements. Comparison is common to all kinds of musical analysis ... comparison of unit with unit, whether within a single work or between two works, or between the work and an abstract 'model.'"[4] Bent concludes that comparison, the act of determining similarity and difference, is "the central analytical act." Therefore, when analyzing Pärt we might build upon a preliminary assessment of the tintinnabuli components – the 'how' – by comparing the results with other possibilities, or by comparing the procedures to other potential or hypothetical ones. In essence, we may investigate the process – the decisions leading to the results – as much as or more than we analyze the results themselves.

Pärt's tintinnabuli music is radical music in need of radical analytical methodologies or, more modestly, radical application of current theoretical tools. Tintinnabuli emerged in the 1970s as a new, original technique but only after Pärt's reacquaintance with and reevaluation of medieval and renaissance music. In the same way, successful analysis of his music might come only after a revisiting of existing methodologies, even those one might not expect to engage when analyzing 'minimalist' music. In order to hasten optimistically the arrival of this success, the first part of this chapter surveys several theoretical and analytical sub-disciplines considering 'how' and even 'how well' each might work when analyzing Pärt. The second part offers a set of deeper analyses, which extend some of these ideas further, investigating Pärt's *process* along the way.

Part 1: analytical approaches

Because the music Pärt composed prior to his invention of tintinnabuli broadly utilizes techniques for which there are currently analytical models (for example twelve-tone technique or collage) they are not under discussion in this chapter. Instead I will concentrate on tintinnabuli itself, which has been the hallmark of Pärt's style since 1976, and has matured into an unmistakable, unique language. It is important, however, to understand the technique as it stands in relation to his earlier music, which was largely serial or aleatoric. The final piece of this earlier period, *Credo* (1968), stands as a compendium of contemporary avant-garde techniques. Tintinnabuli, then, is not just an idiosyncratic dialect imbued with medieval coloring; it is a radical and deliberate turning away from the new and avant-garde as much as it is a reassessment of and reacquaintance with the old and established. To analyze Pärt's music, perhaps one must adopt a similar stance towards old and new analytical techniques. Analysts must devise brand new techniques and, in equal measure, engage existing theories in completely new ways.

What follows is a selection of five distinct analytical methods. Each is considered with an eye towards its possible application to Pärt's music. No complete analyses are provided, but calls for further study are made in each case. Throughout the discussion, 'analysts' are understood to be musicians interested in discovering how Pärt's music works, be they musicologists, theorists, or otherwise labeled. A distinction commonly gets made, particularly in the USA, between the disciplines of musicology and music theory, and most of the ideas represented here fall into the latter camp.[5] Broadly speaking, and despite the considerable overlap between the disciplines, music theory tends to examine the properties of and the relationships between musical components themselves, usually in an abstract, even speculative, manner without respect to any particular composition, while musicology tends towards historical and contextual studies. 'Analysis,' then, can engage both disciplines, using a wide variety of approaches. Those that follow below are just a few of many threads that could be picked up by future analysts of Pärt's music.

Style analysis
Sometimes the application of a single music-theoretical concept to a passage of music offers profound insight into a particular progression of harmonics, a series of intervals, or a complex hierarchy of rhythms. This profundity comes at a cost, however. An insightful theory tends to illuminate a narrow range of musical domains, leaving other elements of the music in the dark, to be investigated by other means. Jan LaRue's expansive

method, described in his landmark text *Guidelines for Style Analysis*, reverses this arrangement.[6] While it may not have the *explanatory* strength of an abstract general theory, style analysis is a most comprehensive *descriptive* technique, requiring the "observation of every nook and cranny of a piece."[7] As its name suggests, it can provide the framework for comparison of music from across genres and across eras. Additionally, it can serve as the background for further analysis, providing vital signs for someone performing a closer examination: "[A]s a point of departure, this style-analytical framework can serve musicologist, theorist, and performer alike."[8]

In LaRue's "nooks and crannies" lurk musical elements that can be sorted into his well-known domains – sound, harmony, melody, rhythm, and growth. While the meanings of the first four are self-evident, 'growth' is LaRue's dynamic replacement for the more static, but more widely understood, term 'form.' Each of these five domains is to be investigated in the 'large dimension' (the overall piece), the 'middle dimension' (the sections or movements), and the 'small dimension' (note-to-note events). There are, thus, fifteen areas of description in a typical style analysis.

In his book, LaRue systematically outlines what kinds of things one might expect to find in each of these fifteen subdomains, and he suggests how the findings might be organized and presented. Of his many recommendations, one seems particularly relevant when analyzing Pärt's music: "The proper test for observation is not 'Is it true?' but 'Is it significant?'"[9] This claim might seem to suggest that the truth-value of an observation is irrelevant in an analysis of style. On the contrary, it calls us not to avoid truth in favor of subjective critique, but to select from numerous possible true statements only those most significant, cautioning readers against drifting into an endless enumeration or listing of facts. The significant facets of a composition are those that are unusual for a composer of that time or place, those that are more or less distinctive to the composer or piece.

To perform a style analysis of one of Pärt's pieces is to compile as many of his distinctive musical elements as are meaningful and to present them in such a way that they can be compared efficiently to the corresponding elements of another's style. Table 5.1 does exactly this with his *Orient & Occident* for string orchestra (2000). On its own, the table ably describes Pärt's compositional style. Surely, anyone familiar with Pärt's music would recognize its description here, even if all references to the composer and his tintinnabuli technique were removed. Its real strength, though, derives not from the observations themselves, but from how those observations are situated in the contexts of Pärt's oeuvre, of minimalism as a genre, and of contemporary music.

A good style analysis invites the analyst to go further. LaRue suggests going beyond description into function: from the 'what' to the 'how.' It is

Table 5.1 *A simple style analysis of* Orient & Occident

	Large dimensions	Middle dimensions	Small dimensions
Sound	Consistent fabric throughout (string orch.)	Texture mostly 4+1, with varied assignments:	*n.v.* passages employ glissando (reflecting titular "Orient"?)
	Some interior sections use *divisi*.	The "4" = two T-voices & two M-voices.	
	Low textural contrast between sections	Crisp alternation between two main fabrics:	Frequently, the "1" in 4+1 = a drone
	Range consistent throughout	*n.v.* = no vibrato; monophonic.	
		espr. = espressivo; T- and M-voices.	
		Sharp dynamic contrast due only to the inter-sectional measures of rest. (G.P.)	
Harmony	(Mono-) coloristic; Static.	Sections distinguished by change in emphasis:	Dissonance is produced by the "passing" of the M-voice between the tones of the T-voice's triad.
	Neomodality (LaRue, 54):	Modal center may shift from D to G.	
	n.v.: D E♭, F♯G A B♭, C♯D.	T-voice triad shifts D–F–A to G–B♭–D.	
	espr.: D E♭, F♯ G A B♭, C/C♯ D.	Drone tone changes from section to section.	
	T-voice on D–F–A or G–B♭–D.	Harmony is consequence of the coincidence of T-voice and M-voice. *espr.* passages often conclude with a sustained harmony, which (coupled with G.P.) suggests a cadential effect.	
Melody	Nature of melody (in M-voice and in *n.v.* passages) consistent throughout.	Melodic fragments (*n.v.* and *espr.* passages) are of varied but short length (1–6 quarter notes).	Each fragment is stepwise and either ascends or descends exclusively.
			(Some descending *espr.* passages, however, have an anacrustic ascending leap.) Slurs in *espr.*; Glissandi in *n.v.*
Rhythm	Uniform tempo: quarter note = 120–132.	Most measures contain three quarter notes.	Within each lettered section, there is an irregular alternation between *n.v.* and *espr.* passages.
	Penultimate section: *più lento* to *lento*.	One could reduce each measure of 6 to two measures of 3, but each longer measure contains only a single sustained chord or tone, which suggests a pause in the hypermeter. (The following rests support this idea.)	Scotch snap used in *n.v.* passages on ascending or descending semitones.
	No time signature, which: (1) is a result of the measures' varied lengths, 3, 6, and 9 quarter notes; and (2) suggests an absence of hierarchy of metrical accent.		

	Large dimensions	Middle dimensions	Small dimensions
Growth	Sections A–L vary in length.	The harmony or pitch class that precedes the section-ending G.P. or rest varies, whether *n.v.* or *espr.* If this is construed as quasi-cadential, then the moment of "cadence" is frequently unpredictable due to the varied natures of both closing harmony and section length.	The tintinnabuli technique insures consistent change in the starting melodic pitches. While mode is consistent, the small ascending or descending fragments project different tones of reference tones in the mode.

the case with some of Pärt's more transparent demonstrations of tintinnabuli that the very descriptions produced by style analysis differ little from descriptions of tintinnabuli itself, so closely bound are the 'what' and 'how.' Once this is acknowledged, however, one can make useful comparisons of Pärt and tintinnabuli with other composers and their procedures. What is more, LaRue does not shy away from subjective evaluation. For him, style analysis "systematically furnishes much of the basis for objective evaluation," and he is as systematic in his evaluative process as in his analytical one.[10] While many analysts of Pärt's music might be reluctant to do any work that may be construed as subjective criticism, such efforts seem desired, even necessary, for at least two reasons: First, Pärt's music is difficult to classify, a fact noted by its supporters and its detractors. To the former the music is innovative, fresh, and rich; to the latter it is derivative, tedious, and empty. Style analysis might be a base-level classification, a starting point for reconciliation of these opposing views. Second, as Pärt routinely is the recipient of *negative* criticism, some well-reasoned *positive* criticism is entirely welcome.

Musical hermeneutics

Music analysis can employ a technical language with terms and concepts utterly foreign to the non-musician. This kind of discourse is essential to the furthering of the discipline, but other kinds of analysis seek to interpret the abstract structures and processes of music using words and ideas familiar to most anyone. While some analyses articulate the form and structure of a composition and, in support of their claims, adduce only the notes in the score or other compositional and theoretical conventions, other analyses look beyond the score to the composer, to nature, or even to the spiritual realm in search of a meaning that transcends the notes on the page. Unsurprisingly, proponents of both methods historically have been at odds with one another. At the turn of the twentieth century, a rising formalism, arguing that the essential core of music was its structure and form, met some resistance in the minds of many for whom form was simply a means of projecting deeper things: emotion and meaning.[11] The formalists didn't deny the existence of emotion or meaning altogether but found such things to be either too nebulous or too subjective to be assessed in a critical, defensible way. Furthermore, if there were such things in music, they existed only in the individual mind of the listener, not as some kind of message from the composer. Insisting that composers *expressed* specific meaning in their music, the dissenters found a voice in musical hermeneutics.[12]

Intended not to explain but to interpret the music, hermeneutical analyses identified the usual elements of tonal structure (phrase and cadence, harmony and counterpoint), but did so in service of the meanings they carried. For instance, melodic ascent and descent might represent, respectively, eager striving and solemn withdrawal. Stability was mapped onto consonance, struggle onto dissonance. Shifts between parallel major and minor keys carried obvious emotional connotations as well. As a result, an analysis could tell a story; it could reveal a drama that unfolded in real time and was a direct expression of the composer. To some this was, moreover, the spiritual intent of the composer, not just the 'story' of the composition. Theorist Lee Rothfarb writes that, for hermeneutic pioneer Hermann Kretzschmar, "music was communicative, and form was merely the 'husk and shell' for communicating a spiritual content."[13] The object of analysis lies beyond the form itself and in the soul of the composer. To better understand Pärt's spirituality, then, one might tune out the unintentionally distracting extra-musical elements and listen to what the formal structure might have to say.

For musical hermeneutics to have any success it requires a reliable, and to some degree predictable, musical language. Major-minor tonality, with its well-regulated conventions of harmonic syntax, dissonance resolution, and metrical hierarchy, offers up an array of phenomena for emotional interpretation. Music from other repertoires could profit from similar analysis but by using hermeneutics of an entirely different sort. Pärt's tintinnabuli makes use of some tonal elements while eschewing others, making it an interesting subject for a hermeneutical approach.

Mein Weg hat Gipfel und Wellentäler (*My Path has its Peaks and Valleys*) for organ (1989) is a good example of Pärt's more advanced technique. Here, there are three M-voices (right hand, left hand, and pedals) each paired with a T-voice, all moving at different speeds. Notably, the T-voices articulate an E-minor triad: E, G, B; while the M-voices move through the fifth mode of A harmonic minor, sometimes known as the 'Phrygian dominant': E, F, G♯, A, B, C, D, E. This creates not only the chromatic clash of G and G♯, but also, as the multiple voices coincide, a broader selection of secondary harmonies than would be found in the simple diatonic collection.

A hermeneutic reading of *Mein Weg* cannot ignore the ever-present tonic triad. Whether it is a moment of ultimate triumph or resolute defeat, the arrival of the final tonic in tonal music is, hermeneutically speaking, the end. To affect this outcome, any number of means have been used by the great composers, but departure and return, to and from the tonic, is at the core of the tonal dynamic. Pärt's piece, on the other hand, is a world without end. Its tonic triad never leaves the listener. Through the ringing of the tintinnabuli, Pärt has removed harmonic syntax from the drama. There is no harmonic progression. Rather, we are presented with an E-minor triad, and dynamism arises not from what happens to that triad, how it is transformed or elaborated, but how the melody, with its strident G♯, behaves in the unflinching face of E minor.

Like most M-voices in the tintinnabuli style, those in *Mein Weg* alternately rise and fall. They first appear in short segments, then in gradually longer swaths, and finally in shorter segments receding into the triad. As the segments rise and fall from note to note, so does the overall series of starting tones for each segment, thus creating ascending and descending fragments nested in other large-scale ascents and descents. How would a hermeneutics of Pärt's music interpret the inevitability of such a structure, whose playing out to completion is largely preordained after the first few measures are presented? Is the listener granted a kind of omniscience here that the listener of a typical tonal piece is not? What is to be made of the seeming indifference of the three voice pairs moving at different rates?

More than just compositional traits, the rising and falling in *Mein Weg* undoubtedly relate to the titular "peaks and valleys" of the poem on which the piece is based.[14] Further, the rhythmic and durational independence of the lines is suggested by the poem's final line: "My road. Yours." While each of us travels a different road, with different highs and lows, the roads are in many ways the same, and they all have the same destination. In tonal music, expectations can be delayed, confirmed, or denied, and the listener is often along for the ride, experiencing the drama first hand, but in tintinnabuli the listener is aware of the outcome. The drama lies in the playing out of a *fait accompli*.

Another twentieth-century hermeneutical methodology appraises the inherent properties of scale degrees in the major and minor modes. By examining how scale degrees tend to behave across a wide range of tonal music (including popular music) and hypothesizing what their patterns might express, Deryck Cooke ascribes an expressive meaning to all scale degrees in major and minor as well as to sixteen common melodic fragments. For example, "to rise from the tonic to the dominant through the major third – or in other words to deploy the major triad as a melodic ascent 1–3–5 – is to express an outgoing, active, assertive emotion of joy."[15] (Rising = 'outgoing'; dominant = 'active'; and the major third is the 'note of joy.')

There is much more to Cooke's methodology; other components of music (pitch, time, and volume) are understood as 'tensions', which interact with the expressive scale degrees to create 'musical energy.' Pärt's music might be explored with Cooke's method, but some interesting decisions would have to be made. Foremost among them would be how to assess those modes which are not the common major or minor modes. The expression embodied by the descent A–G–F–E in E Phrygian mode, for example, must be somewhat, but not entirely, similar to the one embodied by the same four-note descent in A minor. The intervals are the same, but assignments of tonic and scale degree are different. In mapping this kind of analysis to Pärt's music, which of Cooke's expressions should be simply transposed through modal rotation, and which would need to be reconfigured or redesigned altogether? Furthermore, would one need a large body of work comparable to the great tonal repertoire from which one can make general claims about expression and interpretation? These are difficult questions, but Pärt's music often is an investigation of the simple properties of mode and scale, so to ascribe meaning to such rudiments is a worthwhile endeavor.

Schenkerian analysis

The theories of Heinrich Schenker (1868–1935) are theories of tonal music. They offer insight into the structure of individual compositions (primarily works from the master composers of the common-practice era, loosely, from Bach to Brahms) as well as the nature of tonality itself. Schenkerian analysis is concerned primarily with the interrelation of harmony and counterpoint. By relating events on the surface of the music to their contrapuntal underpinnings, the analytical method reveals at least two important characteristics of tonal music: first, that various *hierarchical levels* of structure exist, from the note-to-note surface to a far simpler and deeper fundamental structure, and, second, that certain harmonic progressions at one level of this structure can serve to *prolong* a single harmony at a deeper level of structure (more on this below). We may consider then that composing tonal music is essentially a means of elaboration, and it is the analyst's, and even the listener's, task to deduce the underlying structure (the 'background') from the elaborate surface (the 'foreground'). Finding one's way among the levels in between (the 'middleground') can provide a much richer understanding of the piece and offer a more profound listening experience as well.

Example 5.1 Prolongation: (a) passing tone; (b) passing tone with consonant support (prolongation by intervening dominant chord); (c) passing tones through tonic (prolongation by T-voice)

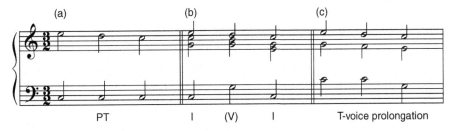

As powerful as the method is, Schenkerian analysis is not appropriate for music that is not constructed in a suitably elaborative manner. Many attempts have been made, however, to apply the technique to medieval, renaissance, post-tonal, and even popular music, with mixed results. While it was never intended to be a universal methodology, some of its graphic tools are nevertheless useful when trying to display other hierarchical structures and therefore are freely adopted and adapted with some success. As for Pärt's music, these tools may be of use, for although his method of prolongation is decidedly non-tonal, his compositions contain extended passages that reasonably can be represented by single, governing tones that together can be graphed in a quasi-Schenkerian manner.

In tonal music, or at least in a view of tonality even modestly informed by Schenkerian thought, a passing tone, when given consonant support by a change of bass tone, is said to give rise to a new consonant harmony, one that *prolongs* the harmony previously embellished only by a passing dissonance. Example 5.1a–b shows exactly this transformation. The dissonant passing tone in Example 5.1a gets supported by the dominant chord in Example 5.1b, a separate, consonant chord, which remains entirely subordinate to the surrounding tonic. Wholly consonant, it can, itself, be prolonged even to the point of its representing a tonal region in the key of the dominant, but it will remain subordinate to the opening and closing tonics, thus preserving the initial hierarchy.

In Pärt's tintinnabuli, prolongation of the tonic is far more literal. Example 5.1c shows another passing motion in the soprano voice. This M-voice is coupled with a second M-voice a sixth below. The passing tones, D and F, however, are not given consonant support. Rather, the T-voice, here in the bass, consistently reiterates tones of the tonic triad. The prolongation of tonic in Example 5.1b exists despite the absence of C or E in the dominant chord. With minimal effort, students of tonal music can learn to understand this, and even hear this, as prolongation of tonic, but it is not always immediately apparent. The prolongation in Example 5.1c, on the other hand, is inescapable. The T-voice's very job is to prolong, literally, the sounding of the tonic triad. The unfolding of the tonic triad is always upfront, at the surface of the music, preventing the passing tones' expansion into a new stable harmony. There are moments, of course, when the T-voice is sounding only one member of the tonic triad. At times like these, when other members of the triad are absent, the non-tonic tones in the M-voice might suggest non-tonic harmonies, even new key areas, but the T-voice always returns soon to the remaining tonic tones.

Because the register of a T-voice is predetermined by its relationship to the M-voice, multiple T-voices might at different points in the piece imply different inversions of the tonic triad, so common is the tendency to view the lowest note in a chord as important in tonal analysis. Apparently, though, the particular inversions matter very little to Pärt; the ringing of the tonic triad's tones is enough. At times the T-voice configuration will suggest a $^6_4$ chord.[16] This certainly should not be considered dissonant, as it might in tonal music, and furthermore should not be considered any less stable than $^5_3$ or $^6_3$ chords. In tonal music, the bass plays an integral role in defining consonance and dissonance, but Pärt's tonic triad is always consonant, regardless of 'inversion.' It is as if the triad's tones are constantly present in all registers, but at any given time we hear only those ringing in the wake of the travelling M-voices. So, while register plays an important role in the drama of Pärt's music, the structure is formed not in a directional pitch space, but truly in a pitch-*class* space, with no ceiling and no floor.[17] While the tonic triad is composed of the first, third, and fifth tones of the mode, there is no evidence, in the T-voice anyway, that the root is somehow more fundamental than the third or fifth pitches. Pärt's triad thus permeates all corners of the environment. This is, of course, quite different from the tonic triad in tonal music.

Schenkerian notation uses notes of various durational values (half notes, quarter notes, stemless note heads) to indicate relative level in the hierarchical structure and beams them together to show large-scale connections. There are, however, two important aspects of tonal music that the notation cannot reveal in Pärt's music. First, while we may uncover a certain hierarchy in the music, there are no *Stufen*. In tonal music, a *Stufe* is a scale step that, when standing in for a prolonged harmony (even tonal areas) at that scale degree, also participates in a harmonic progression governed by tonal syntax. There is no such progression in Pärt's music, but there tend to be distinct large-scale successions of a different sort. Tintinnabuli's M-voice usually moves stepwise to or from (and up or down) a single tone, which may or may not be the tonic tone of the prevailing mode. Throughout a composition in a single mode, the melodic activity may center on various tones such as this. Although melodic elaboration of these tones cannot be

Example 5.2 Background structure of *Missa syllabica*

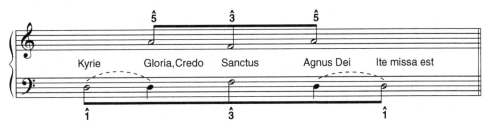

said to be a prolongation proper, the tones themselves do play a governing role in the melodic activity of a particular section of music. The notation, then, can purport to display only these changing centers of melodic
motion. Second, because upward and downward melodic motion is treated
equally, and because a root-position triad is no more fundamental than an
inverted one, stem direction should not be understood to represent participation in either a 'soprano' or 'bass' line. Counterpoint is at the heart of
Schenkerian analysis, so without a clear soprano and bass, the analytical
graph in Example 5.2 cannot properly be called Schenkerian. Nonetheless
it represents a reasonable simplification of the structure of the music at
hand.

In Pärt's *Missa syllabica* for SATB choir and organ, each of the sections
is distinguished by a specific pitch class or pair of pitch classes on which
the M-voices are based. Depending on the particular voice (soprano, alto,
tenor, or bass) and section (Kyrie, Gloria, Credo, Sanctus, Agnus Dei, Ite
missa est), the M-voices move by step up or down, to or from, these pitch
classes. Example 5.2 displays, united in a single background structure, the
pitch classes that represent the various sections of the piece. Stem direction
differentiates the two active voices (when there are two), and dotted slurs
indicate further prolongation of the D.

As argued above, these pitches do not represent harmonies, *Stufen*, or
key areas, but they do represent their respective sections in an important way. Each is the melodic, and thereby textual, focus of its section.
Furthermore, together they articulate the large-scale tonic triad of the
piece's mode, A-Aeolian. The two voices do not play the functional roles
of bass and soprano. They simply, in symmetrical alternation, spell out the
ever-present triad. The tonic triad is an important part of a Schenkerian
background structure, where the passing, goal-oriented motion of the soprano (see Example 5.1b) spurs harmonic progression and prolongation of
key areas. In *Missa syllabica* such deep-level motion is absent. All motion
in the M-voices is subordinated in some way to the tones of the triad. It is
the pervasiveness of the triad, in fact, that exposes a weakness of the quasi-
Schenkerian approach. All melodic motion is in the foreground, and the

triad forms the background, leaving no middleground to speak of. One of the strengths of Schenkerian analysis is how it allows the user to understand the sometimes complex, sometimes conflicting interaction of several different levels of hierarchical structure which is the middleground, but it is often difficult to find such a middleground in Pärt's music. What can be found, and what is part of its appeal, is the stark combination of foregrounded melodies and looming backgrounds, clear as a bell.

Set theory

In the analysis of many post-tonal works, theorists find pitch-class set theory helpful when handling a great deal of (1) collections of tones and (2) transformation of these collections (e.g., transposition, inversion). Its strength lies partly in its one-to-one assignment of integer to pitch-class[18] which enables systematic enumeration both of possible 'chords' and of the relations (whether transpositional or otherwise) between them. Pitch-class sets (pcsets) are quite useful in analysis of the free atonal works of the early twentieth century and can be incorporated fruitfully into certain aspects of twelve-tone analysis as well. On the other hand, music like Pärt's, often limited to a few chords, would normally be an unusual candidate for pitch-class set analysis. After all, if a composition were limited to a single, reiterated sonority, there would be only one pitch-class set to analyze. If one takes into consideration, however, the specific number of times the various pitch classes (pcs) reappear or are reiterated at different points, the details of the set's transformation over time are revealed.

Pärt's *Psalom* for string quartet (1985/1991) features a heterophonic, yet homorhythmic, pair of voices.[19] The voices express the same rhythm simultaneously, but when the lower voice sounds the pitches E, F, G♯, A, or B, the upper in turn sounds E, F, B, C, or D, respectively. The E 'Phrygian dominant' scale is thus divided between the two voices, which share the first two scale steps, E and F. Each voice, however, is limited to its own five-note collection. When labeled with pc integers, the lower voice's collection is notated not as the pitches {E, F, G♯, A, and B} but as the integers {4, 5, 8, 9, 11}. This collection, or set, persists throughout the piece with no transposition or inversion. The melodic segments, however, sometimes include all five pcs, sometimes just a few of them, and frequently reiterations of one or more of them. So while a label such as {4, 5, 8, 9, 11}, if applied throughout, seems to report little activity, the same label, enhanced to show the specific number of iterations of each pc in a given section, would reveal many shifts in emphasis from tone to tone *within the chord*.

Borrowing from mathematical set theory, the pitch-class *multiset* exhibits this multiplicity through a power notation like so: $\{4^2, 5^3, 8^1,$

9^2, 11^0}, where the exponents (superscript numbers) indicate the number of appearances of each pc.[20] Because the five pcs are constant throughout the piece, one may simply detach the exponents from the pcs themselves. Once the pcs are taken for granted, only the multiplicity of each pc is recorded: 23120. This becomes a kind of topographical survey of the chord at a certain point in time. This *multiplicity function* monitors the intensity or presence of each pc. Where 24200 indicates that pcs 9 and 11 are omitted and pc 5 appears four times, 00333 shows an even distribution of pcs 8, 9, and 11, yet no pcs 4 or 5. Throughout *Psalom*, these contours show great variety, from moment to moment or section to section.

Let us consider the broader implications for Pärt's music. To Paul Hillier, tintinnabuli is "music in which the sound materials are in constant flux, though the overall image is one of stasis, of constant recognition."[21] Throughout Pärt's work *stasis* is evoked by the unchanging triad or the repeated scale steps. *Flux*, on the other hand, is a product of the twisting and turning of the triad or the shifting emphases of different scale degrees. To track this shimmering or even undulating quality, one need only keep track of the rise and fall of multiplicity for each pitch class. For example, if the multiplicity functions report a shift from 24200 in one measure to 00333 in another, there will have been the following change in multiplicity: -2, -4, +1, +3, +3. Each entry in this *multiplicity difference function* reports the change in multiplicity of a different pc. Now, even in the absence of transposition, inversion, or similar operations, there is still a meaningful transformation revealed through set-theoretical tools.

In Example 5.3, *Psalom* is broken into its constituent sections, subsections, and sub-subsections, each delineated by a different type of articulation. The slur markings are the smallest segmentations in the analysis, and the first column lists the multiplicity functions for each. The preponderance of zeros indicates that at this structural level at least one of the five pcs is always omitted from the collection. Changes in bowing indications mark off the next level of structure, and the example records the multiplicities within, which essentially add all the multiplicities at the slur level. The third column lists the multiplicities of pcs between rests. The regularity and depth of these rests not only mark another level of segmentation, but also seem to breathe life into the material between them. Had these segments run together, without the intervening point of repose, the shift in multiplicity might be more difficult to perceive. Finally, the largest subdivisions are those marked by grand pauses (points of repose notated 'G.P.') with multiplicity difference vectors running down the right-hand side. Example 5.3 tracks the varying multiplicities of pitch class in these large sections. Take, for example, the last two multisets at the grand-pause level in the lower right. The penultimate multiset is represented by multiplicity function

Example 5.3 *Psalom*. Pc set {4, 5, 8, 9, 11} is listed only by its various five-position multiplicity functions. Multiplicity difference functions appear at right

	Slur	Bowing	Rests	Grand Pause	
m1		10000			
m2		23111	33111		
m4.8		10000			
m5		22120	32120	65231	
m9	10110				+1,+1,0,0,0
m10.2	33001				
m12	11110				
m13.4	22010	66121	76231		
m16		10000			−2,−2,0,0,0
m16.2		44231	54231		
m24	11110				+1,+1,0,0,+1
m26.3	22011		33121		
m28.6	21100				
m30	11011		32111	65232	
m33.3		00100			−3,−2,0,0,0
m34		11121	11221		
m39		11000			
m40		11011	22011	33232	
m43	21100				−4,+4,−1,−1,−1
m44.3	22010				
m45.3	22001				
m46.4	12010	56021	77121		
m49		10000			+1,0,+1,+1,0
m49.2		23111	33111		
m52.11			54120	87231	
m58	11100				−5,−2,0,0,0
m59.3	11010				
m61	01001	12011	23111		
m63	11010				
m64	00100				
m64.6	01010	01110	12120	35231	
m68	21110				−1,−3,−1,−2,0
m70.3	01001		22111		
m73	11110				+2,+1,0,+1,−1
m74.4	21010				
m75.7	11000	32010	43120		

22111. When subjected to the multiplicity difference function <+2, +1, 0, +1, -1>, each entry simply adds to (or subtracts from) its respective multiplicity. This produces the final multiset's multiplicity function: 43120.

The richly varying multiplicity a single pcset can exhibit in a single piece is impressive. Far from a monotonous rumble, the piece shimmers in a non-repetitive manner throughout. The interest lies not just in the pcs themselves but also in their changing numbers. This, perhaps, is the strength of both pitch-class multisets and tintinnabuli. If we aim to dig into the set itself, exploring its multiplicities and shading, we take the pitch classes for granted to a certain degree. Pärt's music often does exactly that; a limited collection of tones exists as a known, finite universe, and the infinite reveals itself in the bustling, vibrant interactions within.

Triadic transformation

Inspired by the work of nineteenth-century music theorist Hugo Riemann (1849–1919), some theorists in the late twentieth century developed tools for analyzing certain transformations of triads and, in some cases, seventh chords. The emphasis is on 'transformation' and not 'harmonic progression' because the variety of possible successions of triads using the only three basic neo-Riemannian voice-leadings exceeds that which is governed by the traditional harmonic syntax of tonal music. The strength of this theory is twofold. First is its comprehensiveness. One may link any two major or minor triads through one or more of these transformations. Second, there is a disregard for the realized inversion of a particular triad, allowing the transformations to occur in a more general pitch-*class* space. Using simple voice-leading one is thus able to account for chord successions outside the bounds of traditional tonal syntax. Pärt's music certainly contains harmonic successions that are unaccountable through tonal analysis. The prevalence of consonant 6–4 chords, for example, suggests operations in pitch-class space without respect to a specific bass line.

Each of the three neo-Riemannian transformations involves the moving of one of a major triad's tones either by a half step or by a whole step, resulting in a minor triad. The operations are reversible, transforming minor triads into major triads. The transformations, which can be seen in Example 5.4, are labeled P (parallel), L (leading-tone, or *Leittonwechsel*), and R (relative).

In his analysis of Pärt's *Beatitudes*, John Roeder takes this one step further, demonstrating how only three triadic transformations undergird the entire structure of the piece. His animated analysis shows these transformations occurring in real time. The transformations are what theorist Julian Hook calls "uniform triadic transformations" (UTTs). Designed to remedy some of the shortcomings of the neo-Riemannian operations and to be more broadly applicable, the UTT simply indicates (1) change (or no change) in mode with a minus or plus; (2) transposition if from major triad; and (3) transposition if from minor triad.

In Roeder's analysis, the prevalent UTT < -, 9, 8 > transforms B♭ minor into G major. (There is a mode change [-] and a transposition of nine semitones [9].) It also transforms G major into E minor. (There is a mode

Example 5.4 The basic neo-Riemannian transformations P, L, and R

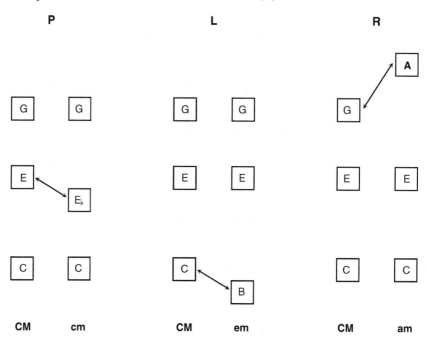

change [-] and a transposition of eight semitones [8].) As Roeder's figure (reprinted as my Example 5.5) beautifully displays, only three UTTs are used throughout *The Beatitudes*, and each lies in a specific position in the visual structure. As the piece unfolds, from the center of the diagram to the edges, one hears the < -, 9, 8 > transformations in the pillars, while the < -, 1, 0 > transformations create new pillars left and right. The < +, 2, 2 > transformations carry us forward as the previous pillars recede into the distance. It is a wonderful example of how a good analysis can visually represent the structure of a piece and also reveal details of its inner workings.

While *The Beatitudes* is well suited for discussion of unorthodox triadic transformations, not all of Pärt's music benefits from this type of analysis. The T-voice so often clearly articulates just a single triad that there may not be any evident triadic transformations at all. In some of the pieces with multiple M-voices however, new non-tonic triads emerge from the texture in spite of the T-voices' prevalence. Sometimes, too, the T-voices will not articulate the entire tonic triad, allowing other distinct triads to emerge clearly. Triadic transformations may then be applied at least to small-scale harmonic successions.

Other approaches

The preceding five approaches are not offered here with definitive or even complete analyses. They stand, however, as five examples of how one

Example 5.5 From John Roeder's analysis of *The Beatitudes*

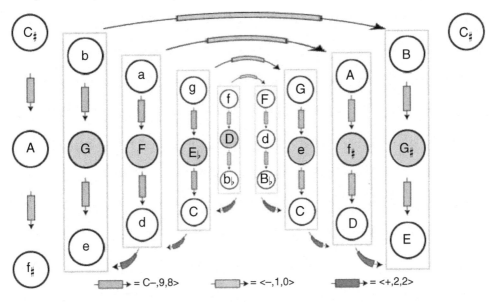

might begin analyzing Pärt using mainstream music-theoretical tools. Advancements in the study of perception and cognition of musical structures; theories of embodiment, semiotics, and gesture; and even study of rhythm all might be brought to bear on the tintinnabuli technique. Finally, in light of Pärt's extended study of medieval and renaissance music, it is not unreasonable to ask to what degree certain analytical techniques employed in the analysis of early music might be profitable in the analysis of Pärt's music. Specifically, an examination of Pärt's methods of text setting might be particularly fruitful.[22]

Following some of the threads set forth above and starting new ones, the analyses below examine the analytical ramifications of the tintinnabuli technique: the multiplicity concealed beneath a uniform surface, the interaction of text and music, and Pärt's personal expression of tonality.

Part 2: multiplicity and process

Multiplicity

In minimalist music there are, to varying degrees, at least two types of process at work. One type, referred to here as the 'rules of the game,' can establish both independent and dependent variables. For example: 'If X happens in one voice, then Y must happen in another.' In such cases, the

Example 5.6 Tintinnabuli technique and built-in diversity. Three-note segments in the M-voice produce unique three-term compositions of three in the T-voice

M-voice:	1	2	3	4	5	6	7	1	2
T-voice:	Fifth		Root		Third			Fifth	

Segments:	1	2	3	4	5	6	7	1	2	R + T + F
	F	F	R							1 + 0 + 2
		F	R	R						2 + 0 + 1
			R	R	T					2 + 1 + 0
				R	T	T				1 + 2 + 0
					T	T	T			0 + 3 + 0
						T	T	F		0 + 2 + 1
							T	F	F	0 + 1 + 2

composer uses other means (outside the process itself) for determining what X is. The other process, referred to here as the 'machine set in motion,' is the result of more comprehensive pre-compositional planning. This process is the unfolding in time of a multiplicity of events, all resulting from a pre-established formula, algorithm, or pattern. One might make the case that the two types differ only in degree not in kind and that it simply is a matter of the structural level at which the composer elects to begin the process. Nevertheless, it can be a useful distinction. Pärt's tintinnabuli compositions, in particular, distinctly exhibit one or both of these types. The process of composing tintinnabuli voices (T-voices) to an existing melodic voice (M-voice) clearly follows 'rules of the game.' Once the rules are established, the T-voice is entirely dependent on the M-voice. As for the M-voice, it might be freely composed or based on pre-existing material. If it is, itself, produced by another systematic process altogether, the M-voice works together with the T-voice as a 'machine set in motion', as multiple subprocesses of a larger scheme. Either type of process can be misconstrued sometimes as a relinquishing of control on the composer's part, but with Pärt we always must consider exactly how closely he controls the process even when it appears entirely automatic.

First let us consider the multiplicity of events that can result from the simplest of processes. The tintinnabuli process, even at its most basic, has an inherent diversity. This is due, in part, to the arrangement of the tonic triad's three tones among the seven diatonic scale steps. Example 5.6 shows one possible pairing of M-voice and T-voice.

Here, the tonic's fifth is coupled with scale degrees one and two, the root with three and four, and so forth. Underneath are the seven possible three-note segments of the scale with a different configuration of root, third, and triad for each. As it turns out, the T-voice, often understood as a static, droning backdrop, represents another instance of permutational diversity.

The small table on the right side of the figure shows the seven resulting combinations of triad members from the segments. There are ten different ways to combine three triad members, and the tintinnabuli scheme provides seven. The three missing ways are three roots, three fifths, and one of each. The disutility of the first two probably needs no comment, but it is interesting that the third one, a simple statement of root, third, and fifth, is impossible in a three-note segment of this scheme. As a result the T-voice is always imperfect, unstable as it floats through and around (but never directly sounds) the core of a piece's tonality – the triad. *Für Alina*, often cited as the piece that introduces tintinnabuli, exemplifies this variety as it breezes through these combinations in only a few minutes.

Most process music is, in essence, an invitation.[23] The listener's initial decision whether to accept or decline is based on the appeal of the proposition itself, even when the details of the musical outcome are unknown. When finally the process is carried out, regardless of whether the listener is rewarded or let down, the results of the original proposition are revealed. Some processes yield a great diversity of results, others a more modest production.

Suppose one were to combine systematically the twenty-six letters of the English with each other: aa, ab, ac, … zx, zy, zz. This simple proposal yields 26 x 26 = 676 results, each one unique. Some would be familiar words, others would be impossible to pronounce, but the invitation to explore each and every one remains. Because the sequence of formulations is predictable – one can anticipate 'ox' while contemplating 'om,' 'on,' and 'oo' – each 'word' can be studied without trepidation or concern for what might be yet to come.

Now suppose we had four quarter-notes and two pitches, high and low. In how many ways may we assign the four durations to two different pitches? The top of Example 5.7 displays, in the language of combinatorics, the five *compositions* of four (rhythms) into two distinct *terms* (in this case, 'high' and 'low' pitch).[24] Each term in the composition represents the number of high ('H') or low ('L') notes in the composition. Below one such composition (1+3) are its possible permutations. Pärt's *Sarah Was Ninety Years Old* for three singers, percussion, and organ (1977) was composed on the cusp of tintinnabulation's debut, yet it displays very few hallmarks of that technique. It does, however, work out in permutational detail one of the results of our simple proposal above, foreshadowing the more sophisticated ways in which his more mature style can produce great variety with simple means. In the first movement, the four permutations of one composition are slowly revealed (see the bottom of Example 5.7). By choosing a composition of four that has exactly four permutations, Pärt establishes four as a governing number for the movement. Each permutation of high

Example 5.7 *Sarah Was Ninety Years Old*, movement 1. Four permutations of a single two-term composition of four. Each term in the composition represents the number of high (H) or low (L) notes in a rhythmic cell.

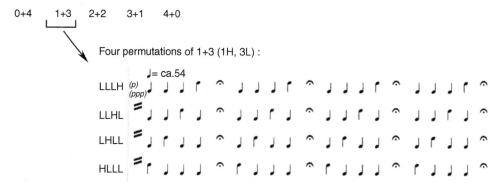

drum and low is repeated four times, separated by rests, before moving to the next permutation. Each is then repeated three times, then twice, then once. Here, one process (the permutations) proceeds matter-of-factly, while another process (diminishing repetition) superimposes a dramatic shape, forcing anticipation of an impending conclusion.

The second movement of *Sarah Was Ninety* achieves maximal multiplicity through similarly simple means. Pärt merges a twelve-note durational pattern with an eight-note pitch pattern, forming a tenor melody.[25] Example 5.8a shows the eight-note melody (a simple ascent and descent: E, A, B, C, D, C, B, A) as well as the twelve-note durational pattern (a variety of note lengths). As seen in Example 5.8b, if one were to assign the first duration to the first pitch, the second to the second, and so forth, the music would repeat itself after only three statements of melody (3 × 8) and two statements of rhythm (2 ×12).

This short cycle does not allow each of the eight melodic tones to pair up with each of the twelve rhythmic durations, but Pärt's clever solution does just this. A quick scan of Example 5.8c reveals how, by repeating the last pitch of one twelve-note rhythmic statement at the beginning of the next, Pärt is able to give each of the eight pitches exactly one turn at each of the twelve rhythmic positions. As a bonus, pitch no. 1 bookends the movement appearing in the first position of the first statement and the last of the last. With minimal materials, Pärt forges maximal variety.

The third and fifth movements are quite similar to the first, and the fourth explores similar permutations, but applied to pitch. In the sixth movement, we find something slightly different. Here there is a series of five harmonic intervals played on the organ. Example 5.9 shows the intervals as scale degrees (in A-Aeolian). In each subsequent system in the score

Example 5.8 *Sarah Was Ninety Years Old*, movement 2: (a) eight-note melody and twelve-note durational pattern; (b) a simple (hypothetical) one-to-one mapping of melody to rhythm; (c) Pärt's repeated-note solution

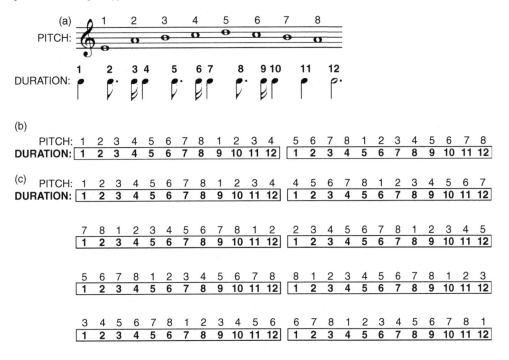

there is a rotation (by two positions to the left or three to the right) of this five-interval series. By system five, the A–B–C–D–E, which started in the upper voice, now appears in the lower. Because the upper and lower voices are out of sync with one another the organ part lacks any suggestion of a cadence; it is cyclical, without beginning or end. Even the recapitulation is not conclusive, because the five-system cycle of interval rotations is out of sync with the two-system cycle of chromatic inflections. Example 5.9 highlights in gray the tones that are inflected sharp by a simple accidental; in one system it is C, in the next it is D, and so on. In system six, the original interval rotation is back, but the inflection is different. This could go on through ten systems, each rotation getting the inflection it didn't receive the first time around. Pärt, however, stops after the seventh system. Perhaps this is to secure an ending on the first and third of the mode (A, C) and to allow systems 1–2 and 6–7 to act as bookending 'A' sections and systems 3–5, a 'B' section complete with a final 'dominant': (E, B).

Sarah Was Ninety undergoes a systematic exhaustion of combinational and permutational possibilities – it employs the 'machine-in-motion.' Pärt's tintinnabuli procedures, debuting shortly after *Sarah*, however, define 'rules of the game' – they suggest a similar wealth of possibilities, never to be exhausted by a single piece. People continue to play new games of backgammon, baseball, and bridge, even though the rules change very little over

Example 5.9 *Sarah Was Ninety Years Old*, movement 6, organ part. Systematic rotation of five dyadic pairs with alternating chromatic inflection

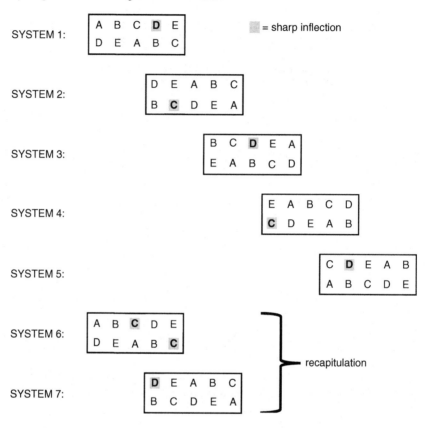

time. In the same way, the tintinnabuli technique allows for a great many compositional possibilities by combining one process with another (e.g., incrementally expanding M-voices, texts governing M-voices, or imitative processes), but many of Pärt's works succeed thanks only to his artful and strategic play within the rules.

Some of Pärt's designs are simple structures in which his strategic choice of elements makes possible the maximization of possibility in some domain. In *Cantate Domino canticum novum*, for four soloists (or choir) and organ (1977, rev. 1996), Pärt sets up a pair of M-voices, the length of their segments determined by the number of syllables in each word of text. When one voice ascends, the other descends. Were both voices to have started or ended on a consistent pitch, there would be only one set of intervallic pairs, as seen in Example 5.10a. After only a few words, the piece's intervallic inventory would be exhausted. What Pärt does, however, is to assign a consistent *starting* pitch to one voice and a consistent *ending* pitch to the other. As a result, every different word length creates different pitch

Example 5.10 *Cantate Domino*: pitch/syllable assignment scheme: (a) hypothetical one-to-one correspondence of upper- to lower-voice pitches. Both lines begin on B♭, offering a limited number of harmonic intervals; (b) correspondence of upper- to lower-voice pitches when first and last, respectively, are held constant

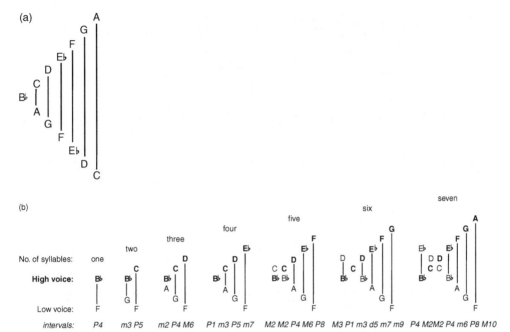

pairings and a different set of intervals. Example 5.10b shows the wedge formations of the crossing lines and lists the multiplicity of intervals below. By coincidence or by design, the largest word of text in *Cantate Domino* contains seven syllables. This allows each of the seven diatonic ones to be combined with each other under exactly one circumstance.

Because intervallic variety in the process established in *Cantate Domino* is dependent on variety of word length, the thirteen verses of Psalm 95 in Latin are a particularly productive choice of text. As Example 5.11 shows, the number of letters in each word and the number of words in each verse both are quite varied. The first half culminates with maximal diversity in verse six, the only verse with six- or seven-syllable words. Verse seven, immediately following, retreats to word lengths of no more than three syllables, much like the first line. With its high concentration of three-syllable words, this verse reasserts the principal tonality: B♭–C–D in the upper voice, A–G–F in the lower.

Individual words govern the inter-voice intervallic content, but the thirteen verses govern the overall form. The verses are arranged in four groups of three. In each group, the first verse is sung by a single voice, the second by a pair, and the third by all four voice parts. Example 5.12 displays their arrangement, as well as the bipartite division between verses

Example 5.11 *Cantate Domino*: tally of word lengths in each phrase

Word length in number of syllables

Verse number	1	2	3	4	5	6	7	Total:
1		///	卌					8
2	///	////	///	/	//			13
3	/	////	///		//			10
4	//	卌	//	//				11
5		卌	///	/				9
6	////	//	/	//	/	/	/	12
7	/	/	卌 卌 //					14
8	///	///	卌	//				13
9	//	///	卌	/	/			12
10	///	//	///	//	/			11
11	卌 /	卌 /	////	/	/			18
12	//	卌	卌	//				14
13	///	///	/	///				10
Total:	30	46	52	17	8	1	1	

Example 5.12 *Cantate Domino*: active vocal parts in each phrase

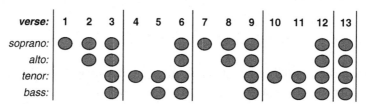

six and seven where the pattern of vocal parts repeats anew. The piece concludes emphatically in the thirteenth verse, where all four voices continue together. As the example shows, *Cantate Domino* patiently and evenly distributes its verses among the men's and women's voices, even as the flurry of irregularly repeating melodic fragments continues throughout.

In all of the foregoing musical examples we see two distinct dimensions at work. One, the *static* dimension, usually is inhabited by elements such as pitch class or mode. The other, the *dynamic* dimension, is where permutational abundance, or even maximization, resides. While the static dimension of Pärt's music is immediately apparent to most listeners, accustomed as they are to ascribing primacy to pitch-class relationships, it is the dynamic dimension that is often hidden, revealed only by careful study or focused listening. In *Sarah Was Ninety*, for example, the minimal materials are clear from the start but, as Example 5.8 shows, there is a systematic effort to combine these minimal materials in maximal ways. In *Cantate*

Domino, too, the most was made out of the fewest of pitch-class elements. The two dimensions, dependent on one another, are necessary for Pärt's music to work, but critics often see only the static dimension. Just as a third dimension is needed to turn a simple line into a vast plane, so must we turn the static dimension 'on its side,' so to speak, and start looking for the dynamism within.

Text setting as process

The setting of sacred texts is foundational to Pärt's compositional style. Even some instrumental works are set to texts that are not sung yet serve as a structural and formal influence. Pärt's vocal music engages the text in at least two distinct, even contrasting, ways, but it turns out that each dramatically foregrounds the words of the text in its own manner. In some pieces the word length and the number of words direct the melodic and formal material, and in others the pitch-melodic machinations are set in motion, acquiring one syllable or one word of text at a time. What follows is an analysis of each approach.

1. When text leads music

In many of Pärt's pieces, one finds both the 'machine in motion,' and various 'rules of the game.' *Cantate Domino* featured both, but the composer carefully insured that each worked according to his intentions. Composed in much the same way, *Zwei slawische Psalmen* (Two Slavonic Psalms) uses a predetermined mode in addition to ascending and descending fragments whose durations are determined by word lengths. It is evident, however, that in the domain in which Pärt had a degree of liberty – the starting pitches of the fragments – he made ideal choices.

The *Slawische Psalmen* use a five-part choir or five soloists, and Psalm 117 is set consistently in the A-Aeolian mode. At any given time there are two M-voices and two T-voices. The M-voices are usually soprano and tenor or alto and tenor, but there is one section where they are bass and countertenor. We do not hear all five voices simultaneously anywhere in the psalm. Like the M-voices in *Cantate Domino*, the M-voices here ascend and descend alternately from word to word, but whereas *Cantate Domino*'s M-voices move in contrary motion, the M-voices in *Zwei slawische Psalmen* are consistently in parallel sixths.

The ascending fragments begin on A in the upper voice and C in the lower, and the descending fragments begin on C in the upper voice and E in the lower. The interjecting "alleluias" diverge from this plan, consistently ascending or descending between E and A in the upper voice and G to C in the lower. This, along with the corresponding T-voice tones, draws attention to the C-major triad, a fitting diversion from the A-minor triad used

Example 5.13 *Zwei slawische Psalmen*, Psalm 117: (a) ascending and descending fragments of the upper and lower voices (arranged in pitch space); (b) ascending and descending fragments of the upper and lower voices (arranged in pitch-class space)

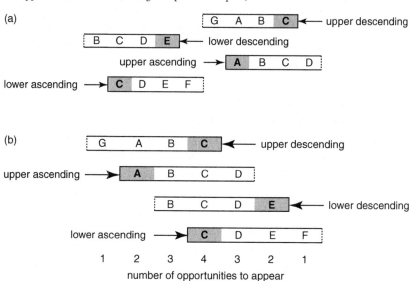

for the alleluias. Furthermore, when bass and countertenor are M-voices the starting tones are swapped. The lower, bass voice ascends from A and the countertenor from C. This is perhaps an acknowledgment of the tonic triad's greater stability in root position in this register. To start the fragments this way was no haphazard choice. First, and most obviously, this configuration insures that starting tones will always be members of the tonic triad, A minor. Second, because no word contains more than four syllables, the fragments, as shown in Example 5.13a, never overlap in the same word. Finally, when the possible pitch classes of each fragment are aligned atop one another, as in Example 5.13b, one can easily see the symmetrical arrangement of the number of opportunities for each pitch class to appear. Pitch class C appears in all four fragments, followed by B and D with three possible appearances each, followed by A and E, then G and F. A maximum word length of five would destroy this elegant pattern. If each fragment extended by one more pc to the right or to the left, the regular 1–2–3–4–3–2–1 pattern of pitch class occurrence would become 2–3–3–4–3–3–2, leaving no pitch class to appear in only one fragment and allowing four pitch classes to appear in three fragments. The inclusion of six-syllable words would even the distribution further, allowing every pc to appear in three different fragments, except C, which would be found in all four.

The arrangement of melodic fragments in Example 5.13b certainly produces diversity in the number of appearances of pitch classes, but it does much more. In the absence of a functional tonality, which utilizes leading tones and tonic/dominant relationships, the varied multiplicity of the pitch classes' appearance serves as a substitute hierarchy. The prevalent pitch C sits atop the hierarchy, and its appearance as both highest and lowest starting tone (see Example 5.13a) further strengthens this role. The F and the G, a fourth above and a fourth below the C, are the most subordinate in the hierarchy. The A and E, while seemingly subordinate in this way to B and D, form a sort of second tier by virtue of their membership in the tonic triad and their ubiquity as starting pitches; even one-syllable words use them. In tonal music, of course, the mere abundance of a pitch, pitch class, or chord has little or no bearing on its position in the hierarchy. In music such as this, however, whose motion is not goal-oriented towards a final 'tonic,' but inwardly directed, the centrality of a tone depends upon its frequent reiteration. Every word of the text, regardless of length, brings the listener back to the central tones. As the words extend in length, so the fragments extend from the triad. It is the absence of a harmonic goal and the reiteration of tones that direct attention to each word of text.[26]

2. When music leads text

In some of Pärt's compositions, the tintinnabuli technique is readily apparent, made plain by the metrically regular succession of M- and T-voices. When text leads the music, lengths of melodic fragments may vary. When music leads the text, however, syllables fall in line according to the compositional design. In a piece such as *Da pacem Domine* (2004), where M-voices and T-voices progress at the regular rate of one note per measure, every syllable of text receives equal emphasis. Although the inherent rhythm of the text is gone, the regularity of the melodic motion might easily inspire meditation upon the meaning of the text. For its part, *Da pacem* does this and more. The piece's polyphonic pattern builds in suspension-like figures that establish a hierarchy of harmonies, and it is the regular succession of tones that makes the interaction of these harmonies straightforward and apprehensible.

   Da pacem Domine is based on the Gregorian chant of the same name, which can be found in the upper of the two M-voices. Example 5.14a makes clear the interval of a third between the M-voices as well as the following of the two T-voices. When F is found in the chant (a frequent occurrence), the other M-voice is on D, which makes a tonic D-minor triad with the T-voices. These 'tonic harmonies' are enclosed in boxes in the example. The 'passing harmonies' are found in between, resulting from the combination of non-tonic M-voices with the T-voices. In this passage such passing harmonies may be major or minor triads, even major-seventh or half-diminished chords. Their stature as passing chords has nothing to do with their empirical consonance or dissonance. They are labeled 'passing' simply

Example 5.14 *Da pacem Domine*, mm. 1–14: (a) the underlying movement of T- and M-voices; (b) the ('T-suspensions') suspensions that result from displacement of the T-voice. Where the overlapping tones are part of the underlying chord, there is no suspension, and a simple arrow is given

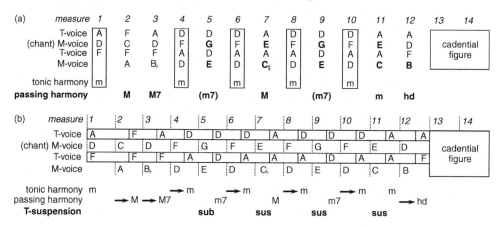

because they are not tonic; they include tones the T-voice is incapable of producing. As a result, this passage produces a mostly regular alternation of tonic harmony and passing harmony, dictated entirely by the original chant and the choice of a third as the interval between M-voices.

The texture of *Da pacem* complicates matters somewhat. After the first measure the arrival of each T-voice tone is delayed by one half of a measure. The chiming of the T-voice consistently lags behind its corresponding M-voice tone, and the two become syncopes, a pair of voices whose regular coincidence of tones has been displaced or made out-of-phase. As a result, each tone in the T-voice extends its reach into the downbeat of the following measure, perhaps even sounding against an M-voice with which it never would have been paired under a simpler tintinnabuli scheme. The downbeat of each measure is now a potential site for a new harmony not derived through standard tintinnabuli procedure. I refer to these moments of displacement as 'T-suspensions.'[27]

The underlying structure in the opening passage of *Da pacem* is largely an alternation of tonic harmony and passing harmony. The use of T-suspensions surely blurs the boundaries between these chords, but it also intensifies the motion from one to the next, heightening the expectation of the subsequent chords in the same way that suspensions in tonal music do. They also give rise to third-order harmonies, resulting from the interaction of tonic harmonies (first-order) and passing harmonies (second-order). Example 5.14b shows the staggering of T-voice against M-voice, and the various orders of harmony are shown below. The tonic and passing harmonies remain, but they are found exclusively on the second, weaker halves of measures. The T-voice is suspended into the strong half of each measure, but in many cases the tones held over are tones included in the ensuing chord. This lessens their suspension-like effect because there is no change in harmony on the weak beat when the underlying chord is in place. Such cases are indicated in the figure with arrows. The true T-suspensions occur on the downbeats of measures 5, 7, 9, and 11. The most striking of these is the C♯/D in measure 7, a combination of tones that wouldn't have formed under the original scheme without displacement. From measure 5 through measure 10 there is a regular, repeating succession of T-suspensions, passing harmonies, and tonic harmonies, intensifying while subtly blurring the constant return to the tonic triad.

Pärt's tonality

As with the pitch classes in *Zwei slawische Psalmen*, a hierarchy arises among the types of harmonic events in *Da pacem Domine*. Neither hierarchy is based on the functions of scale degrees or the functions of harmonies, but they are hierarchies nonetheless, and in each the tonic triad plays a central role. For this reason, Pärt's music is neither strictly tonal nor wholly non-tonal. It is a reworking of tonality.

In *Pari intervallo*, a piece originally for organ, there is, as may be expected, the overarching tonic of the T-voice, but there are other, more local prolongations of a different sort. The piece is divided into six twelve-bar sections, each of which features the M-voices circling near (or hovering around) a particular member of the tonic triad. Each of the triad's tones becomes a kind of reciting tone on which the M-voices concentrate. As seen in Example 5.15, the first three reciting tones in the primary M-voice are G♭, B♭, and E♭. In each section the M-voice begins and ends on the reciting tone, never straying far and moving chiefly stepwise.

The impulse in analysis to reduce complex structures to simple ones leads, in tonal music, to the reduction of a prolonged harmony to a single instance of the harmony by removing the elements that prolong it. The reciting tones in *Pari intervallo* can be simplified in a similar fashion. Example 5.16 shows how reduction of the twelve-measure sections down to their principal reciting tones reveals an underlying tonic triad ascending through the first half of the piece.

In the second half of the piece there is another simplification down to three tones, one per section. I refer to these tones not as reciting tones but *goal tones*. In each of these sections the M-voice traverses a fifth or an octave but culminates in a single tone of the tonic triad: first fifth, then third, and finally root. Central to most conceptions of tonality is goal-oriented motion. A perfect authentic cadence, for example, is not just a harmonic event (dominant to tonic), but one in which the melodic motion reaches its conclusion at scale-degree one. It is clear in *Cantate Domino* and *Zwei*

Example 5.15 *Pari intervallo*: reciting tones. Continuous slur indicates stepwise motion: (a) mm. 1–12; (b) mm. 13–24; (c) mm. 25–36.

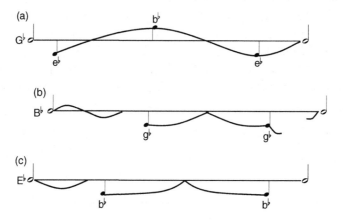

Example 5.16 *Pari intervallo*: reciting tones and goal tones as underlying structure

slawische Psalmen that goal tones and initiating tones are essential to the structure of a composition. They form the anchors that stabilize the activity of the M-voices. In *Pari intervallo*, the twelve-measure grouping is established by the first three ascending reciting tones but is reinforced by the final three descending goal tones.

The final section of *Pari intervallo*, two measures longer than the others, contains a largely descending M-voice, which raises important questions about underlying structure and simplification. The fourteen melodic tones can be seen in Example 5.17a. Immediately apparent is its series of shorter and shorter descending fragments. A common analysis might look like the one found in Example 5.17b: a descent from scale-degree 5, with each tone of the descent bearing its own nested progression. In this reading, the stepwise descent becomes primary, and in a simplification only the five tones of the descent would remain. Example 5.17c is an alternate reading, incompatible with the previous one. Here it is the *end* of each descending fragment that is primary. With relentless emphasis on the final tone, E♭, the diminishing of the fragments is slightly more emphasized. One hears the final tone again and again, echoing faster and faster until the final measure is complete. In the earlier Example 5.12b the goal-oriented motion is large scale, but in 5.17c it is small scale. A simplification would reduce the entire passage to scale-degree 1, which serves as goal tone not only at the end, but also throughout.

Example 5.17 *Pari intervallo*, mm. 61–74. Opposing analyses of the M-voice in the conclusion: (a) the final fourteen notes in the M-voice; (b) reading a descent from scale-degree 5; (c) reading diminishing fragments, all descending to scale-degree 1

Pärt's 'rules of the game'

In 1716, François Campion published a convenient method for the realization of an unfigured bass.[28] Once memorized, the method allowed keyboardists, guitarists, lutenists, and theorbists to play a proper accompaniment from a continuo part that contains no figures.[29] The method simply outlined, in both major and minor keys, the appropriate intervals from each bass tone to its accompanying chord tones. One such realization of an ascending bass line in F major is shown in Example 5.18. In practice, continuo players had to learn many subtle unwritten variations, but Campion's method was a practical place to start.

In much the same way, Pärt's precompositional plans dictate what tones will accompany any given M-voice tone. For example, Pärt might propose the mode of F major (Ionian) with an M-voice centered on C. Its second M-voice might move with the first in parallel sixths and its T-voices at first and second inferior (transposed above the M-voice). That simple proposition predetermines a four-note chord for any given M-voice tone. Therefore one can produce, as Campion did, a set of chord voicings for each of the seven distinct M-voice (bass) tones. Example 5.19 shows the result. While Campion's is pedagogical and practical, Pärt's is purely my theoretical abstraction. Nevertheless, each figure systematically conveys the internal relationship of chord to generating tone to governing scale.

The chords outlined in Example 5.19 are not entirely hypothetical. They form the basis for Pärt's *Spiegel im Spiegel* (1978), originally composed for violin and piano but later arranged for many different instrumental combinations. This 'tonal plan' is merely a foundation, however, and in no way insures the overall success of the piece. It no more predicts the piece than the twenty-four major and minor keys predetermine the notes of Bach's *The Well-Tempered Klavier*. Further decisions need to be made: which instruments

Example 5.18 François Campion's *Règle des octaves*

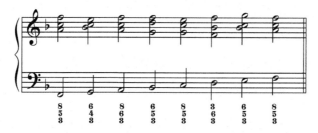

Example 5.19 Possible M- and T-voices in the manner of Campion's *Règle*

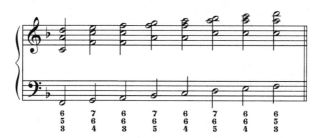

will accommodate which voices? And in which register? Is the central tone an initiating or a goal tone? Ascending, descending, alternating? What about the overall form and repeated sections or fragments? Some defined parameters qualify as 'rules of the game', while others describe the 'machine in motion.' Finding, at the very least, the 'rules' for a given piece would be a convenient shortcut to its analysis since it would provide the mode, the M- and T-voices and their relationships, and the initial and goal tones.

Conclusion

'Process music' does not entail, as some believe, a relinquishing of control by the composer. The control simply resides far from the immediate surface of the music. "The distinctive thing about musical processes," writes Steve Reich, "is that they determine all the note-to-note (sound-to-sound) details and the overall form simultaneously."[30] The composer controls the process, which in turn controls various musical elements. The musical process, more generally, is all about possibility. What seems to attract Reich and others is the possibility of new and even unexpected music. It is not improvisation, nor is it music of chance. After all, the composer has exclusive and complete control over the *design* of the process and, by extension, responsibility for the *results* as well. The difference is that at some point the composer, the listener, and the analyst all share the same role, somewhere between creator and listener. All are called to investigate a surprising and sometimes complex musical world in a single piece.

The tintinnabuli music of Arvo Pärt can be considered process music, but only to a degree. Pärt's process governs (in Reich's terms) the "note-to-note details" more frequently and more specifically than it does the "overall form." In fact, each piece strikes a unique balance of process and invention. The most obvious instance of process in this music is the tintinnabuli technique itself. How the T-voice follows the M-voice is prescribed from the start, and the resulting process is automatic. Sometimes, the words of a chosen text will dictate the entire melodic components of a composition, or even its large-scale form. In fact, quite a few decisions must be made before the process is set in motion: mode is chosen, starting pitches are selected, relationship between T-voice and M-voice is determined, and intervals of imitation are set. But because so many of its elements – instrumentation, small-scale form, freely composed passages – are not generated by an apparent procedure from start to finish, Pärt's music cannot be said to be process music to the extent that, say, Reich's early phase music can.[31] Nevertheless, one thing it shares with pure process music is its ability to produce astonishingly rich 'output' from comparably little 'input.' In this way, to listen to Pärt's music is not simply to await a foregone conclusion. It is to witness the consequences and ramifications of a single idea and patiently to explore the details of the results that emerge.

The foregoing stands in contrast to most structuralist or formalist critiques, which tend to find in minimalism and process music nothing more than simplicity and monotony. Some critiques suggest the low ratio of 'input' to 'output' in the musical process is a sign of intellectual weakness in the composer. Others simply measure the apparently low 'output' with tools completely inappropriate for the job. Suggesting that such critiques are at best misguided, theorist Ian Quinn argues that process music requires an altogether different kind of analysis:

> As long as the practitioner of formalist analysis tries to behave like an Enigma machine, translating the encoded genius of the composer into testimonials in favor of canonization, process music will remain a source of frustration. Minimalism got its start, in fact, when composers decided to cut themselves out of that particular interpretive loop. Rather than writing music with low redundancy and high information content, they began writing music with high redundancy and low information content. Formalist analysis of process music must respond to this challenge by turning the normal function of analysis on its head. Traditionally, analysis aims to reduce the information content of a piece – productively, and however provisionally, temporarily, and contingently – by parsing it relative to some well-understood system of formal conceptual categories.

> Process music comes to the table already digested; its challenge to the analyst-as-interpreter is precisely the minimal challenge it presents to the analyst-as-parser.[32]

In response to this challenge, our task is to go beyond the surface and to examine closely the process itself, whether our ends are hermeneutical or structural, and not to write it off as a cheap trick. Further, we must determine what 'output' a process would produce with different 'inputs,' for the genius of the composer lies not only in the discretion with which a process is used, but also simply in what is chosen as 'input' in the first place.

Even with the best of intentions, one can produce only marginal results when attempting to analyze Pärt's tintinnabuli pieces by drawing exclusively from either of the two principal music theories of the twentieth century. As powerful as they are, neither twelve-tone/set theory nor Schenkerian theory will break down the structure of Pärt's music, which in many ways is, as Quinn suggests, "already digested." One should not, however, disregard them entirely. Pärt's pre-tintinnabuli works display an engagement with serial techniques, and this inclination toward systematic permutation and combination remains in evidence throughout his later works. Although his work is not truly a return to tonality as some might claim, his use of diatonic modes and triads is more than allusion. It is an elegant rendering of tonality that stands only to benefit from judicious application of a modified tonal theory. To analyze Pärt's music, then, one may use elements of tonal and atonal theory where appropriate and must also take care to examine the specific relationship between process and results.

As it rapidly splinters into subdisciplines and profitably intersects with others, the discipline of music theory is thriving, and it ought to be receiving with open arms the music of Arvo Pärt. This is music that displays an astonishing originality and a deep connection with the practices of Western music. Its surface is elegant with broadly appealing beauty, but below that surface fascinating structures lie hidden and ingenious processes are at work. For this reason Pärt's music is, like the music of any other master composer, complex. It rewards the kind of deep study that goes beyond simple listening and consuming. This chapter is a hopeful call for more analytical responses that can rise to meet the imaginative challenges of the music.

Further reading

Allen Cadwallader and David Gagné, *Analysis of Tonal Music*, 3rd edn. (Oxford University Press, 2010).

Timothy Johnson, *Foundations of Diatonic Theory: A Mathematically Based Approach to Music Fundamentals* (Plymouth: The Scarecrow Press, 2008).

Joseph N. Straus, *An Introduction to Post-Tonal Analysis*, 3rd edn. (Upper Saddle River, NJ: Prentice Hall, 2004).

6 Arvo Pärt: in his own words

ANDREW SHENTON

For the Boston and London conferences in 2010 dedicated to his work, Pärt wrote brief letters that welcomed what he described as the serious and substantial discussion of his music that was taking place. He noted that he hoped the insights of the presenters would "provide an inspiration and give me support for my musical ideas." Pärt declined to be formally interviewed at these events and did not participate in public discussions after the papers; however, he observed that these gatherings of friends and scholars were trying to find answers to questions that he had been asking himself for many years, and observed that "dialogue is the main thing." He wrote that during the conferences we should "expect therefore no answers from me!" His own involvement in the proceedings was stated with typical humility: "I think the path that I have searched for and chosen – or maybe it chose me – this path and the many questions that arise from it, this is my contribution."[1] What Pärt is clearly indicating is that he does not view himself as the definitive authority on his own music. As Nora Pärt notes, "Arvo tries very consciously to stay in the shadow of his music."[2] Pärt has also been clear that his public and private personas are separate: "If anybody wishes to understand me, they must listen to my music; if anybody wishes to know my 'philosophy', then they can read any of the Church Fathers; if anybody wishes to know about my private life, there are things that I wish to keep closed."[3]

Obviously there are dangers of over-reliance on what composers say about their own work or of quoting them out of context. Nevertheless, Pärt's comments do reveal, at a certain level, a personal philosophy (or perhaps even theology) of music. His comments collected here are drawn from interviews spanning many years and organized into categories which are intended to complement and inform the other chapters in this book. Some of his remarks are associated with brief descriptions of his compositions in order to offer suggestions for further listening.

Theology

The key to Pärt's personal theology is summarized in this short remark: "Religion influences everything. Not just music, but everything."[4]

Pärt entered the Russian Orthodox Church in 1972 and this branch of Christianity, with its emphasis on chanting, unaccompanied choral music, and bells, certainly informs much of what he writes; however, his music is a rich confluence of both the eastern Russian Orthodox and Western Catholic and Protestant musical traditions. Pärt is not conscious of the root of his theological creativity or the way it impacts his music, but seeks a sincere and authentic act of composition: "I close my eyes, I make gestures. I myself don't know if they are Catholic or Orthodox. If these gestures are genuine, that is everything."[5]

Pärt has not given much detail regarding his own faith, although he has fought against a prevailing view, stating: "I am not a prophet, not a cardinal, not a monk. I am not even a vegetarian. Don't be confused by cheap tabloid information. Of course I am in monasteries more often than in concert halls – but then again, you have no idea how many times I am in concert halls."[6] He hoped that his music was "pleasing in the eyes of God,"[7] and has commented on the need for tolerance towards other people: "There is a good rule in spiritual life, which we all forget continually," he said, "that you must see more of your own sins than other people's."[8] He once remarked that he believed that the sum of human sin has been growing since Adam's time, and that we all share some of the blame. "So I think everyone must say to himself, 'We must change our thinking.' We cannot see what is in the heart of another person. Maybe he is a holy man, and I can see only that he is wearing a wrong jacket."[9]

In a metaphysical statement, he observed that as part of the human condition "Time and timelessness are connected. This instant and eternity are struggling within us. And this is the cause of all our contradictions, our obstinacy, our narrowmindedness, our faith and our grief."[10] But, he has also spoken of the transformative power of the knowledge of God, suggesting that "If people simply hear the word 'God' they become sad; it is sad when it has that effect. But wonders are forever occurring and people who think like that today will feel differently tomorrow."[11] He has also spoken of the richness of the last few moments of life: "It is said that God suffers a person to live only so long as it is important for them to come to know the truth. It is also said that when someone dies, whether young or old, then that moment is given as the best time to die. Therefore the last moments before death are very precious – very important – for at that time things can happen which have not come about during a whole lifetime."[12]

In the early years of the tintinnabuli style most of his music was written for the concert hall and not for liturgical use; however, there are now many pieces that can be used in a liturgical setting. There are more than twenty-five anthems, including the popular setting of *The Beatitudes* (1990/1991) and a wonderfully evocative setting of *Cantate Domino* (1997/1996), Psalm

95: "Sing unto the Lord a new song!" Pärt has set the texts of the *Magnificat* (1989) and *Nunc dimittis* (2001), which are the two canticles commonly sung at Evensong or Vespers, and both the *Berliner Messe* (1990/2002) and the earlier *Missa syllabica* (1977/1996) are gaining popularity as mass settings in a liturgical context. Pärt has also set two other parts of the liturgy that are regularly sung: *Summa* (1977), for unaccompanied SATB choir, is a setting of the Apostles' Creed; and *Vater unser* (2005) for boy soprano and piano, is a setting of the Lord's Prayer.[13]

The creative process

Perhaps the most interesting aspect of any artist is the creative process itself. The way composers channel inspiration, the working methods they use for putting their ideas on to paper, and how they develop both technically and artistically are intrinsically interesting, but they may also shed light on ways to perform, interpret, or appreciate their music.

In an interview in 1988, during his early international success, Pärt was asked specifically why he composed. His answer is revealing:

> For me it's like breathing in and out. It's my life. What does a child do when he plays on his own? He sings. Why does he sing? Well, he is happy about something pretty, inspired by something. That is something quite healthy, quite natural. For adults this state is considerably more complex, for this harmony is smashed into pieces, it's lost. But can I exist without composing, my soul and my spirit? Music is already my language. My music can be my inner secret, even my confession. But what is my confession? I don't confess in the concert hall, in front of an audience. It is directed toward higher instances. The necessity for composing has many layers. They are like bridges, put on top of each other. And you never know which one you are just passing. Some are dangerous and you fall. Most important for me: that I cannot say in a few thousand sentences what I can say in a few notes.[14]

Claiming that music is his life and his language establishes Pärt as someone who composes not out of curiosity but out of necessity. What is perhaps more interesting is his description of composing as his secret or confession. This supports the idea that his music is personal and that his own intention for his music is not for public consumption. By declaring that it is written for a higher authority he confirms his personal religious inclination, but he does so without proselytizing to his audience. His natural ability as a composer means that he can express himself most easily in this medium and this is the most important aspect for him. Elsewhere he has noted, "I'm not a professor – I don't need words to explain."[15]

When asked about his new tintinnabuli technique, Pärt tried to describe his intuitive approach to composition. He explained that sometimes he couldn't find the words to describe his feelings and demonstrated that to his interviewer with a gesture. This, he claimed, was how he wanted to write music.[16] On another occasion he explained that he composed "Mainly in my head, with an inner hearing," adding that "I can't perform my finished pieces on the piano, that's impossible."[17] What he is suggesting here is that since the music was not composed sitting at the keyboard it cannot easily be played on the piano since the notes may not readily lie under the fingers. He is also suggesting that the piano is not capable of fully realizing the nuances of his work in a satisfactory way.

When asked specifically about creativity he said, "What's the meaning of creativity? There are millions of composers who are so creative one is afraid of it. You can drown in the sewage water of our time's creativity. The capability to select is important, and the urge for it. The reduction to a minimum, the ability to reduce fractions – that was the strength of all great composers."[18] For Pärt, creativity is not the most significant part of the compositional process; working with creative ideas is more important. For him, this means being selective and also having the ability to reduce one's inspiration to its essence.

Pärt also believes that the composer should be prepared for the work that they are to undertake. He has repeated a particular story on several occasions which refers to the need for the composer to be emotionally and spiritually ready to compose:

> In the Soviet Union once, I spoke with a monk and asked him how, as a composer, one can improve oneself. He answered me by saying that he knew of no solution. I told him that I also wrote prayers, and set prayers and the text of psalms to music, and that perhaps this would be of help to me as a composer. To this he said, "No, you are wrong. All the prayers have already been written. You don't need to write any more. Everything has been prepared. Now you have to prepare yourself." I believe that there's a truth in that.[19]

Pärt is very visual. Many of his pieces have drawn inspiration from art and architecture, including *Lamentate* (2002) for piano and orchestra, which was inspired by Anish Kapoor's massive steel-and-PVC sculpture "Marsyas," and *Silhouette* (2009/2010) for large string orchestra and percussion, which was inspired by the Eiffel Tower. Of the latter, Pärt observed: "A conductor can see many things in the Eiffel Tower which are similar to a musical structure, with building blocks and the connections between them, the transparency of the construction, and much more. Even the statics, which are a very important aspect of architecture, are also an important element in the construction of a musical form. My work *Silhouette* has become short and light, like a dance, a waltz, creating a light dizzy sensation, maybe like that from the winds that blow through the gargantuan lacy colossus."[20] This visualization of form and of structural elements is key to his creative process. Paul Hillier observed that "for larger compositions especially, Pärt creates a visual map of the work's form which he pins up on the wall of his study. This consists of the text, put into separate verses, with pitch indications and other musical data and the use of different colors to depict voices and orchestration. The result, much more than a mere sketch, encapsulates the entire work at the point where the initial gesture has found its appropriate system."[21]

Hillier provides us with other information about the methods Pärt used during the period after 1968 when he was trying to re-learn how to compose:

> With Gregorian chant as his source, he studied how to write a single line of music. Writing semi-automatically, page after page, filling book after book, he sought to enter a different sense of time, to fully assimilate all that might be meant by the idea of 'monody' [a single line of music]. Sometimes he would draw a shape, such as the outline of wings, or a landscape, and then quickly create a melodic line that would fill that shape. Or he would quickly read a text, set it aside, and then immediately write music to mirror what he had just read.[22]

Pärt was initially interested in the expressiveness of just a single line of music and sought to recreate some of the beauty of the chant he found in the *Liber usualis*, the collection of Gregorian chant he studied in this period. It was an interesting exercise and certainly influenced his melodic writing in the tintinnabuli style; however, it was not the final answer in his search for a new style. Nora Pärt, in her typically succinct manner, evoked an apt metaphor, stating simply: "you need a pair of wings to fly,"[23] and after he had created the note-against-note style Pärt himself declared that "tintinnabuli was my attempt to tackle the problem of polyphony."[24]

Plate 6.1 shows small sketches created by Pärt that give a visual map of some of the early tintinnabuli works. The depiction of *Arbos* (1977) clearly portrays the tree form of the title. This piece depicts the root, trunk, and branches in a clever mensuration canon in which the three different voices play exactly the same music but at different speeds: the second twice as fast as the first, the third twice as fast as the second. For *Sarah Was Ninety Years Old* (1977/1990), Pärt has shown the constant variation of four pitches or rhythms that make up each section of the work, and for *Cantus in Memory of Benjamin Britten* (another mensuration canon based on a descending scale) a widening curlicue depicts the path of the canon as it works its way through the orchestra.

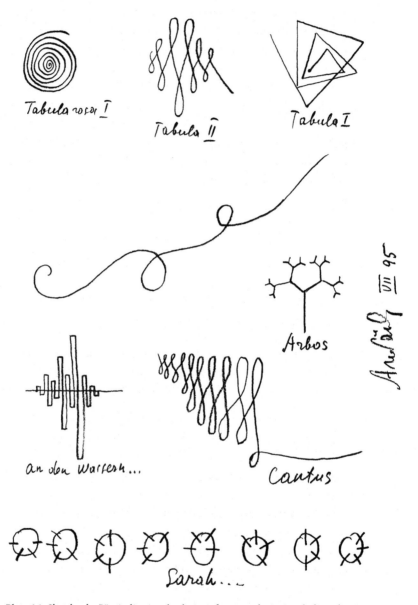

Plate 6.1 Sketches by Pärt indicating the design of some early tintinnabuli works

These simple sketches suggest something of the essence of each piece. This essential element is crucial to Pärt, who has stated that

> I am tempted only when I experience something unknown, something new and meaningful for me. It seems, however, that this unknown territory is sooner reached by way of reduction than by growing complexity. Reduction certainly doesn't mean simplification, but it is the way – at least in an ideal scenario – to the most intense concentration on the essence of things. In the compositional process I have always to find this nucleus

first from which the work will eventually emerge. First of all, I will have to get to this nucleus. Everything depends on which nucleus, or which part of the nucleus, I choose (or am able to choose at a given time) and on the profundity of the consequences.[25]

There are two key points here. First, he notes that reduction doesn't mean simplification. Analysts and critics who refer to his music using this term (sometimes connecting him with other composers under the label 'new simplicists'), are often unaware of the complex processes at work in the construction of even the shortest pieces. Second, by finding the nucleus of the work, the musical cell from which the rest of the work will grow, Pärt is able to develop the music in many ways. Nora Pärt observes that

> There is a link between Arvo's attempt to find the nucleus of a musical expression and the profusion of aspects of the final work. It is thus that many people can find something in his music which is surprising to Arvo. Music grown from a root can develop in multifarious ways unpredictable at the start of the compositional process. The flower developing from this root has innumerable facets. Each one of them attracts a particular person reacting to a particular aspect … This is probably also the reason why the people who appreciate Arvo's music are so diverse.[26]

The extraordinary beauty of the tintinnabuli style is the diversity of the blooms which can grow from these musical cells. Pärt himself said: "A composition comes as a single gesture which is already, in essence, music. The path to this is hard; you descend to the lowest spiritual plane, the bottom of the world, not knowing what will be found. The only thing you know is that you don't know anything. If this gesture, like a seed, takes root, it must be cultivated with extreme care so that it may grow; meanwhile you are oscillating between heaven and earth. The compositional task is to find the appropriate system for the gesture."[27] Pärt has also suggested that in getting to the core of a musical work a composer has to relinquish what he describes as "ballast": "eras, styles, forms, orchestration, harmony, polyphony" so that the composer can ask the question of its musical essence: "Is it truth or falsehood?"[28]

The true genius of Pärt is his uncanny ability to find the appropriate system for these cells. Pärt explained that the process is not easy, adding, "It is one's capacity for suffering that gives the energy to create." Using the metaphor of a conductor beginning a piece, Pärt describes the content of this nucleus, and repeats that the process is often hard and sometimes unfruitful:

> I imagine the conductor having an upbeat, when the whole thing starts.
> We can't hear anything yet. And the people in the concert hall don't know

what's coming. Then the conductor makes the upbeat. The upbeat, the moment when he raises his hand actually contains the formula of the entire work. Its character, dynamics, tempo, and plenty of other things. The conductor and the musicians know it from practicing together. I guess the composer is in a similar position before he starts writing. He must have the knowledge or a perception of what's coming when the hand goes down. What is the first note? And what is the second one? The first step is everything, decisive. Sometimes it comes easily; sometimes it doesn't come at all. Every time I feel I have to start from scratch.[29]

When asked about his own compositions, Pärt has been consistent in being able to offer no opinion. As early as 1978 he said: "I have no standpoint related to my own compositions at all, especially to those written so long ago. I haven't any contact with them. I have lost intimacy with them, the body warmth. They're like birds that will fly away after being incubated. Sometimes they seem to come back, because sometimes you happen to listen to some performance or you happen to see the sheet music. Generally, I try to forget all that."[30] On another occasion he used a metaphor to try to explain the difficulty of asserting the primacy of one piece over another: "When one has for example ten children, how does one view the third child, or how does one view the seventh child? How does one answer this?"[31]

Questioned about discernible developments in his own technique, or similarities between older and newer works, he replied:

One can only see such things with time … It's like taking a blood test of my music from today or ten or twenty years ago: one can tell that it's my blood, but today you'll get one answer from the test and tomorrow another, depending on what you've eaten and your general condition of health. There could be great differences between the two; such things are in a constant state of change. Much more so than a change of style … One can never say that one has reached a point of perfection, that one is completely right and that what one is doing is stronger than something else. One needs distance to see that. I can say with hindsight that I've lost almost all contact with my earlier music. I sometimes hear it and I feel it's not my music – I've forgotten it all. But that isn't my problem; what's more important is what I have yet to discover.[32]

This continual quest for new discoveries accounts for obvious development in Pärt's music since 1976 and for the highly individual character of each of his pieces.

When asked if he thought tintinnabulation was a system that could be used by other composers, Pärt replied that it would not be the same way as he used it and indicated that there was an essential theory behind what he had created: "Still, I would formulate and sum up the theory one day should the opportunity arise. This theory has the same clarity as the structure of breathing. It is so simple and tangible. I have internalized this formula. And with it there are innumerable creative realizations possible."[33] To date only a few composers other than Pärt have experimented with the tintinnabuli technique. This is perhaps surprising since Pärt has had such success with it; however, it could also be that it is Pärt's remarkable genius that allows him to create such beautiful music using these tools. Whatever the case, at present the tintinnabuli style is always recognizable as Pärt's work.

Tintinnabulation

Tintinnabulation was devised after a period of reflection during which Pärt studied composers such as Machaut and Josquin, and writers such as Dante and the medieval poet Shota Rustaveli. Pärt also studied Gregorian chant and explained that this music "has taught me what a cosmic secret is hidden in the art of combining two, three notes," adding "That's something twelve-tone composers have not known at all. The sterile democracy between the notes has killed in us every living feeling."[34] Although he had himself composed using twelve-tone techniques, he had concluded that "if the human has conflict in his soul and with everything, then this system of twelve-tone music is exactly good for this … But if you have no more conflict with people, with the world, with God, then it is not necessary. You have no need to have a Browning [gun] in your pocket, or a dagger."[35]

This period of reflection came to a close when Pärt realized he had to start again from scratch and create a personal means of expression. "And maybe there was one point when I said, 'Stop with this old music as a composer.' Now in this place must be born something of mine – from everything that I have learned in old music, in religion, in life, and how much I was able to see my own sins and imperfections, and to repent it. To say, 'Yes.' And if you do, then it is like when you are on a computer, and you write a text and then you press something and it is empty. But it is a good thing. Begin from zero, from nothing. It's like if there is a fresh snow and nobody has walked [on it], and you take the first steps on this snow. And this is the beginning of new life."[36]

Pärt wanted a return to an "economy of expression" and sought pure beauty in that expression.[37] He confirms repeatedly that "at times it was enough to hear just one or two chords and a whole new world was opened up."[38] He claimed: "I have discovered that it is enough when a single note is beautifully played. This one note, or a silent beat, or a moment of silence, comforts me. I work with very few elements – with one voice, with two voices. I build with the most primitive materials – with the triad, with one specific tonality. The three notes of the triad are like bells. And that is why I call it tintinnabulation."[39]

His most frequently quoted comments about tintinnabulation suggest that it is not just a compositional technique but also a way of viewing the world. He tends to give metaphysical rather than physical descriptions of the music and has depicted tintinnabulation as "an area I sometimes wander into when I'm searching for answers – in my life, my music, my work," and describes the search he faces: "In my dark hours, I have a certain feeling that everything outside this one thing has no meaning. The complex and many-faceted only confuses me, and I must search for unity. What is it, this one thing, and how do I find my way to it? Traces of this perfect thing appear in many guises – and everything that is unimportant falls away. Tintinnabulation is like this. Here I am alone with silence."[40]

Silence is important for Pärt. For him, it is not empty or vacant but so vital that his principal concern is: "How can one fill the time with notes worthy of the preceding silence?"[41] Silence as a compositional device contributes to the sense of stasis and stillness in much of his music, and this in turn contributes to the numinous in his music – that is to say, the sublime or mystical element, or the sense in which it evokes a supernatural presence. Commentators have likened this to hesychasm, a prayer tradition of the Eastern Orthodox Church which invites people to retire inwards, to keep stillness, in order to experience God. Pärt has been clear about what this silence means for him: "My music has emerged only after I have been silent for quite some time, literally silent. For me, 'silent' means the 'nothing' from which God created the world. Ideally, a silent pause is something sacred ... If someone approaches silence with love, then this might give birth to music. A composer must often wait a long time for his music. This kind of sublime anticipation is exactly the kind of pause that I value so greatly."[42]

For Pärt, his short piano piece *Für Alina* (1976) was "the first piece that was on a new plateau. It was here that I discovered the triad series, which I made my simple, little guiding rule."[43] When one interviewer suggested that the melodic line was like "a child tentatively walking," and the tintinnabuli part was like "a mother with her hands outstretched to ensure her toddler doesn't fall," Pärt jumped at the metaphor and exclaimed: "This is the whole secret of tintinnabuli. The two lines. One line is who we are, and the other line is who is holding and takes care of us. Sometimes I say – it is not a joke, but also it is as a joke taken – that the melodic line is our reality, our sins. But the other line is forgiving the sins."[44] He has phrased this in similar ways on other occasions:

> The M-voice [the melodic line] always signifies the subjective world, the
> daily egoistic life of sin and suffering; the T-voice [the triadic tintinnabuli
> part], meanwhile, is the objective realm of forgiveness. The M-voice may
> appear to wander, but it is always held firmly by the T-voice. This can be
> likened to the eternal dualism of body and spirit, heaven and earth; but the
> two voices are in reality one voice, a twofold single entity.[45]
>
> One line is like freedom, and the triad line is like discipline. It must work
> together.[46]

From the modest beginnings in *Für Alina*, Pärt developed a wide range
of processes to develop the nucleus for each piece and this has produced some large-scale compositions including *Miserere* (1989/1992), a
30-minute work for SATB choir, instrumental ensemble and organ; and
Litany (1994/1996), a work of similar length for soli, SATB choir and
orchestra.

If a listener is familiar with some of the dazzling complexity in a work
such as *Passio* (1982), one of Pärt's longest works at around 75 minutes, it
would be natural to question his claim for reduction and simplicity in his
music. When asked about the use of well-formulated principles of construction in the tintinnabuli works, Pärt replied that he did not see any
contradiction since, as he put it,

> everything in the world is numerically arranged in one way or another.
> There are definite rules everywhere – it has to be so. But my principle is
> that they must not be the most important part of the music. They must
> be simple – they fall away and are only a skeleton. Life arises from other
> things. When things are simple and clear, they're also clean. They are
> empty; there is room for everything. It is more important than these
> principles of construction. If one plays one or two notes beautifully in
> an austere and clean combination, then that's good – we have two good
> things.[47]

Pärt believes that "Style is a mathematical abstraction – an all-em-
bracing, unifying figure," and that "Each style has its own driving paradigm and its own weapons."[48] It is also important to note that over time
Pärt has been less strict in his application of procedures to his music.
Nora Pärt observed that "The first period was very strict … It was very
important for Arvo to give himself a system, rules and discipline. And
over time, Arvo had more and more freedom."[49] Pärt himself added
a note of caution regarding the lack of self-imposed restrictions: "I
believed in myself more and more … It can be good or bad. It is dangerous, this freedom."[50]

The nature of Pärt's tintinnabuli style has naturally likened him to a
group of composers called minimalists whose compositions are based on

minimal use of musical material. When asked how he felt about this, Pärt replied: "I don't know – it's not something that concerns me. When I listen to a piece of music, whether it's Steve Reich or anyone else, I never think about whether it's minimal or repetitive; that's not important, except, perhaps, for analysis. But I don't need analysis to elucidate these things. I'm not a professor – I don't need words to explain."[51]

Critics of Pärt's work sometimes liken it to New Age music, which superficially shares some of the same characteristics of the tintinnabuli style, including modality, consonance, and the use of quiet repeating patterns to create relaxation. However, as Nora Pärt has correctly observed, New Age music strives to be free of conflict, whereas "Pärt's music may be calming but it also contains pain and compassion and this is what makes it essentially different to New Age music."[52]

Pärt's catalog contains numerous examples of pieces that exist in different versions and people sometimes wonder if this is a marketing strategy to sell more copies and get more performances. Pärt has a much more elegant explanation: "For me," he says, "the highest value of music is outside it. Special instrumental timbre is part of the music, yet it's not a primary quality. That would be my capitulation to the secret of music. Music has to exist by itself ... Two, three notes. The secret must be there, independent of any instrument. Music must derive from inside, and I have deliberately tried to write such music that can be played on a variety of instruments. It does make a difference to me from which instruments to which I change, though. I do see qualitative levels there."[53] So *Spiegel im Spiegel* for example, which currently exists in twelve versions ranging from the original violin and piano piece from 1978 to a version for saxophone and piano in 2011, is in Pärt's view only superficially colored by the timbre of the instruments. The real essence of the work is contained in the notes themselves.

Despite Pärt's claim that his music is contained only in the notes, he has an ear for imaginative and interesting sonorities. *De profundis* (1980) for men's voices, organ and three percussion instruments ably depicts the text of the penitential Psalm 130: "Out of the depths I cry to you, O Lord!" *Tabula rasa* (1977) and his setting of the *Te Deum* (1984–85/1992) both use the sounds of a 'prepared' piano (which employs screws and other objects placed on the strings to modify the sound), and the *Te Deum* also uses a pre-recorded tape as part of its timbral language. *L'abbé Agathon* (2004/2005) was first conceived for soprano and eight cellos, and *Fratres* (1977) currently exists in seventeen different versions as diverse as brass orchestra (2004), and guitar, string orchestra, and percussion (1977).

Text-setting

Text is often the fundamental generative agent for Pärt's music. He stated that, when he is composing, "the words are very important to me, they define the music," and goes on to confirm that "the construction of the music is based on the construction of the text."[54] Initially this dominance of the text on his compositional rules was misunderstood by people who had not examined the music closely enough to see how it worked. Back in 1999 he complained: "My claim to let words write their own music makes some people laugh, particularly musical journalists. They do not take it seriously."[55] Now, however, his work is seen as paradigmatic of the symbiotic relationship between words and music.

The techniques Pärt employs differ from piece to piece. Most of the words are set syllabically, which is an aid to clarity of expression and therefore comprehension. For *Kanon Pokajanen* (1997) he wanted to "allow the word to be able to find its own sound, to draw its own melodic line."[56] For *Passio*, his setting of St. John's description of the final day of Christ's life, it is actually the punctuation of the text that sets the scheme according to certain rules based on the use of three relative note values: short, medium, and long. For example, in the last word of a phrase ending with a comma, the stressed syllable is medium; whereas in the last word of a phrase ending with a colon or period, each syllable is long. In the first word of a new sentence (or phrase beginning after a colon), the stressed syllable is medium and in the last word in a phrase ending with a question mark, each syllable is medium. All other syllables are short. Furthermore, phrases are grouped in pairs, and in each pair of phrases the first ends on a dissonance, the second on a consonance.

Many of these principles can be seen in Example 6.1, which shows a passage sung by the Evangelist from the start of the work. The part of the Evangelist is sung not by a solo male voice, as might be expected, but by an SATB quartet accompanied by four instruments: violin, cello, oboe, and bassoon. The text is divided into four main sections which begin with a single melodic voice and then add T-voices and M-voices one by one in various combinations up to eight parts, before reducing them part by part until there is a single voice again. What is remarkable is the way Pärt manages to elucidate the text by his subtle manipulation of those elements which are not governed by his strict compositional procedures.

Most of the texts Pärt has set are religious. He explained: "I've always been guided by texts that were particularly close to me and full of existential importance for me," and he suggested that humans have not changed much in the last two thousand years, "which is why I believe that the sacred texts are always very topical. In this view, there are no significant differences

Example 6.1 *Passio*, Figure 3, demonstrating some principles of text-setting

between yesterday, today and tomorrow, because there are truths that continue to have validity. Man feels now as then, and has the same need to free himself from his mistakes."[57]

The majority of Pärt's choral works are in Latin, the universal language of the church. Pärt believes "Latin is nice ... because it is not an everyday language," and explains that "I would like to have distance with everyday language if I write music."[58] He brings the same sensitivity and creativity to whichever language he uses. The following is a list of languages Pärt has set, with a representative example of each:

Church Slavonic	*Bogoróditse Djévo* (1990) for unaccompanied SATB choir.
English	*The Deer's Cry* (2007) for unaccompanied SATB choir.
Estonian	*Meie Aed* (1959/2003) for children's choir (SSA) and orchestra.
French	*L'abbé Agathon* (2004) for soprano and eight violoncellos, and in two other versions.
German	*Es sang vor langen Jahren* (1984) for alto, violin and viola.
Italian	*Cecilia, vergine romana* (2000/2002) for SATB and orchestra.
Latin	*Cantate Domino* (1977/1996) for SATB choir and organ.
Spanish	*Como cierva sedienta* (1998/2002) for soprano and orchestra.

Performers and audiences

The direct influence of groups such as Hortus Musicus, The Hilliard Ensemble, and The Estonian Chamber Choir on Pärt's music is of great importance both to his compositional process and to the popularity of his recordings, and is discussed elsewhere in this collection. Like many composers, Pärt has revised his work during rehearsals and, as the dates of composition suggest, he has often made revisions and corrections at a later date.[59] His published scores are often sparse, especially the orchestral parts of his works, which do not indicate what else is happening in the piece. This means that performers have to grapple with exactly how one or two notes should be "beautifully played." Thanks to some outstanding recordings, notably the 'authorized' recordings on the ECM label (many of which were recorded in the presence of the composer), a performance practice for Pärt's music has evolved which encourages exactly the intentional, meticulous, and tuneful playing that is required.[60]

With regard to performance practice, one interviewer suggested that there were, broadly speaking, two ways to perform Pärt's music: "One is the strict, detached kind, with the notes placed one after the other. A different way is the more romantically influenced style, with agogic [accentual] impetus." Asked which way he preferred Pärt replied: "Romantic or detached … that makes no difference to me. Something else is important: interpretation must live, it must breathe and convince us. Only that has a value and importance. Everything else is to my mind mere theory." Pärt went on to describe what it's like to hear his own music, likening it to an open wound which always aches when you touch it, but he countered this comment with an anecdote about Neeme Järvi conducting *Cantus* less differently each time he performed the piece: "He lives and changes and so does his interpretation … I have learned that each performance is a unique version in which every bit has its own place."[61]

In one scene in Supin's film *24 Preludes for a Fugue,* Pärt thanks a group of performers who are playing his music and remarks that a composer is nothing without them. He demonstrates this by holding up his coat and letting it fall to the ground, noting that without a person, it is useless. He has also acknowledged that his music is not actually his, but that he and the interpreter are collaborators in a process: "Then suddenly an interpreter comes along, who plays something out of this empty space in such a way that you feel within yourself that this is no longer your music. In fact, it isn't my music. The music is simply a bridge between us, and what the interpreter does is very beautiful."[62]

A good relationship with performers is key to the production of an authentic and satisfactory version of the piece being performed, but a relationship with the listener is also vital. Pärt has not cultivated audiences himself by any special means, preferring to let the music speak for itself. He describes his relationship with his audience using the metaphor of passing trains: "Moments of recognition between composer and listener happen somehow like sitting in two passing trains. You only make out the person in the other train during a fleeting glance through the window. We composers have our path to follow, and the listeners theirs. The artist is also just a traveler, like the listener too. And still, we meet … through music, let's say."[63]

Human rights

It is important to remember that Pärt spent a significant part of his life in a Soviet state and that this has had a profound impact on him. When asked if early in his career he wanted to be famous and whether he thought he might achieve it with the tintinnabuli music, he replied that he was not aware that he developed a musical technique that would be so fertile, nor was this his primary concern. He claimed, "I just wanted to stay alive."[64]

He has spoken of oppression, but speaks too of the human spirit: "It would not have been difficult for the Apostles to have lived in the Soviet Union. And there are wonderful people like that there. Heroism can flower in that climate. But it is not absolutely necessary for people to live under such conditions. Perhaps it is more important for something to happen with us, out of our own free will. It makes a difference in the way one thinks if one is hungry or full. Should we all for that reason go hungry? There exists a higher level for us than just being hungry or full. We would not allow ourselves to founder on these two extreme alternatives."[65]

He contrasts his own experience with what he perceives as a general disposition of people in the West: "People here are very sleepy; they are satiated with so many things – everything is available to them. People have no worries and become very passive. What activity there is, is of a super-ficial kind: a bodily activity, a sort of aggression. One must be active and above all not hibernate like a bear, but all this activity is not really pure or full of life – it is not linked to the spirit. Everything here is far more theoret-ical, unlike the life and death situations that one experiences in totalitarian states. There is no danger here: you can write, say, and do what you want, but in totalitarian states you can only do what is allowed, and important things aren't allowed."[66]

Pärt has always been concerned for human rights and although he acknowledges his place as a musician in the scheme of things he has recently been using his power and influence to highlight specific cases of injustice. In 2006–07 he dedicated all performances of his work to Anna Politkovskaya, a human rights activist who was assassinated in 2006. His Symphony No. 4 is dedicated to Mikhail Khodorkovsky, a former oil oli-garch accused of business crimes, and also to "all those who are impris-oned without rights in Russia." As part of the program for the British premiere of the piece Pärt wrote a forceful and strongly worded message entitled "David and Goliath," in which he describes what is taking place in the Moscow courtrooms as a "lynching." He expressed his admiration for Khodorkovsky: "I bow before Mikhail Khodorkovsky's fortitude and composure, before his intellectual productivity in such unthinkable condi-tions." Pärt regrets that he personally does not have "a viable opportunity to help him and his associates" but hoped that his music would be a carrier pigeon that might reach Khodorkovsky in prison in Siberia one day.[67] In his own way, Pärt has become an effective advocate for human rights and has modeled a humanistic response that encourages everyone to participate in a stand against injustice.

Legacy

The International Arvo Pärt Centre is located in Laulasmaa, a village about 40 kilometers west of Tallinn. The Centre currently has two buildings: the main house contains the administrative offices, and the garage building has been converted to a climate-controlled archive and also contains space for the many people who are conserving and cataloging the collection.

The aim is to preserve and present Pärt's creative heritage by digitizing, systematizing, and storing materials for the future. Although not slated to open fully until 2015, the Centre has a web site which details its principal goals:

> From 2015, the centre will include a research institute, an education and music centre, a museum, a publishing facility, and the basis for all this will be a completely up-to-date archive, which is being created at the instigation of the composer's family.
>
> The centre will offer opportunities for study and academic research into Pärt's work and music. It will provide a complete overview of the composer's work and allow access to the essence of his creative contribution and written material. The centre also plans to issue grants, publish material relating to Pärt and his work, as well as organize conferences, concerts and master classes.
>
> The archive contains the composer's hand-written musical diaries, manuscripts, notes, quotations, notes with comments by the composer, documents and correspondence, photographs, the composer's equipment, tape recordings and cassettes, an audio collection, vinyl records, a video collection, research papers, awards and dedications, programmes, posters, media coverage, books, musical instruments and more.[68]

Created in 2010 by Pärt and his family, the Board consists of Pärt's wife Nora and their two sons, Michael (the Chairman) and Immanuel. There is currently a staff of five and many volunteer team members. Modeling its work on the Schoenberg archive, the Board has been thorough in its two principal objectives: to archive Pärt's work and to make it accessible in imaginative ways to the public. We are fortunate that this diligence will preserve Pärt's legacy so that future generations can hear him speak in his own words.

7 Bells as inspiration for tintinnabulation

MARGUERITE BOSTONIA

Many descriptions have been employed by musicians and popular media to characterize the austere, timeless qualities of tintinnabuli. Being both a spiritual and artistic métier, its most quintessential declaration is often quoted from Arvo Pärt himself: "The three notes of a triad are like bells. And that is why I called it tintinnabulation."[1] What Pärt describes as something "like bells" is a musical essence that transcends its own comparison. The full reference from his debut ECM recording provides us with a fuller context:

> Tintinnabulation is an *area* I sometimes wander into when I am *searching* for answers – in my life, my music, my work. In my dark hours, I have the certain feeling that everything *outside this one thing* has no meaning. The complex and many-faceted only confuses me, and I must *search for unity*. What is it, *this one thing*, and how do I *find my way* to it? Traces of *this perfect thing* appear in many guises – and everything that is unimportant falls away. *Tintinnabulation is like this.* Here I am alone with silence. I have discovered that it is enough when a single note is beautifully played. This one note, or a silent beat, or a moment of silence, comforts me. I work with very few elements – with one voice, with two voices. *I build with the most primitive materials – with the triad, with one specific tonality. The three notes of a triad are like bells.* And that is why I called it tintinnabulation.[2]

Self-identifying his technique from *tintinnabulum*, the Latin word for 'little bell', Pärt discerns a unified, pure sound that can permeate both the ear and external space. A single bell retains a natural, unchanging tonal complex that is unbound by style conventions, which predates functional harmony, and which persists through modern times in its primitive manifestation. Along with the aural symbolism of a bell, Pärt also affords equal import to two other aspects: a search for a perfect place, and for unity. "Tintinnabulation is like this," he declares, and for him it symbolizes all three elements.

Pärt's interviews across the years provide additional characteristics of this "one thing" that is like bells, which he seeks so intensely. It is also clear from the documentary *24 Preludes for a Fugue* that this quest began at a young age, and is unashamedly spiritual as well as artistic.[3] His personal pilgrimage, his need for a place that is cloaked by the stasis of a single tonality, yields a music that possesses the lucidity of monophonic chant in a musical dimension where this pure sound flourishes. In an interview in 1998 he described the innate simplicity that underlies complex entities: "All important things in life are simple. Just look, for example, at the partial tones of the overtone scale: the initial, lower overtones are perceptible and easily distinguishable, whereas the upper ones are more clearly defined in theory than audible."[4] By evoking ancient attributes of *musica universalis*, this former sound engineer turned intuitively to the scientific origin of sound in order to refine sound to its purest elements.[5] If anything divine exists in music, it was to be found in this natural essence, not by man-made layers of contrived complexity. "Tintinnabuli is like this."

A great debt is owed to Paul Hillier, who has had the advantage of many collaborations with Pärt, and has engaged in the formidable task of exegesis for Westerners; that of describing the mysteries of Orthodox beliefs in Pärt's life and their intimate links to tintinnabuli. Implicit is the distinctly Eastern praxis of *theosis*, or the lifelong searching of believers to share in the divine nature, often through silence and repetitive prayer.[6] In Pärt's words, "Religion and life – it is all the same."[7] Hillier enhances our understanding of innate bell qualities in language that mirrors Orthodox beliefs and tintinnabuli's polarity of prayerful stasis versus purposeful quest:

> If a single bell is struck, and we contemplate the nature of its sound – the *Klang* at impact, the spread of sound after this initial gesture, and then the lingering cloud of resonance – what we hear takes us to the heart of tintinnabuli. A finely wrought bell makes one of the most mysterious and creative sounds: a sound that certainly 'rings out' and reaches towards us, yet at the same time pulls us in towards it, so that soon we realize we are on the inside of it, that its inside and outside are in fact one and the same.[8]

Before leaving Estonia, in an interview with music critic Ivalo Randalu, Pärt mentions a numinous quest when asked, "Let's take, for example, 'Tintinnabuli.' What do you try to discover or find or achieve there? That keynote and the triad; what are you looking for there?"

PÄRT: Infinity and chastity.
RANDALU: ... What is "chastity" in this context? By the means of sound?
PÄRT: I can't explain, you have to know it, you have to feel it. You have to search it, you have to discover it. You have to discover everything, not only the way how [*sic*] to express it, you have to have the need for it, you have to desire to be like this.[9]

How desperately Pärt seems to struggle with the magnitude of his search! Abstractions of timelessness, purity, or *theosis* are not easily articulated, but the "desire to be like this" is a pursuit that intersects many religious ideologies. Since "Traces of this perfect thing appear in many guises,"

Pärt sought a spiritually pure art music that impels the composer towards a new paradigm, and compels the listener to respond. Undertaking his search involved years of exploration, outside the confines of cathedral and concert hall. From the time of the pivotal work *Credo* (1968) to the brief and modest *Für Alina* (1976), Arvo Pärt privately reclaimed his faith and transformed his artistry, emerging with a new compositional voice. He refers to this time as seeking his way out of a "creative deadlock" which was like the road to Calvary.[10] We are escorted on a journey where "this one pure thing," symbolized by bell sonorities, resonates in ways he needs not explain to the spiritually minded. 'Holy minimalism,' a commercial term ill-used to describe a group of postmodern tonal composers of sacred content, cannot begin to portray Pärt's solitary pilgrimage, which took place during the 1960s, isolated and far from the urbane American and British minimalists.

In Supin's documentary, Pärt speaks with numerous vivid comparisons: "like two people whose paths seem to cross … like a blade of grass has the status of a flower … like communication between two friends … like embracing … like a blessing." Rhetorically speaking, use of the word 'tintinnabuli' goes beyond simile and metaphor and is a fully engaged metonym: a figure of speech in which the name of an entity is borrowed to define another, where both share innate characteristics, musical and spiritual. "That is why I call it tintinnabulation."

A final characteristic that reinforces this metonymy is brought to light by Hillier: tintinnabuli was a nameless intuitive development in pursuit of a new synthesis of musical materials. Nora Pärt first discerned the subliminal connection between the triadic techniques and the resonance of bells. While all musical instruments are known to possess natural overtones, bells alone are composed of an audible, triadic structure, lengthy resonance, and inherent inharmonic qualities. The name 'tintinnabuli' was suggested a number of years after the blossoming of the style, and has then been consistently adopted for program notes since 1977.[11] Once this association was drawn by Nora, the composer's use of an acoustical characteristic to identify a complete compositional system reflects musical simplicity, the aptness of metonymy, and the perfection of christening his style *tintinnabuli*. The Pärts caution against taking the name literally. Nora shares that "It's poetical, and the sound of the word is musical."[12]

One might recall that numerous other composers have been inspired by bell sounds, through borrowing, quotation, and allusion. Russian composers are known for overt imitations of bell ringing.[13] The organ repertoire is filled with chime works. The dramatic symbolism of bell signals are also frequently exploited in staged works and symphonic poems.[14] Allusions to bells are present in abundance among romantic and modern program music, particularly in the piano repertoire. Pärt's composition teacher, Heino Eller, composed a popular piano work titled *Kellad* (The Bells) which is still performed in Estonia.[15] Pärt uses actual bells rather sparingly in his own works, with *Cantus in Memory of Benjamin Britten* being the most noted example. For his seventy-fifth birthday celebrations in his childhood home of Rakvere, he composed *Kyrie*, a brief work for the five bells of the Church of the Holy Trinity. His most consistent evocation of bells, however, is as a newly organized tonal presence throughout his works.

Having a final voice in the tintinnabuli legacy is the new *International Arvo Pärt Centre*, repository of his creative work, which stresses that the underlying building blocks of his works remain the core of the process, and the inseparable whole of the melodic and triadic union within tintinnabuli technique can generate "a form of polyphony [which] is built out of tonal material drawn from beyond the paradigms of functional harmony."[16] Tintinnabuli has emerged not as imitation of bells but as a new paradigm, seemingly inimitable, which is capable of depth, complexity, and large formal evolution without compromising simplicity and spirituality, in that place where "everything that is unimportant falls away." From the aspect of spirituality, the aforementioned holy minimalists have also emerged with ritual music that appears to transcend their liturgical roots, beckoning the greater church as well as the unchurched.[17] Many of their works are tonal and liturgically based, but more suitable to the concert hall than liturgical settings. Tintinnabuli, however, seems to stand alone as a new organic nucleus, often described by Pärt as a new gesture; as *Auftakt*.[18] It is intended to be the vehicle of a spiritual essence, going beyond any surface attraction of bell timbres. It beckons; it "pulls us in towards it," according to Hillier.

Bells are an ancient musical instrument, usually cast in the 'primitive material' of bronze. The authoritative writings of campanologist Percival Price illustrate the presence of many varieties of bells in all cultures.[19] Once cast, a bell is virtually impervious to manipulation by performers or composers; even 'style' is dependent upon materials used, and tower structure, and tempo of execution is limited by its mass and mechanisms. Our unanswered question remains regarding tintinnabuli: how genuine is the evocation of bells for Arvo Pärt, and, if it is genuine, what kind of bell or essence is he aiming to produce? Since most of the early champions of Arvo Pärt's music outside the Soviet Union were British, early articles and studies refer to English bells and change ringing as inspiration for tintinnabuli. This includes Paul Hillier's articles and his biography.[20] In order to determine a bona fide bell effect, it is necessary to learn what working bells existed in Estonia when Pärt was resident there and what other bells he may have heard.

Plate 7.1 The bells at St. Mary Lowgate, Kingston upon Hull, Yorkshire, England in the 'up' position

Within Europe, there are three distinct bell-ringing styles: English, Dutch, and Russian. While all countries can have any number of random-sized peals and tolling, England has had a unique change-ringing style since the seventeenth century. Five to twelve bells on 360-degree rotating wheels are rung – actually swung – in ordered mathematical permutations. Teams of ringers – one to a bell – learn to pause their bells at the top of the wheel just long enough to let the next bell drop first, allowing the free clappers to strike inside a swinging bell. Their ropes are connected to the circular wheel, not to the bell (Plate 7.1). The bells themselves are roughly tuned to a diatonic scale. No doubt, Pärt has experienced English change ringing during many visits to Great Britain, but there is no evidence of English change ringing in Estonia.

A second type of bell and style of ringing originated in the Low Countries: the carillon. This instrument, developed in the fourteenth century, consists of skillfully tuned bells in full chromatic scales, numbering from twenty-three to as many as seventy or more. The Dutch perfected closely guarded tuning secrets which were lost until resurrected by modern acoustical technology.[21] The instrument is operated by a baton-style keyboard, and each baton is connected to a clapper by tracker action and

Plate 7.2 Theodore C. Butz Memorial Carillon, Chicago Botanic Gardens, USA

linkages (Plate 7.2). Carillons are capable of melody, harmony, articulation and dynamics, and have a large body of repertoire. Nevertheless, the World Carillon Federation lists no carillons installed anywhere in Estonia.

Plate 7.3 Church of St. Nicholas, Ozeretskoe village, Moscow region, Russia

Russian bells are a type of peal with several distinctions from other European bells. The name for a set of Russian bells is *zvon*, and it is an Orthodox aural icon of Pärt's adopted faith. Within the Russian Orthodox Church, the *zvon* represents the expression of the joy and triumph of God's church; is capable of touching hearts, of encouraging the faith of believers; and reminds all within earshot of what is transpiring during Divine Liturgy (Plate 7.3). The *zvon* can number from a small group of three to five, to as many as thirty or so bells. Most important is that Russian bells are always untuned, left in their naturally cast state, causing them to sound less traditionally harmonious than a tuned carillon.

Zvoni are assembled by size, and grouped as bass, alto, and treble, never arranged in a scale. The playing style is also unique: it is primarily additive rhythmic patterns rather than melodies. Another distinction is that the bells are hung dead and not moved; the clappers are moved with ropes. With no need to swing the bells, there is less stress on tower structures, and Russian foundries created some of the largest bells in the world. The world's largest bell is the Tsar Bell, which broke after casting, was never rung, and is enshrined at the Moscow Kremlin. One impression of a visitor during Easter Week (*Pascha*) was that the sound of Moscow's 5,000 bells was "the most impressive aural display in Christendom," with the Kremlin bells shaking the ground. Before electric amplification, no other instrument in history could produce so loud a sound as the large Russian bells.[22]

Heavy clappers or 'tongues' limit the speed of bass ringing, but the smaller treble bells are capable of rapid jingling. Alto bells often create 'upbeat' patterns. The final distinction of the *zvon* is that it is the only musical instrument used in the Russian Orthodox Church, other than the human voice, and the Church *Typikon* provides strict instructions for liturgical ringing.[23] A ringer, or *zvonar*, is usually a cleric, and with training can ring multiple bells with ropes, foot pedals, and other wooden levers. Layered patterns of repetitive rhythmic ringing are indicated for holy days, parts of the liturgy, and as call to worship, ranging from somber and simple to complex and riotous.

With Estonia being a former Soviet Republic (1944–91), it is important to determine whether Pärt experienced Russian bells in the soundscape of Tallinn. Estonia was historically an occupied nation, by Scandinavians, Germans, and eventually Tsarist Russia. This accounted for the influx of Russians and the Russian Orthodox Church from which Estonian branches of Orthodoxy were formed. After a brief period of national independence between the world wars, Estonia was again subsumed into the Soviet Union after World War II. During Estonia's brief independence, the 1917 Russian Revolution was cause for a cataclysm of liturgical oppression, church destruction, and murder of clergy. This included a bell holocaust: tens of thousands of bells were destroyed, including approximately 2,300 in Moscow. For over seventy years, Russians were forbidden to practice their faith and were robbed of the comfort of hearing *zvoni*. Prior to perestroika, only five classic (pre-revolutionary) *zvoni* survived:[24]

1. Rostov Veliky (Rostov the Great) was home to the Uspensky Cathedral. Its horizontal belfry contains fifteen bells which were preserved by the Soviet Union for culturally historic purposes. It is located north of Moscow, on Lake Nero.
2. Vologda was home to the Cathedral of the Resurrection, having twelve to fifteen bells, and one of only 500 churches preserved intact out of nearly 60,000 destroyed. Vologda is called the city of churches and is an architectural center north of Moscow.
3. Danilovsky Monastery is one of the first monasteries built in Moscow during the thirteenth century, and was the first returned to the Orthodox Church in 1983. It is the residence of the Patriarch and spiritual center of Russian Orthodoxy, originally housing thirty-five bells. Seventeen bells were saved from destruction by Charles Crane, of Harvard University, in 1930 (before Pärt's birth) and installed in Harvard's Lowell House, where they remained for over seventy-five years. (After much negotiation, the bells were returned to Moscow in 2008, with Russian bell replicas cast for Harvard.)
4. Pskovo-Pechersky Monastery is today located very near the Estonian border, in Pskov. However, Pskov was Estonian territory during the Russian Revolution, thus completely spared from Soviet destruction. When Estonia was later

annexed by the Soviet Union, years had elapsed since the 'bell killings,' and the thirteen bells were spared. Pskovo-Pechersky is also a center for liturgical arts and icon painting, and Hillier notes that Pärt visited many Orthodox centers during his time of religious conversion and study of early music.[25] Close proximity to Estonia makes Pskov a likely destination for Pärt, with its treasures of icons and *zvon*.

5. St. Alexander Nevsky Cathedral, with eleven bells, was dedicated in Tallinn, Estonia, in 1900, and is the most recently cast of the surviving classic *zvoni*. Even during Soviet years, its bells remained in continual use.[26] Indeed, Arvo Pärt's inspiration from Russian bells was genuine, as he was within earshot of the *zvon* of St. Alexander Nevsky – enjoying bells long denied the Soviet faithful.

Since perestroika, there has been a resurgence of Russian church activity, and a rebuilding and recasting of replacement bells. Valery Gergiev of the London Philharmonic, and artistic director of the Mariinsky Theatre, inaugurated the Moscow Easter Festival in 2002, filled with concerts, operas, and the return of *Pascha* bells. With so much of the art lost, acousticians studied the few surviving bells as models for this long-awaited restoration, and about eight new foundries have already replaced thousands of destroyed bells. When the Pärt family first immigrated to Berlin in 1980, years after the beginnings of tintinnabuli, they would have only experienced roughly tuned bell peals that survived World War II. Berlin's three existing carillons were newly built eight or more years after their arrival.[27]

Having confirmed the survival of authentic Russian bells in Estonia, an exploration of the sound spectrum is appropriate. From acoustical studies, the unique *zvon* overtone series has been documented, consisting of the fundamental frequency (actually the second partial) and an inharmonic minor third above it (tierce). Farther above the tierce is the fourth partial, sounding approximately a fifth above the fundamental, called the quint. Even further above are shorter-duration thirds, sevenths and ninths (see Figure 7.1). Most interesting in bells is the first partial approximately an octave below the fundamental, known as the hum tone; Hillier's "lingering cloud of resonance." The famous bass bell of Rostov, named 'Sisoy,' weighs 36 tons, with a 1.1-ton clapper, and has a hum-tone reverberation of over 2½ minutes![28] The constancy of Pärt's triadic T-voice, along with frequent drones or long durations, seems to emulate the natural hum-tone presence. The bells' untuned state means the intervals are not equally tempered, and could be diminished or augmented fifths, along with sevenths or ninths for the octaves. The inharmonic quality of untuned bells became a beloved characteristic of beautiful color and timbre, often referred to as 'red,' or 'raspberry.' (These tritonal qualities could be the origin of a Russian compositional preference for tritones.) Figure 7.1 compares the typical harmonic series of strings and bells.

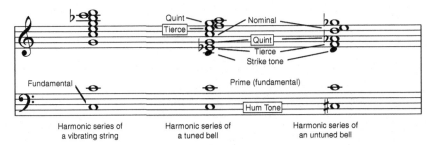

Figure 7.1 Harmonic series of a string, tuned and untuned bells (strike tones of bells included)

The strike tone, a resultant tone which is not part of the overtone series, becomes reconciled to unison with lower frequencies in tuned bells. In the Russian untuned bell, the more intense strike tone is inharmonic to frequencies closest to the triad structure. In the example of an untuned bell in Figure 7.1, a diminished triad is formed by the strike tone, tierce, and quint. When multiple bells (and multiple imperfect triads) are combined in a festive *zvon* pattern, such welcome inharmonicities are inadvertently colorful and cacophonous. Pärt does not attempt to completely emulate the multi-sized bells of a *zvon*. His intuition leads him instead to limit his tonal center and triads to one choice, and to judiciously change or combine tonal centers in larger or more complex works in carefully preplanned fashion. Unquestionably, treatment of the omnipresent T-voice in tintinnabuli compositions shares the innate character of a bell triad and tonal hum note in Pärt's new musical applications.

'Dissonant chords' or 'non-functional harmony' are often descriptive of vertical tintinnabuli sonorities which incidentally result from the expanding melodic M-voice interacting in union with the triadic T-voice.[29] Evoking the modal monody of Gregorian chant injects dissonance and momentary tensions which are carefully controlled by devices of T-voice positions, parallel doubling, or other metrical devices and expansion schemata. Pärt described his inseparable voices to his biographer, Hillier, as the wandering and subjective M-voice, representing ego, sin, and suffering joined to the monolithic T-voice portraying forgiveness and objectivity; the "eternal dualism of body and spirit, earth and heaven." Nora Pärt famously elucidated this duality as "1+1=1."[30] Pärt himself views this as a mystical manifestation: "Hidden behind the art of connecting two or three notes lies a cosmic mystery."[31] Having arrived at the name 'tintinnabuli' for this technique, Pärt rarely discusses bells again. The majority of his more recent discussions focus on the union of pure, neutral elements, on the image of the journey, and hidden meanings; all of which remain symbolized by the character of a bell. All instruments have finite ranges; a bell is simply more reductive than most in its tonal capacity. Minimal sonic structures and economy of means are characteristics that are shared with American minimalism, which results in multiple spontaneous discoveries, musically exclusive of each other at the time of their origins.

According to Orthodox aesthetics, the untuned *zvon* as icon expresses the joy of the Resurrection, calls the faithful to prayer, and banishes thoughts of sin and weakness. "The bronze voice of Orthodoxy" is a sounding icon of the voice of God.[32] Centuries on Orthodox heritage exist to uplift believers via meditation on aesthetic archetypes, all of which are essentially anonymous. Orthodox musical scholar Kurt Sander eloquently describes the Orthodox integration of iconography, hymnography, chant, and architecture as the "ultimate interdisciplinary philosophy" which unifies the worship of the communion of saints in a "heaven on earth."[33] Liturgically speaking, tintinnabuli is not only musically figurative, but a liturgical window to spirituality, another point of contact for an Orthodox believer as well as the worldly audience. This iconic dynamic further distances tintinnabuli from minimalist processes. Pärt chose bell-like qualities to symbolize "this one thing," and he crafts his artistry in the same careful Orthodox manner as the painted icons embody the spiritual essence of saints rather than their earthly likenesses. Echoing the "eternal present" of the Divine Liturgy, Sander also indicates aesthetic differences between the "beautiful," which is worldly and sensual, and the "sublime" which reflects spiritual mystery and timelessness. M- and T-voices mirror this liturgical polarity, and guide listeners to Pärt's cosmic "hidden world." For the Orthodox composer, Sander concludes, "the process of creating the musical icon, like the Christian struggle for salvation, is driven by a vision of perfection. With such a vision, the process of creation becomes itself an icon, the quest for artistic perfection symbolizing the greater human quest for Divine perfection."[34] For Pärt's struggle, the process has become the icon, the quest is aimed towards the Divine, and the 'area' of the search is tintinnabuli. Music and liturgy are one: "There is no border that divided ... Religion and life – it is all the same."[35]

During a recent conversation with Pärt, I expressed curiosity about the introduction and coda of the organ work *Annum per annum*. The thundering, rhythmic patterns seem like the famous large bell peal of Speyer Cathedral, for which it was written. Hearing my thoughts, Pärt brightened and smiled, saying, "Good! That is what it is to *you*. Very good." His intention was to frame the work, and when asked what it symbolized, his quick response was "Joy, just joy in the celebration," implying something as obvious as *zvoni* thunderously pealing the joyful news of *Pascha*.[36] He seemed genuinely pleased that intuitive points of contact for composer and listener could be realized through his music.

Tintinnabuli is an archetype that is as non-egoistic as chant and icon painting, drawing others toward it. Seemingly sacred, illusively minimalistic, branded as holy, rich in universal symbolism, tintinnabuli has indeed achieved spiritually iconic proportions and the worldly pinnacle of artistic integrity. In the documentary *24 Preludes for a Fugue*, Pärt is seen alone at his piano, marveling at the infinite expressions possible – for as many people are in the world, "there are different prayers and sighs." Another scene, of a teaching seminar in Estonia in April of 1999, concludes with his demonstration of the "one perfect thing" in very poignant language: "It [tintinnabuli] makes such a heart-rending union; the soul yearns to sing it endlessly."[37]

Further reading

Irina Aldoshina and A. Nicanorov, "The investigation of acoustical characteristics of Russian bells," paper presented at the 108th Convention of the Audio Engineering Society, New York, February 19–22, 2000.

James H. Billington, *The Icon and the Axe: An Interpretive History of Russian Culture* (New York: Alfred A. Knopf, 1968).

Leonid Ouspensky and Vladimir Lossky, *Meaning of Icons*, translated by G. E. H. Palmer and E. Kadlouvbosky (Crestwood, NY: St. Vladimir's Seminary Press, 1982).

Percival Price, *Bells and Man* (Oxford University Press, 1983).

Kallistos Ware, *The Orthodox Church, new edition* (Baltimore, MD: Penguin Books, 1997).

Edward V. Williams, *The Bells of Russia* (Princeton University Press, 1985).

8 Arvo Pärt and spirituality

ROBERT SHOLL

I Orientations

This study examines the ways in which Arvo Pärt's music may be experienced as spiritual or even religious. Pärt's music embraces both a secular spirituality (understood as a personal experience of, communication with, or belief in the divine), as well as such experiences within the context of institutional religion.[1] The multivalent agency of his music, situated between what the philosopher Charles Taylor has identified as conformity and unbelief, is essential to its communicative power and appeal.[2] This study, therefore, offers a perspective on how the complexity of this musical agency and the spiritual experience of Pärt's music can be constructed, articulated, and evaluated.

Spirituality is a construct that is focused around specific technical and aesthetic concepts that can be related to the secularity and complexity of modernity. This relationship can be understood in the following way:

Modernity	*Spirituality*
Progress	Staticism
Materialism (external)	Spiritualism (internal)
Disenchantment	(Re)enchantment
Decay (death)	Transcendence, transformation (life)
Contingency (anxiety, now)	Permanence (eternity)
Anxiety	Centeredness (calm)
Knowledge about (science, rationalism)	Knowledge of (intuition)
Alienation (desensitization)	Integration (resensitization)
Desubjectification (institutions)	Awareness (person)
Fragmentation	Holism

This dualist conception is consonant with the ways in which spirituality, especially from the 1960s onwards, has been perceived as a counter-cultural panacea to modernity that has also absorbed a social psychosis of self-substantiating belief without recourse to religious or political authority.[3]

Both modernity and spirituality, conceived in these ways, however, have represented a search for an understanding of God as much as a resistance to the constrictions (doctrine and dogma) of formal religion. Some recent well-publicized books by Richard Dawkins, Christopher Hitchens (and others) are symptomatic of modernity's resistance (even disavowal) of God. These commentators put God under the microscope, examine God by human standards of post-Enlightenment rationality, and find God wanting.[4] Spirituality, however, rather than resisting or disavowing God, enacts a search to understand God despite such 'rationality.' It is not a form of escapism from modernity. Rather, spirituality is a consciousness that has absorbed and even reconfigured the problems of modernity through alternative and sometimes equally rational discourses.

Spirituality can therefore be imagined as a relationship in which humanity is looking for God (through all means at its disposal), even though (from a Christian perspective) God already loves us, and has already found us. Music acts as a context for this relationship, and, more specifically, as an agent in this complex negotiation of searching and of realization. Arvo Pärt's music, as much as it espouses a unity with God, is symptomatic of humanity's search for God, and, as such, it is a self-conscious and modernist form of political vanguardism that relies on a productive engagement (rather than any antipathy) with modernity.[5] His music, more pertinently, points to an excruciating gap between humanity and God that, in unexpected ways, is an exhortation to participate in and even bridge this liminal space.

This study examines the nature of this participation through the complementary strata of Pärt's music. It examines his musical language, and its resonances in associated aesthetic concepts and meanings that apply to modernity, spirituality, and religion. An understanding of the content and structure of Pärt's tintinnabulation music (after 1976) forms a preface to a discussion of cultural and musical narratives of death and mourning, and enchantment and embodiment that inform Pärt's musical search for God, and identify it as a soundtrack of our age.

II Language and resonances

Philosophy and theology have traditionally attempted to explain that the source of musical inspiration derives from God, the soul, or some secular 'noumenal' region.[6] All of these explanations point towards, and attempt to describe, in some sense, the reason for the music's existence and, as a secondary phenomenon, the composers' own experience of their music: what they were trying to do or to say, and what they want people to experience when they hear it. The desire to explain music in the twentieth century – a strange sojourner in a strange land – was an imperative for many of the major twentieth-century composers. Arnold Schoenberg, Igor Stravinsky, Olivier Messiaen, Pierre Boulez, John Cage, Karlheinz Stockhausen, and John Tavener, amongst others, have written extensively about their own music and the music of others.

Arvo Pärt has not written or said very much about his own work, but his music has been defined around certain key concepts: tintinnabulation, icons, silence, and simplicity.[7] These concepts derive from an attempt by the composer and others to explain the source of his inspiration, and how his imagination has been articulated in his music. They are linked to the composer's own involvement with the Russian Orthodox Church, and they form a constellation of ideals that help to configure his music as spiritual.[8] Although these concepts are described elsewhere in this volume, what follows is a brief explanation of these formative aspects of Pärt's musical language and its spirituality.

Pärt's music has come to be understood as spiritual since the advent of the tintinnabulation technique in his short piano piece *Für Alina* (1976). At its simplest, tintinnabulation is a counterpoint between two lines: the M- or melody voice (which is often modal) utilizes notes from the 'tonic' mode, and the tintinnabulation or T-voice arpeggiates notes from the 'tonic' triad against the M-voice. Pärt understands these voices, which effect a subtle and kaleidoscopic shift between consonance and dissonance, as an idealist dialogue between the melody (or M-voice) as the subjective, "egoistic life of sin and suffering" and the tintinnabulation (T-voice) as the "objective realm of forgiveness."[9] The subtle sense of tension and release imparted by this technique creates the quintessential quality of Pärt's music. In order to understand the significance of this idea for spirituality in music, the background of this concept requires some explanation.

Tintinnabulation represents an engagement with and transformation of traditional ideals of creating a sense of musical narrative and structure. In this ideal (germane to the symphonies of Beethoven, Brahms, and Bruckner, for instance), a formative musical idea or motive undergoes a gradual (or organic) transformation, appearing in sometimes radically different but recognizable guises throughout a movement or a work. This motive is usually presented in the tonic (chord I), at or near the opening and again at the closure of the work, and the sense of this tonic is created by a dynamic opposition with other related chords, principally the dominant (chord V). In this idea of musical development, the main motive of a work undergoes processes of compositional manipulation: embellishment, augmentation/diminution, inversion, extension (addition and subtraction of material), and timbral and registral recontextualization. It is transformed through time and through presentation in different keys that are related to the tonic. This creates a developmental musical narrative that is dependent on the way in which consonance and dissonance are used to create short-term (localized) and long-term (structural) senses of tension and release.

This is sometimes understood as an 'organic' musical development that enables a structure that grows (like a tree) from a root (with the motive understood as the musical seed) towards long-term goals of resolution. In order to escape this kind of 'common practice' ideal of musical development, many composers in the twentieth century (Stravinsky, Messiaen, Cage, György Ligeti, and Steve Reich, to name a few) composed music that creates its own kind of musical narrative through the juxtaposition of blocks of material. While it is tempting to see this ideal of musical development as distinct from common-practice principles for ideological, heuristic, cultural, or even racial reasons, in fact these composers have found their own ways to join or make connections between blocks of sound in unique ways that refine or allegorize the narrative and developmental functions of traditional music.

Arvo Pärt's music belongs to this latter tradition. While Pärt's music does not develop using the traditional methods described above, he does find ways – usually through accretion of material (adding and subtracting voices for instance), and using the tension and release inherent in the tintinnabulation method – to create his own coherent forms of musical architecture.[10] His music is sometimes called minimalist because it repeats material, but such an interpretation of this term is misleading: the procedures of Pärt's music have little in common on a technical level, and even less on an aesthetic plane, with the type of energetic and pulsating rhythmic repetition found in the music of the American minimalist composers Steve Reich and Philip Glass that is, as Robert Fink describes it: "inseparable from the colourful repetitive excess of post-industrial, mass-mediated consumer society."[11] Pärt's music may use repetition, but it is certainly not minimalist in this sense.

Its use of musical material is actually self-referential, formally hermetic, and deliberately limited (immanent) in its exploration of the motivic implications of his ideas. Each work, and each section of a work, is generally characterized by a certain repertoire of dissonances and consonances, and a selection of textures and sounds that provide a stable identity to that particular work. In fact, given that the tintinnabulation technique is so simple, it is a testament to Pärt's originality that he has created so many different contexts for it.

That Pärt uses a minimum amount of material means that he must tread a fine line between repetition and monotony. Indeed, because the sense of change within this material is often achieved with great subtlety, it is possible to hear the evolution of the material through time, and aspects of expectation and fulfilment (if not long-term tension and release in his music) that are analogous to the common-practice procedures described above. Crucially, however, the degree to which one experiences new events as new is minimized. Because his textures have minimal but varying information, density and flux, the sense of change and direction, and even a sense of progress, when certain works are examined closely, are carefully controlled to create a sense of narrative particular to each work.

In short, Pärt's music demands a certain kind of listening that might referentially call to mind other traditions of musical structure. However, the desire to explain the effect of his music has led to various problems. Because it uses blocks of material, it is sometimes identified as 'static' art, in contradistinction to the 'dynamic' common-practice model described above. In this sense, staticism is a musical and ideological construction that configures the meaning of the music as a panacea to the sense of dynamism, drama, and progress associated with modernity. This perceived staticism of the music has led to a description by Paul Hillier of the music as a "sounding icon." The music has therefore been inextricably linked to the devotional art associated with the composer's own Russian Orthodox faith.[12]

As a visual metaphor, the icon is a powerfully representational way of describing (and criticizing) Pärt's music. An understanding of the spirituality of his music requires some explanation of icons and the ramifications of using this concept. Icons are painted images made as an aid to worship. Through fixed contemplation of such an image, the viewer is drawn into a greater sense of understanding of him- or herself, and into an understanding of the meanings and significance of the Christian faith. Central to this genre of images is the figure of Christ. There is no existing factual and universally recognized image of Christ. Perhaps because of this, artists throughout the last two millennia, with certain exceptions, have been empowered to imagine a standard iconography of Christ's image. So, because nobody knows what Christ looks like, each artist must recreate a new image, and each icon therefore remains incomplete. The icon's self-conscious resistance to realism, or even anti-realism, an expression of the Ten Commandments' prohibition of images, demands another representation that still remains allusively incomplete.[13]

Icons are therefore ideal and idealist representations made to inspire the mind to imagine the real presence of Christ. The imagination is empowered to bridge the gap between representation and reality, and even to create a new spiritual reality: a sense of being with Christ that is akin to faith. For the Christian, this can never happen until after death, however strong the sense of any visual experience might be. This is of course deeply subjective, but the idea that humanity can be empowered by icons to continually reach beyond its own mortality in a process that could be called transcendence presents a powerful vehicle for the understanding of Pärt's music. Transcendence here can be understood as the ways in which the listener is taken on a journey both into the nature of an alternative or deeper reality (perhaps an intuition of Christ's goodness, God's healing presence, or the glory of creation) and into a more profound understanding of him- or herself within these paradigms. There is therefore a dialogue between external perception and internal awareness. Contemplation, like meditation, is not done to achieve or 'get' something, but to experience something.

If through its staticism Pärt's music can be understood as a sounding icon, then this has profound ramifications for the way in which it is understood as spiritual music. Put another way, it means that the forms and structures, and the language that is used to describe them, are configured in a concept (the icon) that allows Pärt's 'static' music to be perceived as spiritual or religious. So, how is this sense of contemplation, of absorption and possible transcendence, created in Pärt's music? In *Fratres*, three phrases in increasing numbers of quarter-note beats per bar (7 – 9 – 11) are subtly varied and intensified through a simple strophic form.[14] The extreme slowness and the irregular phrase structure, and the absence of an upbeat or a downbeat, engender a sense of timelessness, assisted by a musical narrative which is created through the recognition of varied repetition. This aspect of varied repetition and intensification creates a depth to the music that could be likened to the way in which the iconostasis (a continuous screen of icons separating the nave from the sanctuary in Orthodox churches) points the viewer towards the sanctuary and the sacraments beyond.[15]

In the following two examples the sounding bass of the chord is the drone of violin II, and the string harmonics give a thinner, more liminal quality to the sound.[16]

In the opening of the work (including the two-measure introduction that introduces the prominent G-minor modality), violin I and the cello have the M-voices consistently in tenths, while violin II and the viola have the T-voice (Example 8.1).

Compare this with Example 8.2a and 8.2b: the beginning of the second and third verses. In both these examples, the cello has the main M-voice, counterpointed by the M-voice in the violin. The consistent intervallic relationship (in tenths) between these instruments in the second verse disappears in the third verse, where there is an increased level of dissonance between both the M-voices and with the T-voices. Whereas in

Example 8.1 *Fratres*, opening

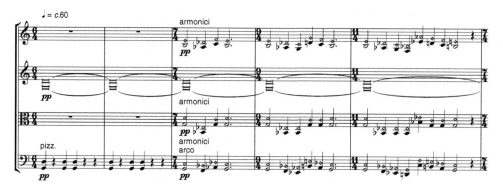

Example 8.2 *Fratres*: (a) mm. 11–13; (b) mm. 19–21

Example 8.1 there is a clear sense of G as a tonic (without any strong polarity with any other chord such as a dominant (V) or subdominant (IV) which would imply a traditional sense of tonality), in Example 8.2a and 8.2b, there is a more intense but subtle sense of conflict between the outer M-voices, which return respectively to a focus on E♭ major and C minor, and the T-voices in G minor.[17]

So, even without tonality (traditionally created by a dynamic opposition of tonic and dominant chords), Pärt employs a symbiosis of related chords and tonal regions. Through the repetition of blocks of material a

Example 8.3 *Fratres*, mm. 27–29

subtle sense of musical change is promoted, along with an increase in tension, and a sense of progression and of narrative. This is taken a step further in the fourth verse, which intensifies the material yet again by registral change (violin and cello M-voices in tenths again), with increased dynamic levels, while also preserving and enhancing the sense of antipathy between the M-voices and the G-minor T-voices. In Example 8.3, violin I plays the same notes (an octave higher) as the cello in Example 8.2.b. The sudden absence of string harmonics in this fourth verse creates a further intensification of the sound.

In Examples 8.2 and 8.3 Pärt focuses the music on different nodal points: on E♭ in measures 11–13, and then on different focal points of C minor in verses three and four. In measures 19–21 it is C, and in measures 27–29 it is A♭ projected against the G–D drone in Violin II.[18] So, although the material has not developed according to the norms of common-practice harmony, there is a sense of a shifting perspective on a limited amount of material, and a changing level of density (voicing) in the texture. The increased intensity of the material also provides a sense of progression and movement within a supposedly 'static' structure. To complete the metaphor, the subtle but inexorable quality of change in the music is akin to the gradual but increasing absorption into an icon, and it is this aspect of narrative and changing subjectivity that is important to an understanding of the work as spiritual.

Fratres is a piece of absolute music: music without a text that does not have any kind of extra-musical narrative program that could be implied by the title or the contents. The sound of this music (with its use of string harmonics) is decentered, allusive, on the verge of the audible, and between presence and absence, in a way that implies a notion of spirituality as ineffable, almost intangible, searching and unfulfilled without reference to any concrete spiritual or religious narrative.[19]

In *Trisagion* for string orchestra (1992, rev. 1994), Pärt makes an explicit link between the homophonic chords in the piece and religious meaning by writing an (unheard) text directly underneath each system of the music; the syllables of the text line up with the chords. Pärt therefore encourages the listener to believe (when using the score of course) that there is a meaningful link between the sounds and the religious substance of the text, which is an invocation of the humble and penitent soul's response to Christ's sacrifice on the cross, and concludes with the Lord's Prayer.

The repetitive form of *Trisagion* implies a set of variations, even though the degree of harmonic and textural variance is limited and carefully dilated. The relentless E-minor quality of the music is never broken, but is subtly stretched from within by changes of instrumentation, timbre, and register, most particularly by a variance of the density and intensity of sound. The plasticity of the phrasing in *Trisagion* allegorically gives a sense of tension, release, and even goal-directedness without tonal mediation, and the aural sense of certain music events or markers orients the listener (through the subtle use of repetition, chromaticism, dynamics, and register), and gives the music a sense of progression that somewhat undermines the absolute implications of the term 'staticism.' So, given that there is a subtle sense of variation, development, and even teleology in *Trisagion*, the work can be understood as enacting a personal and quasi-liturgical sense of devotion and absorption, as though standing before an icon in an intensification of prayer that is part-narrated, and partly experienced as embodied in the music.

In a salient critique of the music of the so-called 'holy minimalists' (a pejorative term that encompasses the music of Pärt, John Tavener, and Henryk Górecki), the Scottish composer James MacMillan rehearses an axiomatic critique of this music:

> I find their music very beautiful ... but it's a music that is deliberately monodimensional. It's a music that sets out to be iconic. It sets out to have no sense of conflict. It's a music that's in a kind of transcendent state and that's why it's beautiful. But that's also why it exists in one level, there is a deliberate avoidance of conflict, and people like Tavener make very convincing claims for why his music should be that way: an avoidance of the dialectical principles that have been in Western music through Beethoven and before ... my whole compositional philosophy thrives on conflict and ambiguity ... so that there is violence in my music whereas with these other composers there is not, and that sometimes surprises people who think that music of a spiritual dimension should not have violence ... Perhaps the downside of the zeitgeist for spirituality in music is this need to retreat from the world. That's never been my concern.[20]

Although drawing a personal creative distinction, MacMillan's critique is somewhat tendentious: one might as well criticize Mark Rothko's panel paintings for not having the figurative detail and sense of conflict found in Pablo Picasso's *Guernica* (1937) or, more poignantly, the drama of Caravaggio's violent canvases (an ultimate expression of Tridentine Baroque Catholicism). They are patently different things, and made for different purposes.

MacMillan is effectively defining an opposition between spirituality and religion: the transcendent opposed to the dramatic and worldly. He is also echoing a long-standing theological (Neoplatonic) idea that associates temporal staticism with eternity, contrasted with worldly (progressive) time.[21] Certainly, by espousing the icon as a visual metaphor, with its ideal of staticism, Pärt's music can be linked to an experience or intuition of eternity, and can be understood as spiritual in this sense. The theologian Jeremy Begbie supports MacMillan when he states that

> the music of composers such as Tavener and Pärt ... is characterized by a highly contemplative ambience and often labelled "spiritual" ... I have suggested one way of accounting for at least part of the immense popularity of this music: it offers a cool sonic cathedral in a hot, rushed, and overcrowded culture. And I spoke of what I think are its potential benefits. But I also questioned the implicit assumptions about God and time that seem to be at work (and are sometimes articulated): in particular, the belief that the more deeply we relate to God, the more we will need to abstract ourselves from time and history.

Begbie continues:

> We can press the point further. If Christ has embraced our fallen humanity, including its fear, anxiety, hunger, loss, frustration, and disappointment, and these have been drawn into, indeed, become the very material of salvation, can we be content with a vision of the spiritual that is unable to engage just these realities, with a cool cathedral that bears little relation to life on the streets? To focus the point further still: God's engagement with our time climaxes in a hideous and ugly death. Any concern for the spiritual cannot evade this (1 Cor. 1:18–25). As we saw, this is what lies behind MacMillan's suspicion of the New Simplicity movement, that it plays too easily into a world-denying (time-denying) distortion of Christianity in which God's cross-centered involvement with humanity is marginalized.[22]

This is a fascinating critique in a number of ways, and unpacking it affords a glimpse of certain fundamental concepts germane to an understanding of Pärt's music as spiritual. Essential to both MacMillan's and Begbie's critiques is the notion that seriousness in music (in technique and aesthetic intent) is synonymous with complexity, and this is in turn synonymous with value. That complex music should be prized over simpler music is itself a reflection of traditions of writing about music, sometimes traceable to the composers themselves. This preference also reflects the demands of academia for increasingly complex cultural, musical, analytical, and interdisciplinary critiques that support the association of modernity with complexity. This is understandable and even commendable: much modern music is complex and demands to be met at least on its own terms. But while Pärt's music does not espouse the level of technical complexity of MacMillan's music, the richness and the intensity of the experience it affords cannot be concomitantly downplayed in this way.

The distinction between the "cool sonic cathedral" and the "hot, rushed, and overcrowded culture" that Begbie ascribes to Pärt's music plays directly into the kind of demarcation of spirituality and modernity outlined at the outset of this study. Pärt's music is anything but 'cool' or objective. Its over-riding effect of lamentation and of grief is so appealing, from a Christian worldview, precisely because it does not ignore but takes up and attempts to heal what Begbie describes as "our fallen humanity, including its fear, anxiety, hunger, loss, frustration, and disappointment." Pärt's music embraces the horror of Christ's death (in *Trisagion*, *Miserere*, and *Passio*, for instance) through its own sense of musical drama, which has at its root the intensification of minimal sound materials, to take the Christian listener towards a deeper understanding of his or her own role in the endgame of salvation.

Pärt's music may therefore benefit the Christian who must surely believe that Christ was the son of God, and that as God made man, Christ suffered and died on the cross to save the sins of humanity and that he rose again on the third day, thus providing a talisman of the great Christian hope and, crucially, a focal point in history for the faith that humanity will also be resurrected. For a believer, the iconic or ecstatic quality of Pärt's music can act as a devotional aid, or more, as an intimation of what it would be to live *as if* resurrected.

But for those not content with the somewhat circular and predicated answers of Christianity or Christian theology, the (ec)staticism of the music may, in a similar vein, act as medium for understanding the transcendence of suffering in the world that is at the core of the Christian message of hope. Even if Pärt's music, at its best, operates within a limited emotional spectrum, the poetic of lamentation, desolation, and even pity for humanity is surely accessible to the agnostic, the atheist, the non-Christian as much as the Jew or the Buddhist.

Perhaps the most insidious of the criticisms by Begbie and MacMillan is that somehow because the music is not 'complex', it is also not 'critical' of our time, and that it is not 'socially responsible.' Leaving aside the issue of whether music should do this at all, Pärt's music has been used, in films for instance, to excavate deep social, ethical, and emotional responses. While it could be argued that the beautiful sunlit images of a Ukrainian forest, the site of a Nazi massacre, and the voice of a survivor describing the event, are sentimentalized by Laurence Rees's choice of *Spiegel im Spiegel* (1978) as background music in the first episode of his documentary *Auschwitz, the Nazis and the 'Final Solution*,' such a critique would circumscribe the complexity of the experience offered. At this moment, the viewer is called upon not just to lament the inhumane action of others as contrasted with the beauty of the natural world (this might indeed be sentimental), but to imagine that this beauty existed as the event took place. Pärt's music therefore provides a space for the construction of our own presence at the event itself. It empowers the imagination to reflect on what we might have done in that situation, and even how human nature has not greatly altered in our own time (Kosovo, Rwanda). This poetic of mourning is another episode in the story of Pärt's spiritual music.[23]

III Death and mourning

It is surely an irony that in the twentieth century, when music had reached its zenith of dissonance, that so much was made – by Anton von Webern, Cage, Messiaen, and Tavener for example – of the role of silence. Silence is the ultimate antipode of sound, and it is linked in spiritual terms in Pärt's musical aesthetics to an ultimate state of self-realization, and to death.[24]

Modern culture has been obsessed with death. This is unsurprising considering that in the last two hundred years the ideal of the secular rationalist state has, while attempting to guard the citizen's rights, also been an enthusiastic agent for humanity's bloodlust, and has encouraged the invention of more cruel and industrial ways to achieve specious goals.

The Marxist philosopher T. W. Adorno's dictum that "To write poetry after Auschwitz is barbaric" has many ramifications, but here I am only concerned with two aspects.[25] On a musical-technical level, for Adorno, the music from late Beethoven onwards represented an attempt in music to work out the consequences of motivic material that, while using the ideal of development presented above, also tends towards fragmentation. Adorno understood this as a metaphor for the increasing desubjectification of the individual through industrialization, mechanization, and institutionalization (what the sociologist Max Weber called 'disenchantment').[26] The utopian promises of the Enlightenment were therefore a sham for Adorno, and art that is authentic reflects this social reality. For Adorno, the resultant breakdown of tonality – or what Schoenberg more positively called "the emancipation of the dissonance" – was a symptom of the way in which (socially responsible) art reflected a disenchantment and an obsession with death (reification) that led straight to the gas chambers.[27] So, if the sort of common-practice musical development discussed above is synonymous with progress, then it is also a reflection of (and even instrumental in) the decline of humanity. The other implication of Adorno's dictum is that, after the industrialization of killing in Auschwitz, the metaphysics of hope are no longer valid: hope has no hope.[28] In this climate, it is surely no longer possible to aestheticize death, to pity it, to iconicize it, or to make it quasi-heroic in the way that is done in the song cycles of Schubert, Schumann, and Mahler.

In some senses, the history of twentieth-century music (and art) is like a corpse that will not die. The predominance of '-isms' in the twentieth century, as well as political and artistic factions (often with their attend-ant manifestos), has provided an ever-expanding constellation of artis-tic ideals and endeavour that, like small-scale suns, arise and continually burn themselves out to form part of the living museum culture of history.[29] Whether one sees this flux as symptom of decline, or indeed as proof of a blind sense of hope essential to the poetics and rhetoric of modern music, the music of Arvo Pärt once again breathes life into the corpse of modern-ity, but it also inhabits this body.

It is no surprise then that, given the use of theological imperatives as metaphors, our museum culture should also be interested in resurrections. The resurrection of past music, performance techniques, and instruments, and the music of pre-Enlightenment composers were an obsession of the twentieth century. Pärt's discovery of the tintinnabuli method, partly as a response to the challenges of form and coherence created by the "eman-cipation of the dissonance," was preceded by years of silence, and study of such early music.[30] His interest in renaissance polyphony, plainchant, mode, and rhythm is symptomatic of a desire to revive modern music with the enchanted and unsullied material of pre-Enlightenment, pre-ration-alist artisanship. On one hand, this kind of conscious use of preexisting material speaks of a drowning culture clutching at straws, but it was and is also a way of connecting contemporary music with a tradition (thereby giving a sense of authenticity to originality). This sense of mourning for a lost and an unreachable utopia is essential to the spiritual poetics of Pärt's music, and expresses with exquisite poignancy something of the quandary of modernity and humanity after Nietzsche's pronouncement on the death of God.[31] The same poetic dialogue between painful remembrance and uto-pian (even Christian) hope is enshrined in the tintinnabulation technique (the engagement between consonance and dissonance), which promises the possibility of fulfillment (salvation).

If, as musicologist Daniel Chua has pointed out, "in replacing God" humanity must "succumb to its own critique" and die, then any sense of re-enchantment (new aesthetic life) must be essentially temporary.[32] A spiritual music, in effect, becomes a glorification of this contingency. It enacts a tension between a modernity that, as a corpse that will not die, continually strives for re-enchantment, but it also makes a Christian eschatological claim on what that new life should be. The sense of lamentation, pity, and desolation in Pärt's work, expressed through a language grounded in musical stasis, therefore iconizes death as a spiritual absolute. The image is not frozen, however, but, like an icon, it is made to be contemplated, absorbed, and taken up by the living.[33]

IV Enchantment and embodiment

The historian Michael Saler provides the following useful definition of disenchantment:

> This view, in its broadest terms, maintains that wonders and marvels have been demystified by science, spirituality has been supplanted by secularism, spontaneity has been replaced by bureaucratization, and the imagination has been subordinated to instrumental reason.[34]

It is indeed tempting to understand this disenchantment as a symptom of a pervasive and underlying nihilism inherent to secular modernity. Re-enchantment through art must offer opportunities other than glorification or escape from disenchantment. It provides a space for originality, and for the search for an authentic expression. In Pärt's case it is clear that his pre-tintinnabulation compositional silence was a result of a dissatisfaction: a mismatch between what he felt was an authentic voice, and what the prevailing wallpaper of the 1960s musical avant-garde thought were legitimate historical and ideological methods of expression. However, like Górecki and Tavener, Pärt stepped aside from one kind of vanguardism to take up another.

Such a break undoubtedly took self-belief and artistic conviction, but, as Pärt's output has shown, iconoclasm is no guarantee of consistent quality or intellectual energy. Certain pinnacles in his oeuvre have, however, perhaps unlike many works within the vanguard of (high-)modernism, captured the imagination of the listening public and performers alike. So what is it that is attractive about this music? At a certain level the equation of simplicity = profound, and spiritual = release/escapism seems plausible. For a populace saturated and overloaded with information and particularly with the imposition of aesthetic signification, a music that seems to denude itself consciously of labels provides humanity with an opportunity for emptiness, for clarity, and to recognize something of its spirit or essential nature.[35]

Even if this were true, and it is clear from the above discussion that the spirituality of Pärt's music comes with its own complex ideological baggage, this perspective still locates music and spirit as external agents that do something to a person. When Pärt himself states of tintinnabulation that he had "discovered that it is enough when a single note is beautifully played," and that "one note, or a silent beat, or a moment of silence, comforts me," it seems that he is speaking not of external stimuli but of an internalization of sound, and an internal response.[36] What, then, if the spirituality of Pärt's music can be located in the body itself? Through its delicacy, and its sensitivity to the preciousness and freshness of organized sound itself, his music could be understood and experienced as embodied. Pärt's music invites the listener to listen more intently not just to the music, but to oneself, and in this sense a work such as *Pari intervallo* (1976) may, for the first minute or so, seem strikingly boring. That the listener is induced to alter his or her metabolic rate is essential to its poetics, but this does not fully explain this embodied experience, which does not just entail something being done to the listener, nor a response or reaction, but a form of active, somatic participation, and even a making of the sense of spirituality.

In their book *The Embodied Mind*, Francisco J. Varela, Evan Thompson, and Eleanor Rosch identify the 'folk meanings' of meditation as:

> (1) a state of concentration in which consciousness is focused on only one object; (2) a state of relaxation that is psychologically and medically beneficial; (3) a dissociated state in which trance phenomena can occur; (4) a mystical state in which higher realities or religious objects are experienced. These are all altered states of consciousness; the meditator is doing something to get away from his usual mundane, unconcentrated, unrelaxed, nondissociated, lower state of reality.[37]

Behind this kind of dialogue is the theological trope of 'fallenness,' which Pärt attests to himself when he describes tintinnabulation as a perpetual dialogue between the self and forgiveness.[38] Jeremy Begbie is right to be suspicious of the implications of this convenient theological ideal when he cautions against "the belief that the more deeply we relate to God, the more we will need to abstract ourselves from time and history."[39] But any belief that meditation, as much as Pärt's music itself, is not undemanding would be misleading. If indeed Pärt's music asks us to reflect on our own state, it might indeed also embrace, in a theological sense, what Begbie poignantly describes as "our vocation to share in Christ's sufferings (Romans 8:17)" as part of "what it means to be conformed to the image and likeness of Christ

Example 8.4 Symphony No. 4, opening

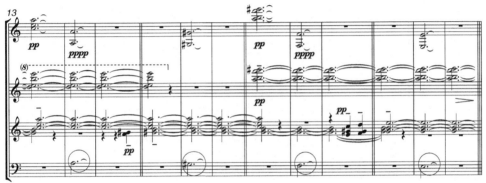

(2 Cor. 3:18)."[40] An embodied experience of Pärt's music is of course possible for Christian and non-Christian alike, and may be one in which mindfulness is both somatic and transcendent, contingent and searching.[41]

The opening section of Pärt's Symphony No. 4 "Los Angeles" (2008) attests to what this experience might be. The sense of becoming and overcoming, linked to the ideal of traditional development, is weakened throughout. Instead, the tintinnabulation technique blurs two chords (the 'tonic' A minor and the 'dominant' E major) to effect a shifting density and intensity of consonance and dissonance. This contingency works in tandem with a searching descending A-minor scale in the bass that implies direction and fulfillment (notes circled in Example 8.4). However, the irregular appearance of the scale steps, their (later) registral displacement, and a plateau of relative harmonic stasis in measures 68–81 within this section fulfills such a promise. A mindful experience of this music might be one in which the listener experiences and participates in the dialogue of stasis and progress in this music. This passage might also provoke memories or a realization of pain and a resignation to the world, together with the creation of a renewed utopian desire that it should be otherwise: all essential elements of Pärt's spiritual poetics.

The sense of the sublime (implied by Pärt's performance indication) is one in which the self is not passively sublimated in the sound, but rather embodied and active. Varela, Thompson, and Rosch describe this embodied experience as a "reflection in which body and mind have been brought together ... reflection is not just on experience, but reflection is a form of experience itself – and that reflective form of experience can be performed with mindfulness."[42] Put another way, the disenchantment linked to modernity offers rational knowledge *about* the self, the world and even God, while the spirituality of Pärt's music is associated with an intuitive knowledge *of* these things, through a consciousness that is "open to possibilities other than those contained in one's current representations of the life space."[43] This is not merely a "dance of sympathy" as Roger Scruton calls it, in which, as Jeremy Begbie explains "when music moves us, a significant part of what we are doing is responding to musical embodiments of bodily movements."[44] Participation is more than mediation of musical structure and cultural meanings through kinaesthetic mimesis.[45] It would involve the way in which past memories, sensations, and feelings (of oneself and the world) are taken up to inform new meanings, new possibilities, and new realities, that, even in a therapeutic vein, may entail new qualities of alienation and excess congruent with spirituality.

As such, one of the purposes of Pärt's music would be to show humanity, in a Christian sense, what it would be like to live as though it were possible to be resurrected. Through the imagination, humanity is required to realize something of and beyond itself. This is the essence of the music's enchantment. It is not necessary to be a Christian to understand this sense of transcendence, or indeed to enjoy the music of Messiaen, Pärt, or John Tavener, any more than it is necessary to be a Buddhist, Hindu, or Jew to feel the power of Buddhist chant and bells, the sanctity of a Hindu temple, or the sincerity and sanctity enshrined in the incantation of the Torah. But to be more than a cultural tourist, knowledge about the technical, cultural, and aesthetic aspects of Pärt's music is a precondition for the contextual knowledge of its spirituality.

The spiritual enchantment offered by Pärt's music is deeply consonant with a search for a more rational, harmonious, and profound way of living that is part of a planetary ecology of revival sometimes regarded as 'new age,' but which is in fact another reactionary tributary of modernity. It has been argued that Pärt's music is even commodified to promote this counter-cultural spiritual purity, or what Pärt calls "the neutral."[46] That such music is a threat to the critical orthodoxy and core values of modernity is etched in some of the more critical responses to this music.[47] Undoubtedly, however, the degree to which spirituality is interpreted as manufactured (and for what purpose) may be contentious for some. Likewise, the degree to which a seemingly secular work such as the Symphony No. 4 can be understood as a sacred work (inspired by Christian religious texts), or a manifestation of a secular narrative of sacralization (as a protest or lament considering its dedication to Mikhail Khodorkovsky and "all those imprisoned without rights in Russia"), will depend largely on the images, iconography, and language that are attached to it.

For many, however, the transcendent experience of Pärt's music might be described most closely as that of the sublime.[48] The romantic experience of the sublime was bound up with images and constructions of the artist as divine mediator, as well as heroism, nature, and death. It was an experience that, culturally conceived, pointed to a peak human experience that was a secular substitute for God. Late twentieth-century studies of peak human experience in sports or the arts, known as 'flow,' point in a radically different context, to an experience of the sublime as embodied.[49] Through engagement with a specific activity, a person experiences himself or herself and the world free of constraints, and with a sense of an expanding or infinite horizon of possibilities.

Experienced in this way, the spirituality of Pärt's music would be life-enhancing.[50] Perhaps Pärt's music is deeply comforting to the living because it provides an intimation of, indeed a preparation for, our own death. If this is so, then surely it can prepare us and show us how to live our lives.[51] The contingency of enchantment that I have identified as essential to Pärt's music and modernity is commensurate with an embodied experience of the music that is fragile, vulnerable, and human. To experience this is to exist on a fulcrum, or a tipping-point that both embraces and may transfigure a resistance to the transcendent, while embodying a desire and a search for the divine that is intrinsically modern. As a soundtrack of our age, the significant popularity of Pärt's music may be attributed to its intimation that life with, or knowledge of, the divine is not only for the unspecified future, but is a pathway for the here and now.

Further reading

Mario Beauregard and Denyse O' Leary, *The Spiritual Brain: A Neuroscientist's Case for the Existence of the Soul* (New York: HarperCollins, 2007).

Jeremy S. Begbie and Steve Guthrie (eds.), *Resonant Witness: Conversations between Music and Theology* (Grand Rapids, MI and Cambridge: Eerdmans, 2011).

Peter Conrad, *Creation: Artists, Gods & Origins* (London: Thames and Hudson, 2007).

Jonathan Harvey, *In Quest of Spirit: Thoughts on Music* (Berkeley and Los Angeles: University of California Press, 1999).

Jonathan Sacks, *The Great Partnership: God, Science and the Search for Meaning* (London: Hodder & Stoughton, 2011).

Hent de Vries (ed.), *Religion: Beyond a Concept* (New York: Fordham University Press, 2008).

Robert Wuthnow, *Creative Spirituality: The Way of the Artist* (Berkeley and Los Angeles: University of California Press, 2001).

9 The minimalism of Arvo Pärt: an 'antidote' to modernism and multiplicity?

BENJAMIN SKIPP

Curious and well-organized people are often characterized by the desire to group things together. As musicologist Jim Samson has contended, a tendency to classify objects according to a set of shared properties allows knowledge to be both "manageable and persuasive."[1] This is as true for the music of everyday life as it is for the rarities which form the subject of arcane typologies; in all circumstances people feel the compulsion to analyze the music they enjoy. Anyone who has worked in schools will know that few subjects ignite debate between young people as much as the eternal delineation of popular music genres. The arguments that rage between those in the know about the differences between 'dubstep' and 'grime' are motivated by the same spirit of enquiry that leads those in other more institutional spheres to discuss the categorization of Arvo Pärt as minimalist or 'holy minimalist,' modernist or postmodern. In recent years, however, these labels, like a moth-eaten cardigan, have begun to wear slightly thin in academic discourse. Useful and enlightening criticism is often deferred in favour of tortuous defining, redefining, and qualification of these irksome terms to the extent that many academics simply sidestep them. There is a section of the audience, however, for whom the words modernist and postmodern may yet prove helpful to their appreciation of music. Many of us care deeply for music but sometimes the ability to identify and articulate why this is the case lies beyond our competency. In grappling with these words, and with the meanings which orbit them, we may begin to understand what it is about Pärt's music that makes it precious to so many listeners.

My purpose here is to show how Pärt's minimalism corresponds (or clashes) with received notions of modernism and postmodernism. Given that there is a rich and vast literature already on these terms, this chapter cannot hope to be exhaustive, but it is my intention to provide a (small) number of observations which show how Pärt's music is set apart from familiar theoretical models of elite modernism and the multiplicity of postmodernism. No doubt, my portrayals of both terms are characterizations; brief by necessity, but hopefully not skewed or unhelpful in providing a sketch of the way that Pärt's ideas and approach fit into the landscape of new musical aesthetics.

Pärt's status today as one of the world's preeminent composers should not obscure the fact that, in the grand scheme of music, his compositional career is remarkably recent. Although he composed throughout the middle of the twentieth century, tintinnabuli emerged in the 1970s and it has only been since the 1980s that this particular compositional system has become popularly and internationally acclaimed. Pärt's success has been dependent on his audience's ability both to register his particular voice in the jostling tumult of contemporary musical culture, and to follow it. Indeed, he has a fan base of considerable size and fidelity, a characteristic that is readily recognizable in the consumption patterns of pop. Arguably this is because his strong individual idiom – his *style* – has served as a compass for audiences, enabling them to navigate the unfamiliar realm of new music, even within a short space of time.

The idea of style in the early twenty-first century is itself problematic. Writing in relation to the music of previous ages, the late theorist Leonard Meyer defined style as "a replication of patterning, whether in human behaviour or in the artefacts produced by human behaviour, that results from a series of choices made within some set of constraints."[2] Meyer's definition articulates the presence of two central and competing forces within style: forces of human choice (which are relatively unrestrained creative actions), set against constraints of culture (which take the form of 'unbreakable' rules). A style may be said to exist when such constraints are established by artistic consensus, which, at certain times in music's history, have resulted in the limitation of personal choice. In the case of the classical style of the late eighteenth century, for example, the rules of composition were "especially coherent, stable and well established."[3] Of that age, Meyer asserted that it was a relatively simple task for the style to be taught and internalized, which explains the prodigiousness of a figure such as Mozart, for whom only a "small portion of his choices could have involved a deliberate decision among possible alternatives."[4]

This may have been true in pre-Enlightenment Europe, but today 'style' has resulted in a paradox, for, while the desire to categorize other things (including music) and other people is strongly felt by most intelligent beings, so too is our contemporary resistance to *being* categorized. Very few of us enjoy being grouped together as merely one example of a standard model, just as a small number of composers appreciate the labels which are thrust upon them by theorists or journalists. To have one's music aligned with that of another implies that a similarity has been registered, and similarity or – worse – imitation remains the enemy of originality.

Pärt is connected to the idea of 'style' on a variety of levels. Across the corpus of his own works, he has developed his own personal style since 1976 in the form of tintinnabuli. As a form of musical grammar, tintinnabuli relies on the repetition of certain rules regarding the M- and T-voices. Critic Wolfgang Sandner, writing an explanation for *Tabula rasa* (the recording which announced Pärt's entrance into the Western musical consciousness in 1984), conceived the blend of individual characterization within an overarching generic style, tintinnabuli, as the "curious union of historical master-craftsmanship and modern 'gestus."[5] By this he suggested that the individual works are conceived with the goal of presenting a recognizably unified attitude, each resembling a single strand within a thicker compositional fabric. Similarity between works is essential to Pärt's broader artistic aim, but it has meant that he is in constant danger of being perceived as the dupe of powerful capitalist agents, mass-producing works of identical value and character, and sacrificing his originality to a template sanctioned by an insidious recording industry.

On a second level, his style is often associated with the works of composers John Tavener (b. 1944) and Henryk Górecki (1933–2010) as part of the New Simplicity, and by extension as part of the global phenomenon that is minimalism.[6] The term 'minimalism' has courted almost entirely negative responses from those artists and musicians who are saddled regularly with it, and clearly Pärt does not conform to the most widely held understanding of that term as music of constant, fast-moving figuration and generally sporting "bright tone colours and an energetic disposition."[7] This style, associated with Steve Reich (b. 1936) and Philip Glass (b. 1937), was nurtured by them in the urban centres of the USA and is in many ways the exact opposite of Pärt's far less frenetic handling of rhythm. If minimalism is understood, however, as a broad aesthetic distinguished, according to musicologist Elaine Broad, by "the conception of the *non-narrative work-in-progress*," then Pärt can be grouped in a minimalist category.[8] In any case, the association with music of limited material has subsequently shaped Pärt's standing within the narratives of twentieth- and twenty-first-century culture. Often his labelling as a 'postmodern' composer is the result of the casual assumption that minimalism in its entirety is anti-modernist. An authority on the subject, Keith Potter, characterized minimalism as a "major antidote to modernism," and Pärt has been invested with some of that anti-modernist feeling.[9]

So what kind of sickness is modernism that requires such an antidote? A simplified image or even caricature of what it means to be a modernist composer continues to influence contemporary musicians both within and outside high-cultural institutions. When people talk in general about an idealized type of composer, they are most often referring, unconsciously perhaps, to the modernist figures of the early to middle twentieth century. It was, after all, these personalities who had the rigid self-belief to re-fashion the fundamentals of music so audibly at the beginning of the twentieth century. This caricature is a conflation of Schoenberg, as the figure most commonly associated with such an attitude, with any number of *enfants terribles* – Stravinsky, Boulez, Birtwistle – who populate accounts of the twentieth century. Forcefulness, typical both of modernists' characters and their music, is like an intoxicant to their supporters who regard the more abstruse compositions as evidence of some magical and secret power. Modernists are proud, bordering on the arrogant, and concerned principally with their own creations without too high a regard for their public.

As with many popularly held ideas, the sense that modernist composers are sustained by a self-belief in their inherent rightness without the need to bend their style to a public is not entirely without proof, as borne out by the writings of some of the most prominent modernist composers. It would be negligent to overlook Milton Babbitt's contention that composers are comparable to specialists in physics, working within their own secluded laboratories without the obligation to explain their inner workings to the amateur. "The time has passed when the normally well-educated man without special preparation could understand the most advanced work in, for example, mathematics, philosophy, and physics. Why should the layman be other than bored and puzzled by what he is unable to understand, music or anything else?"[10]

It is somewhat ironic that the word 'modernism,' whose Latin root (*modo*) implies 'just now,' is still employed today, even though it is associated with compositional attitudes which were 'just now' a century ago. The label modernist, or 'high' modernist, continues to conjure the same aura of avant-garde originality that still shapes the reception of Schoenberg and his contemporaries. At the same time, modernist implies institutional respectability. Michael Nyman, himself a composer whose style is not always embraced by the institutions of high culture, classified the following as the central avant-garde column of the post-renaissance tradition: Boulez, Kagel, Xenakis, Birtwistle, Berio, Stockhausen, Bussotti.[11] Their music continues to be thought of as hard, complicated, and at the cutting edge even while most are now in respectable late age or deceased.

Musically, the modernist composer is at total liberty to compose works that are bizarre to the innocent listener, for this only strengthens their standing. Such a listener, who may wish to partake in modernist music but has neither the education nor the benefit of musical literacy, will find the creation of a musical sound-world that embraces the unfamiliar a source of bemusement or, potentially, of offence. An infamous example of such effrontery occurred at the first performance of Harrison Birtwistle's strident work for solo saxophone and drum kit with wind orchestra, *Panic*. Performed for the traditionally conservative audience in attendance at the 1995 Last Night of the Proms concert in London, it was greeted with howls of derision. "Unmitigated rubbish" was the *Daily Express*'s headline, and it was "an atrocity of epic proportions" according to *The Spectator*.[12] Noise, it was assumed by the concert-going public, is a different thing from music, unworthy of the cost of a ticket. According to Babbitt, the confusion which is felt outside of the profession need not be lamented, but the movement from incomprehensibility to hostility in the minds of the public is less forgivable. He wrote that "it is only the translation of this boredom and puzzlement into resentment and denunciation that seems to me indefensible."[13]

At times in his history, Pärt himself has composed music that seemed to adhere to a modernist attitude, closer to a headstrong radicalism which is commonly (if perhaps incorrectly) identifiable with the likes of Birtwistle or Babbitt. As an example, Pärt's *Collage über B–A–C–H* (1964) obeys its own rationality at the expense of its audience, who, almost the object of a joke, are presented with a baffling alternation of reorchestrated Bach and twelve-note heterophony. In this work, the Sarabande (instrumentally modified) from Bach's *English Suite in D minor*, BWV 811 is juxtaposed with twelve-tone clusters that ape the characteristic rhythmic pattern of this stately dance. *Collage über B–A–C–H* comes from a period before the decisive turning point of Pärt's career in which he stepped back from the constant production of new works in order to reflect deeply on his development. The result was a fashioning of the system for which he is best known, tintinnabuli. The pre-tintinnabuli period is often described in Pärt's biography as more explicitly 'modernist' because of his adoption at this time of a collage principle which mingled music from the past with his own, and it is difficult to deny the strangeness of these works, or to ignore the alienating effect they have on their audiences.

The identification of Pärt's earlier compositional life as modernist is made problematic, however, in light of the fact that he was working in a political environment which inhibited the kind of innovation which is regularly associated with the term. A decade after Pärt's birth the tone of Soviet aesthetics was set by one of the most important directors of cultural policy, Andrei Zhdanov, in his concluding speech at the Conference of Soviet Music Workers, in which he described modernist music as a second, unhealthy alternative to healthy progressive principles:

> The other trend [modernism] represents a formalism alien to Soviet art, a rejection of the classical heritage under the banner of innovation, a rejection of the idea of the popular origin of music, and of service to the people, in order to gratify the individualistic emotions of a small group of select aesthetes.[14]

While Zhdanov's prejudice against what he termed "formalism" was the result of an overpowering nationalist ideology, this does not mean that his comments were totally unperceptive. The commitment to composing music that satisfies the "individualistic emotions of a small group of select aesthetes" is a fair description of the motivation for many modernist artists. Pärt has not always been celebrated by as broad an audience as today, and he was castigated by the authorities for his *Nekrolog* (*Obituary*), which was basically reliant on twelve-tone technique.

To support modernism is, however, to accept not only that certain music is composed, performed, and sustained by a small minority of people in comparison to the broader audience, but that this music is seen as a more advanced stage of musical development conducted by specialist musicians who have been highly trained for the task. Specialization, according to philosopher Jürgen Habermas, is one of the distinguishing aspects of modernity, occurring within three autonomous spheres: science, morality, and art. Such a separation became necessary for eighteenth-century thinkers in light of the collapse of a unified world conception of religion and metaphysics, in whose place was erected the specialized domains of scientific discourse, theories of morality and the production and criticism of art. Habermas suggests that

> This professionalized treatment of the cultural tradition brings to the fore the intrinsic structures of each of the three dimensions of culture. There appear the structures of cognitive-instrumental, moral-practical, and of aesthetic-expressive rationality, each of these under the control of specialists who seem more adept at being logical in these particular ways than other people are.[15]

The project of the Enlightenment was dependent upon a necessary division between expertise and everyday praxis, but it had as its ultimate aim the filtering through of the 'cognitive potentials' of those three specialized domains to the betterment of the organization of everyday life. While a form of elitism is inevitably bound up within the specialized languages of modernity, accumulation of specialized culture was intended as the means of enrichment for everyday existence, to further an understanding of the world and to promote the happiness of human beings. Unfortunately, few would argue that modernist music, which is generally supported financially by a small number of wealthy institutions such as university composition departments or 'research laboratories', has managed to fulfil its utopian goal. The experimentation which takes place within IRCAM, for example, remains hermetically sealed from the majority of its neighbours who populate the streets of Paris.[16]

It is principally for this reason that Pärt's music after 1976 seems to resist the modernist moniker. Unlike many new compositions, tintinnabuli has become ubiquitous through a wide range of channels and, significantly, is a musical style well-loved by the non-academic press. The shift after 1976 in Pärt's style is often understood as an about-turn. His music before this date is commonly understood as 'modernist' because of his exploration into the tenets of his own musical language, experimenting with serialism, collage, and pastiche. Consequently, tintinnabuli, as with minimalism generally, is situated as a counter-modernist reaction.

Defenders of modernist music cannot accept such a minimalist style on the grounds of its simplicity. For example, a composer such as Robin Holloway asserts that music should be constructed by its composer with "all the skill and experience he can command."[17] To Holloway, artistic maturation, as with academic and emotional development, is a process through which the individual learns from experience and is able to deepen his or her response. "Why should intelligent people prefer anarchy over order, destruction over construction, frivolity, portentousness, arid vacuity over genuine content and palpable significance?"[18] He describes Pärt's music as "simplistic wallpaper" as a means of drawing attention to the minimal and recurring palette in use.[19] A more extreme reaction to minimalism is that of Elliott Carter, who views any musical style based on incremental variation as contributing to the gamut of objects and ideas that make up evil ideologies: "about one minute of minimalism is a lot, because it is all the same. One also hears constant repetition in the speeches of Hitler and in advertising. It has its dangerous aspects … In a civilized society things don't need to be said more than three times."[20]

Composer David Matthews, while not an advocate of the purely musical techniques of Pärt and Tavener, does at least recognize that their music might be valuable, even if their value lies outside of the 'pure' musical experience. He writes that theirs "is a somewhat artificial stance, though the strength of [their] religious convictions gives a depth to their music which might otherwise sound dangerously thin."[21] Indeed, because Pärt's music is founded on theological belief, it could be understood as a recoil to a previously uncivilized and unenlightened society. Pärt particularly bemoans this situation and the inevitable shadow cast on his own work as a result, remarking that "if people simply hear the word 'God' they become sad; but what is sad is when it has that effect."[22] Pärt's somewhat flimsy standing within certain enclaves of the intelligentsia is the result of his exclusive reliance after 1976 on a religious framework, a connection which was dependent upon both his acceptance of key commissions and his development of a 'spiritual' musical language, tintinnabuli. This only adds to the sense among skeptics of Pärt that his use of religion is a substitute, and not just a motivation, for musical creativity.

While the language of faith can hinder a purely empirical discussion concerning music's construction, it can also lead to new theological discussions which may elucidate the real value of a work. In relation to Pärt, the term 'holy minimalist' is particularly deserving of discussion because of the gamut of possible meanings implied by the indefinite epithet 'holy.' The drive to be precise over spirituality is indicative of a period in which issues of religious identity are becoming increasingly tangible through the political language in which they are couched. Conflicts fought as an expression of religious intolerance have characterized the turn of the millennium, as has the cry to examine and identify national and racial alliances, with the result that much self-analysis as to the question of faith has appeared in the media. As a recent notable example, Pope Benedict XVI's tour of the United Kingdom in 2010 spawned a national public debate on the relationship between, in his words, "secular rationality and religious belief."[23] His words seem to underline a central discourse concerning identity formation in the twenty-first century, and one which must be faced by a civilization undergoing shifts at a rapid pace not only in religious matters but throughout the whole of its social fabric. As urban geographer Robert Beauregard puts it, we live in a "world becoming simultaneously disarticulated and rearticulated under the onslaught of corporate globalization, ethnic social movements, state violence, massive waves of immigration, and intellectual upheaval."[24] Consequently, it seems vital to distinguish *religion* as the shared use of ritual which leads to cultural identification with a particular group, in contrast to the language of *spirituality*, which is contingent upon the individual.

It is emblematic of the generally liquid manner in which postmodern belief now operates that while Pärt is confirmed within a specific religious tradition, Orthodox Christianity, his music is simultaneously heard as an example of eclectic, spiritual mysticism. To be sure, from a casual listener's viewpoint, there is a confluence between the styles of Pärt and Tavener, a perceived parity which, regrettably, is too commonly echoed by composers and critics.[25] Tavener's tendency to engage with a broad collection of sources, librettos, or texts, however, casts doubt on the validity of drawing the two composers together under a single description. There are some similarities between the two Orthodox composers in generic musical processes, not least in their continual reliance on repetitive verse-forms, pedal pitches, and espousal of modality.[26] All of which have contributed to the perceived quality which is central to their success; namely, their provision of "oases of repose in a technologically saturated culture."[27] Aside from these techniques, however, the two composers are characterized by substantial differences in their personal understanding of religious dogma, which has resulted in clear musical contrasts. Crucially, and unlike Pärt, Tavener perceives his acceptance of numerous musical styles as the necessary counterpart to a spirituality which is equally plural, commenting that "I do feel that music cannot be exclusive, neither can religion be exclusive anymore."[28]

The slogan of holy minimalism covers up differences in approach but it has aided Pärt's popular reception just as it has benefited a number of composers: Henryk Górecki and Georgian composer Giya Kancheli (b. 1935), for example, whose styles may be only tangentially connected to each other. The commercial success of this 'brand-name' can best be understood in the context of spirituality as it developed in the second half of the twentieth century, a period in which interest in pre-Christian paganism in Western Europe and the USA grew as the result of a reaction against both Christianity and capitalist modernity.[29] Spiritual non-exclusivity owes much to the expansion of various forms of New Age practices that exist in a symbiotic relation with capitalism, the media, and public figures who champion them. This 'neopaganism' is the result of various social factors which anthropologist Brian Morris lists as:

> the drug cultures of the 1960s and 1970s; an increasing interest in non-Western religions coupled with a general disenchantment with Christianity; a search for new forms of spirituality in an era of global capitalism when nihilism, consumerism, and instrumental reason seem to be all-pervasive; the rise of the human potential movement with its emphasis on counselling, self-help, and self-realization; and finally the feminist and ecology movements that have critiqued the dominant tendencies of Western capitalism and its culture.[30]

The holy minimalists are often marketed as prophets for the postmodern, but while this image suits Tavener, it is in tension with Pärt's own view. Tavener presents himself as a figure that has exposed the religious neuroses of Western modernity, and actively engages with numerous subjects in a manner which shows him to be an itinerant explorer, rather than a monotheistic believer. Tavener's preference for the 'East,' a term he uses to embrace Christian Byzantium, Sunnism, and Hinduism, is one example of this ideological inclusiveness, which can be understood as a vital aspect of Western postmodernism.[31] This is also the context of Tavener's popularity, which is of a different kind of support than Pärt receives from his patrons. Tavener's 2007 royal commission by his 'close friend' Prince Charles, entitled *The Beautiful Names*, was a setting of the ninety-nine names for Allah and courted much press coverage.[32] Contrastingly Pärt, living an incongruously humble existence "cares little for fame or fortune, preferring to live quietly and simply in a leafy suburb of Berlin ... [composing] in absolute isolation."[33] His purposefully barren style serves to bind him to a message of monastic discipline.

Hillier employs the term 'hesychastic' purposefully to suggest the absolute control over the passions which can only emerge through tranquillity.[34] The word, which stems from a name for a sect of fourteenth-century quietists on Mount Athos, suggests that this discipline is a facet of Pärt's Orthodox affiliation. "The term 'hesychasm' implies stillness, silence, tranquillity, and also stability, being seated, fixed in concentration. As early as the fourth century it was used to designate the state of inner peace and freedom from bodily or mental passion from which point only one might proceed to actual contemplation."[35] For Pärt, passions are to be controlled rather than yielded unto, in order that God may have a receptacle through which to speak. This suggests a measure of impartiality and detachment while maintaining the potential to be moved by suffering and prayer. While the temptation to caricature Pärt as a hermit removed from modern life should be resisted, he does not conform to images of progress and egoistic glory which infuse numerous strains of modernity. The kind of artistic therapy in which Tavener allows his passion free flight is not encountered in the detached approach of Pärt. A familiarity with Pärt's religious scores reveal that, as with Stravinsky, he is a composer who prefers to create within strict limits rather than being directed by his own emotional response.

The image of the icon is pertinent here for, like the painters behind the production of those objects, Pärt continues to grapple with the challenge of creating an artwork which may express divine beauty without allowing it to become the focus of a form of artistic idolatry. Artists who are sensitive to the theology of their work continue to be confronted by the human follies of creativity – the egoism of the artist and the decadent sensuousness aroused in the body – in contrast to the super-human purity of God, which is part of the object of their adoration. Tavener has countered this by actively striving towards resolution in Eros, producing music that is unashamedly luxurious in sonority. For those committed to the patristic tradition, however, music continues to act as a lure away from the metaphysical. The human body is tempted by music when, as voiced originally by Saint Augustine, it resonates with the physical nature of longing.

> When I love you [God], what do I love? Not the body's beauty, nor time's rhythm, nor light's brightness … nor song's sweet melodies, nor the fragrance of flowers, lotions and spices, nor manna and honey, nor the feel of flesh embracing flesh – none of these are what I love when I love my God. And yet, it's something *like* light, smell, food, and touch that I love when I love my God – the light, voice, fragrance, embrace of my inner self, where a light shined for my soul. That's what I love when I love my God! (*Confessions*, Book X: 6, 8)[36]

From Augustine's words it is clear how un-texted music could become the instrument of the mind's manipulation by the body for the early church. Paradoxically, the strongest analogy for loving God was rooted within a language of the senses because, like God, these drives operated unconscious of linguistic constraints; at the same time, suspicion was cast upon the physical and sensual aspects of religious devotion because they were in danger of leading the mind astray to worldly passions. Music, flowers, and flesh had the capability, therefore, of affecting the body in the same manner as religious devotion but with a less redemptive purpose. Augustine's deep attraction to music, which he articulated through the language of doxology, was therefore intermingled with an inherited platonic suspicion of physicality and the body. This is a conflict which has previously been encountered by Russian Orthodox composers who attempted to combine the strictness of Eastern liturgy with artistic values incorporated from the West. Rachmaninov's *All-night Vigil* has, in the past, been an unpopular work in the Western choral repertoire because "for some, its restraint effaces the composer's public identity, a hindrance to an artist in an age of individualism."[37] Likewise, Tchaikovsky's *Liturgy of St. John Chrysostom* is uncharacteristically muted due to its intention as a liturgical work. In part this is due to the Augustinian trepidation of composing music which works against the liturgy. One audience member at Rachmaninov's version of the *Liturgy of St. John Chrysostom* remarked that it was "absolutely wonderful, even too beautiful, but with such music it would be difficult to pray; it is not church music."[38]

Pärt is equally aware of the possibility of overpowering his audience with virtuosic sonorities that might propel his own artistic personality into the work. For example, with the exception of the opening and closing choral sections, *Passio* exists as a work founded on subtlety rather than grand gestures, in an effort to subjugate its own musical materials to the Christian narrative and text. Arguably the rhetorical power of the *exordium* and *conclusio* is necessarily grand in order to construct a frame that throws into relief the sacramental words of the Gospel. Only in these outer, clamorous sections does Pärt permit himself to produce music in which can be glimpsed a more human desire for an excessive emotional gesture in comparison with the spirit of humility, which is to be found in the pared-down forces of the gospel narrative. Even in this outer framework, however, the retention of tintinnabuli means that the 'message' of humility in the face of a larger form is never totally abandoned, or, as Wilfrid Mellers described it, "the total effect is grand, yet pain-ridden."[39]

While discipline lies at the centre of Pärt's musical character, its significance is often papered over by the success which his and Tavener's music has attained in a popular sphere, a situation which has perhaps caused his critics to be too hasty in consigning him to the abyss of ambient music. Pärt's dissatisfaction with serialism has led Hillier to position tintinnabuli as one of the "forces displacing the hitherto central language" of modernism, yet his reliance on processes that operate on mathematical principles elevates him above the level of a casual dilettante and moves him towards a modernist attitude.[40] His admiration for Webern, which is audible in his fascination with the smallest qualitative changes in sound, challenges his reception as an abstruse mystic. On the contrary, Pärt's development was reliant upon his encounter with serialism, for it was here that he discovered an earnestness in the purpose of art which he himself shares:

> Why is Webern's music so highly regarded by contemporary composers? Because it's so simple; disciplined and rigorous, but simple. (That isn't to say that there aren't also very complex things in his music.) Unfortunately, however, composers often think that because they think a lot they have something to say ... Underneath all this complexity is only a lack of wisdom and no truth. The truth is very simple; earnest people understand this to be so.[41]

Here is encapsulated Pärt's approach to composition, which is directly connected to his broader understanding of faith. The "truth" to which he refers above is a religious truth, namely a belief in the existence of an exclusive relationship between God and humankind through an incarnate Christ.

The belief in an absolute truth sits uneasily with relativist notions of spirituality, and Pärt's insistence that his music gives voice to a single Christian truth is a significant reason for questioning his labelling as essentially postmodern. In this sense, the minimalism of Pärt's music stems from this theology, itself a kind of 'minimal orthodoxy' that treats anything outside of the relationship as needless and self-indulgent. Having undergone a transformation from his earlier secular modernism to this new sacred stage, Pärt speaks with the authority of a convert and recognizes that the intense freedom of technique found in his earlier works emphasized the skills of human creativity rather than the beneficence of God in bestowing such skills. Serialism, through its heady fascination with its own intramusical techniques, draws attention away from a work's greater metaphysical claim. Pärt's minimalism, meanwhile, provides a "cool sense of purity and discipline" as a counterbalance to the "decades of intense expressionism that characterised high modernism."[42]

It is a purity formed through technique (tintinnabuli), and through subject (the narrative of Christianity). In this sense, to experience Pärt's music is to partake in the reenactment of medieval music and to become part of a catholic community which has existed throughout history. According to Hillier, tintinnabuli provides a counterbalance of values in a cultural marketplace of excessive speed and variation.

> A culture that attempts to live without the sustaining power of myth is a culture that is not whole, that has no connection with the past. And it is in this manner that we may understand Pärt's sense of purpose: as an attempt to reconstitute art within a sense of past and future time, to fly in the face of the disconnectedness of postmodernism and seize a cultural meta-narrative from time so distant, yet so potently realized that it has the force of new life.[43]

In positing a musical subject which is unified and integrated, Pärt's project is essentially an old-fashioned one, encouraging the convergence of critiques of capitalism with religious philosophy in a manner which is rare outside of the pulpit. Tintinnabuli is an indictment of the detritus of contemporary living; it regards musical complexity as vanity and eclecticism as the symptom of boredom, and underlines the tragedy of a society whose majority exalts in brief and snappy tunes. The theologian and ordained minister Don Saliers is one of the small number of thinkers today to cling to the possibility of music retaining a utopian and redemptive core: "Surely it is still the case that what moves us most deeply (rather than merely entertains us) has both contemplative and prophetic powers, and is visionary, carrying with it a 'sense' of life and world."[44] The daubing of 'mere' entertainment in such negative tones recalls a Kantian philosophical heritage which adhered to the belief that art should achieve something beyond decoration, a quality termed *sacramentality*:

> This [sacramentality] can occur when we cease to be interested in music only for entertainment or 'back-ground' purposes, and begin to pay attention to how music points towards the deep elemental facts of our existence. Music may point, for example, to our mortality, our capacity for love and suffering, or to a sense of mystery beyond the commonplace or the mere appearance of things.[45]

The language employed here by Saliers to describe the potentially elevating properties of music is drawn from an attitude which is no longer current in musicological thinking, namely one which rests on the notion that music should aim to contain the values of love and suffering in its structures.

It is one thing to accept that music should be sacramental, but in practice it is much harder to conceive how music might be able to embody such values. Is it, for example, purely a question of dissonance? It is too crude to claim that the most abrasive and unremitting dissonance symbolizes the value of suffering, and neither can love, as an unbounded and profound emotion, be reduced or pinned down to being heard in only one form of musical structure. Values such as love and suffering emerge musically in an infinite number of ways just as creativity – and humanity – are infinitely variable. It is not my intention (nor Saliers's) to claim that only one type of music can be sacramental. In the case of Pärt, however, there are qualities of his music which seem to ask for a specifically sacramental interpretation.

Crucial is the way in which Pärt treats the perception of time within the structure of his music. It is characteristic of his minimalism that dramatic contrast, and particularly rhythmic contrast, is eschewed, a feature which is typically viewed as a weakness:

> Pärt's *Passio* (1982) is a setting of St. John's version of the Passion Story in which each vocal part moves along its same few pre-allotted notes for the entire 70 minutes. All voices move together in the same rhythm, and all the rhythms are built from the same basic cells. Thus the piece sounds remarkably consistent from beginning to end; what comes out of your CD player on 'Scan' is not much different from what comes out on 'Play.'[46]

It is disconcerting that *Passio* can be portrayed in such a way. Firstly, it is a distorted presentation of the material to imply that difference does not exist, since the various figures in *Passio* (the Evangelist, Christ, Pilate, and the crowd) are distinguishable from each other through the use of contrasting tintinnabuli voices and rhythmic patterns specific to each character. A more worrying aspect of Fisk's characterization, however, is the absence of a considered opinion as to why Pärt deliberately 'measures time' and draws it out over a relatively long period. The answer, I would suggest, lies in the qualities of love and suffering, which are themselves temporal. Unlike the fleeting stab which accompanies a stubbed toe or the elation of a holiday romance, suffering and love are both subject to endurance.

My understanding is not a wholly isolated one. The appropriation of Pärt's music in a variety of contexts reveals a common association between the enduring temporality enacted through his style with the notion of 'deep' emotion. A significant example from recent years is the television play *Wit* adapted by Emma Thompson and Mike Nichols from the stage play by Margaret Edson. The narrative of *Wit* follows the final illness and death of Vivian Bearing, a notable John Donne scholar, as she undergoes aggressive medical treatment. Of interest from a Pärt perspective is the regular use of *Spiegel im Spiegel* as an aural backdrop for the subject of Bearing's suffering. This music emerges at various times of both emotional anguish (as when Bearing re-lives memories of her time with her father), and physical distress (as the illness eventually and painfully overtakes her body).

The very presence of music within a television play which deals with this subject might be considered crass since it serves to detract attention from the epicenter of human suffering, which is otherwise presented with almost documentary objectivity. Furthermore, the choice of this particularly beautiful Pärt work is suspect, presenting the experience of the cancer patient in a perversely prettified light. Consequently, the music potentially turns the viewer into a charlatan, relying on the film as an *excuse* for emotion rather than centering genuine emotional intelligence towards it.

While these reservations may be true of the use of some music in films with a highly emotional subject, it is worth considering whether *Spiegel im Spiegel* operates technically in the same way that other music regularly does within film. Unlike conventional film scores, minimalist music tends not to comply with the contour of the narrative and in fact is more inclined to obey its own abstract momentum: once the musical process begins, not even the visual imagery of the film can affect it. As Mervyn Cooke has written,

> The mechanical nature of such repetition [minimalism], in which the music sometimes pursues a path quite independent from the suggestions of the visual image, could readily foster emotional neutrality and distanciation.[47]

This is particularly notable in Nichols's reliance on Pärt's *Spiegel im Spiegel* in *Wit*.[48] This work is constructed from sixteen phrases which develop from an initial interval of a rising second. Each couplet of phrases includes an inversion, with the pitch 'A' as the plane of reflection. The piano writing accords to tintinnabuli with a chord of F major in ordered inversions providing a constant harmonic sonority. The cycle of events (by which I mean the sequence of movement from one note to next in the melodic part, the point at which the tintinnabuli note is articulated and the sounding of notes at the extremity of the keyboard) accords to a fixed rhythmic ordering within each phrase. The process once initiated runs autonomously. It is this regularity, the series as it were, of the music which is the route of attraction in certain kinds of minimalism. The purity of the structure as it evolves through cellular growth provides an enjoyment which is experienced across a wide number of disciplines, not least mathematics, but is also derived from artistic cultural moments that emphasize grace, regularity and good construction.

What saves the use of *Spiegel im Spiegel* within the film from crass sentimentality is its relationship to time. It does not contain contrasts or dramatic melodic content that would make the passing of time into a dynamic and enjoyable experience. Instead, the crotchet pulse is unwavering, marking time without decoration. The passing of time is made inescapable, as well as cyclic, and therefore the double-edged nature of existence as something at once beautiful but also inextricable is underlined. This is fitting for the subject. As Professor Bearing, lying in her bed, narrates while *Spiegel im Spiegel* is played:

> You cannot imagine how time … can be … so still.
>   It hangs. It weighs. And yet there is so little of it. It goes so slowly, and yet it is so scarce.
>   If I were writing this scene, it would last a full fifteen minutes. I would lie here, and you would sit there.[49]

Pärt's music is not sentimental, but it does represent a form of unflinching honesty and in this, perhaps, it fulfils Saliers's understanding of sacramental significance. Life, not only that of the individual but of humanity across time, is wrought from the persistent interplay of suffering with love.

Both a modernist form of music criticism and recent 'theo-musicology' emphasize the importance of transformative potential in music. In each it is a requirement that music is examined and evaluated through a particular mode of specialized listening. A passivity of listening, which results from the commoditization of musical works, is not appropriate for perceiving the depths of human experience, its complexities and near-infinite thought processes, which are enabled through this artistic medium. Jonathan Harvey alights on this idea when he suggests that "we [society] need more acknowledgement of the state of *receptor* in the Arts – the wide-open consciousness Buddhists call 'suchness' where everything that happens is vivid and important."[50] While Harvey's position is not singly Christian, his attitude is in alignment with Saliers, who upholds the idea that in order for music to be the bearer of theological import, there must be a sensibility for hearing music "*as* revelatory."[51] This accords strikingly with a modernist vision of music: Babbitt "demanded increased accuracy from the transmitter (the performer) and activity from the receiver (the listener)," and in his *Introduction to the Sociology of Music*, the arch-modernist Theodor Adorno described a number of increasingly sophisticated listening approaches with the intention of discovering something 'revelatory' about society within musical structure.[52] Such modernist theo-musicology asserts the need for receptivity in the listener to the theological and social potential in music, which is predicated on the "reciprocity of sound and life through time."[53] This involves listening to the musical content in such a way as to hear in its development a representation of the processes which shape spiritual and social development. As Saliers asks, "could it be that music offers, in both its structures and its improvisations, an image of how life may be lived?"[54] This is the same challenge which Adorno posed in an entirely non-religious context but without hope of a resolution. On the contrary, for Saliers, the belief in a Christian teleology means that "the venerable terms beauty, goodness and truth still hover over us."[55] It is these values which Pärt's music strives to make audible.

Pärt's music leads us to reconsider the contours of the contemporary music landscape. While there are confluences of outlook with serialism (the best-known example of modernist aesthetics), it is also apparent that Pärt's music is shaped by a paradigm of accessibility of material, stemming from his belief in simple truth, rather than an evolving complexity. He thus challenges an antagonistic reading of modernism and postmodernism, instead conforming to John Barth's model in which specialized and accessible elements coincide:

> My ideal postmodernist author neither merely repudiates nor merely imitates either his twentieth-century modernist grandparents or his nineteenth-century premodernist grandparents. He has the first half of our century under his belt, but not on his back … He may not hope to reach and move the devotees of James Michener and Irving Wallace – not to mention the lobotomised mass-media illiterates. But he should hope to reach and delight, at least part of the time, beyond the circle of what Mann used to call the Early Christians: professional devotees of high art.[56]

What seems vital to this understanding of postmodernism is the replacement of an oedipal complex (or anxiety of influence) with the ability to hold on to elements of modernism while transforming them, indeed to exist betwixt and between them. This multi-directional capability to look back towards the shore of modernism as well as towards the line of an unbreached horizon means that Pärt's music is intrinsically optimistic. It contains the possibility of being part of a 'sacral community' (a membership which alienating music thwarts) and, through the surety of its form and theology, it offers a promise of release from the confused plurality which characterizes the postmodern.

Further reading

Christopher Butler, *Postmodernism: A Very Short Introduction* (Oxford University Press, 2002).

Jonathan Cross, "Writing about living composers: questions, problems, contexts," in *Identity and Difference: Essays on Music, Language and Time*, ed. Peter Dejans (Leuven University Press, 2007).

Paul Griffiths, *Modern Music and After: Directions since 1945* (Oxford University Press, 1995).

Stuart Hall, "The question of cultural identity'" in *Modernity and its Futures*, ed. Stuart Hall, David Held, and Tony McGrew (Cambridge: Polity, 1992).

Jonathan Kramer, "Beyond unity: toward an understanding of musical postmodernism," in *Concert Music, Rock and Jazz since 1945: Essays and Analytical Studies*, ed. Elizabeth Marvin and Richard Hermann (University of Rochester Press, 1995).

James Meyer, *Minimalism: Art and Polemics in the Sixties* (New Haven, CT: Yale University Press, 2001).

Ivan Moody, "The mind and the heart: mysticism and music in the experience of contemporary Eastern Orthodox composers," *Contemporary Music Review*, 14/3 (1996), 65–79.

Boris Schwarz, *Music and Musical Life in Soviet Russia, 1917–1970* (London: Barrie and Jenkins, 1972).

Roger Scruton, *Culture Counts: Faith and Feeling in a World Besieged* (New York: Encounter Books, 2007).

10 Arvo Pärt in the marketplace

LAURA DOLP

In Michael Moore's documentary about the attacks on the US in 2001 (*Fahrenheit 9/11*, 2004) the screen suddenly cuts to black, leaving its disoriented audience with the threatening sounds of physical impact at the site of the Twin Towers. Another wrenching edit introduces hand-held footage of bystanders staring upwards in disbelief. Instead of reuniting images and sound in this moment, Moore makes a crucial aesthetic decision and one that serves as the catalyst for this chapter: he aligns one of the most challenging events of the new millennium, in its surreal horror, with the ethereal sound world of Pärt's *Cantus in Memory of Benjamin Britten* (1977). From an empirical standpoint, *Cantus* plays an incongruous and short-lived role in the film; it has little in common with Jeff Gibbs's original score or the pop and rock songs that Moore later stated were responsible for sustaining him and the crew through the filming process.[1] Yet Pärt's music fulfills a potent role in its narrative and critical function. Like so many filmmakers since the early 1990s who have utilized Pärt's precomposed music – especially the tintinnabuli style – Moore capitalizes on its effectiveness to express a singular, sustained idea within a narrative process.[2]

The story of Pärt's inadvertent involvement with *Fahrenheit 9/11* is not only a lesson in the potency (some would say coerciveness) of his music in the hands of one filmmaker. It is also a decisive moment in the story of Pärt's reception, a story that has been shaped increasingly by film and new media. In a strange twist of fate, Moore's audience for *Fahrenheit* was the largest ever in American documentary film. Its release was a highly publicized event because the Walt Disney Company had retracted its initial support and later forbidden its subsidiary Miramax to distribute the film, citing its partisan nature.[3] Images of the scene with Pärt's music had saturated the media in graphic detail. By mid-summer of 2004 Nielsen EDI had declared that *Fahrenheit* was the most popular feature-length documentary ever, with sales in North America upwards of $80 million dollars.[4] In effect, it placed Pärt's music front and center in a heated discourse involving a paradigmatic political shift of a generation, and it created an aesthetic connection between Pärt's music and violence in its myriad forms.

In retrospect, it was the incongruity of Moore's pairing, rather than its specific content, which has become a recurring theme in Pärt's relationship to contemporary media. Professionals and amateurs alike have recognized that laying down a soundtrack of Pärt's music does more than 'dislocate,' or make the unfathomable manageable. While it allows a certain distance from public and personal cataclysm, it also intensifies our emotional engagement with it. This dual mode of critique and its translation into commercial and artistic terms has become a significant factor in Pärt's cultural currency.

This chapter examines the historical themes of Pärt's marketable identity and their relationship to current politics and modalities of his reception. In particular, it traces the vernacular meanings of Pärt's music in the marketplace, which have broadened from assertions of religiosity and autonomy in conventional recorded formats, to more public and creative ownership in film media as an aesthetic agent of something "unattainable, forgotten or dispossessed."[5] This process has been characterized as a move from carefully controlled market share to a broader, more inclusive engagement that is no longer governed by proprietary claims.

ECM and the branding of Arvo Pärt

In the years following Pärt's move to Western Europe, his work was often marketed as a centralizing aesthetic force on both sides of the Atlantic for a loosely associated group of Northern and Eastern European composers that included Giya Kancheli, Peteris Vasks, John Tavener, and Henryk Mikolaj Górecki.[6] For millennial America, Pärt's combination of artistic choices and reclusive, austere persona captured a place in the commercial imagination precisely because it ran counter to prevailing notions of excess and quick fixes. In the mid-1980s, the Munich-based ECM Records was the first commercial entity to develop a brand reflecting the composer's private stance. Pärt's early commercial success and the long-term shaping of his public identity are attributable to ECM's realization that his 'elemental' style could be developed as a cohesive and appealing product. From the onset, their strategy proposed several themes: the notion of piety, the ideal of the individual spiritual seeker, and the valuation of a symbolic, non-narrative form of story-telling. These themes were introduced in Pärt's debut album *Tabula rasa* (1984, ECM New Series) and subsequently infiltrated the discourse of his reception. This rhetoric has broadened and become more complex, but ECM's framing has continued to function as a rhetorical point of contact for artist, product, curator, marketer, critic, and consumer.

The partnership between Pärt and ECM has been fortuitous, since the aesthetic predispositions and aspirations of both parties are closely aligned. Manfred Eicher (b. 1943) founded the company Editions of Contemporary

Music in Munich in 1969. Eicher, who is also producer, publisher and editor, was trained at the Berlin Academy of Music and first established himself professionally as a recording assistant with Deutsche Grammophon. He is widely admired in his field and his list of professional accolades is extensive, including a 2006 Grammy award for Best Classical Producer for his work with five ECM New Series albums released in 2001.[7] As a sound engineer, Eicher's goals are both technical and philosophical. He views himself as a kind of meta-artist whose curatorial impact is realized in holistic terms, stating that his preference is "towards that which has to do with lucidity, transparency and the movements of sound. It's not only the notes but the thought behind them that sculpts the sound."[8]

ECM was founded as a jazz label but the company later extended its outreach to include other types of contemporary music, recorded poetry, film soundtracks, and printed material. The label had its first big commercial success with a 1975 live solo recording entitled *The Köln Concert* featuring the pianist Keith Jarrett. In 2004 the company marked the thirty-fifth anniversary of its founding as well as the twentieth anniversary of its New Series division, which Eicher established in order to record and promote a broad range of contemporary art music and for which Pärt's music played an inaugural role.

From the onset, it was clear that ECM did not consider themselves merely a recording company but also exemplars of a distinctive type of visual design. The company maintains a careful aesthetic established by Eicher and his longtime collaborators, the graphic designer Barbara Wojirsch, her husband Burkhart Wojirsch, and the photographer Dieter Rehm. Their packaging designs have a reputation in the industry for their elegance and minimalist vocabulary, including a sparseness and attention to structural outline.[9] Moreover, ECM's designs endured several decades of technological change. They translated well between LP and CD formats and provided a distinctive and dispassionate environment in the frenetic context of the web. The company's stated philosophy – that music with integrity requires integrity of approach – led to restrained business practices. Before they began releasing their recordings for online delivery in the mid-2000s, their website FAQs explained that the lack of sample sound clips was justified because the company was not in the sound-bite business. This supported their long-standing defense of what they termed the 'character' of a contemporary composition and the 'dramaturgy' of their jazz productions.

The formal promotion of their design took shape in 1996 when the Swiss publisher Lars Müller, in collaboration with the in-house team, produced a glossy monograph entitled *Sleeves of Desire: A Cover Story*. The book documents the visual evolution of the ECM catalog and discusses how music,

Recording:

Fratres
October 1983, Basel

**Cantus in memory
of Benjamin Britten**
January 1984, Stuttgart

Fratres (for 12 celli)
February 1984, Berlin

Tabula Rasa
November 1977, Bonn
(Live recording by
West German Radio, Cologne)

Recording engineers:
Heinz Wildhagen
Peter Laenger
Eberhard Sengpiel
Dieter Frobeen

Photos:
Kalju Suur
Juri Gurewichs

Cover design:
Barbara Wojirsch

Production:
Manfred Eicher

An ECM Production
℗ © 1984 ECM Records

Plate 10.1 ECM New Series *Tabula rasa* (1984).

title, and image played a role in the design process.[10] Midway through the
book Pärt's *Tabula rasa* appears with little fanfare, belying its seminal role
as the first recording released under the New Series label. The album featured three of Pärt's compositions: the title track (a work for orchestra, and
solo piano and violins), two versions of *Fratres*, and *Cantus*.[11] Its visual
design was characteristic of ECM's visual style, with its subdued colors and
simple geometric layout (Plate 10.1).[12]

When asked about their consistent aesthetic, the designers attribute it
to intuition rather than the requisite calculation of a corporate enterprise.
In an accompanying commentary to *Sleeves of Desire*, Steve Lake writes
that to his knowledge no one at ECM had ever "wasted a moment trying to
fabricate a 'corporate identity' for the label" and attributes any distinctive
or coherent ECM style to their intuitive allegiance to the music.[13] Likewise
the publisher reiterates Lake's stance, claiming that "authorship, intuition
and a designer's emotional commitment nullify all the decrees of marketing and graphic design."[14] Fifteen years later the project of documenting
ECM's work resulted in another volume of cover art entitled *Windfall: The
Visual Language of ECM* (2010). Most of the content is photographic and
its formal organization is described as a type of "visual score," where the
flow of album covers creates individual aesthetic experiences. Through
these publications ECM has not only staked a claim in the history of modern music but also demonstrated its intent to synthesize the visible and the
audible in CD formats.[15]

Although recordings of Pärt's music are promoted with the same understatement as other ECM artists, Pärt is a star and holds a special place in
the history of the company. Eicher's enthusiasm for Pärt's music is evident
in his dramatic public statements; where he likens his first experience of

hearing *Tabula rasa* to "a meteorite falling from the sky."[16] Eicher's advocacy has clearly brought commercial benefit and critical acclaim to both parties. The first notable success of their partnership came in 1993, when *Te Deum* was released and became a Top Five classical hit.

From the beginning, ECM's tenacious and comprehensive marketing strategy has sought to promote Pärt's music to an increasingly varied audience. In anticipation of the release of *Litany* in 1996, they used endorsements from Michael Stipe, the lead singer of REM, in their promotional materials and hired an independent publicist who specialized in alternative and pop press.[17] The album was serviced to over six hundred radio outlets, including college, public, and commercial classical stations. At the time of *Litany*'s release, ECM's label manager Paula Morris highlighted the significant number of Soundscan sales – about 70,000 units, which represented more than 80 percent of those shipped. Morris claimed that this was evidence of the broad and diverse nature of Pärt's audience; not only 'hardcore' classical buyers but listeners who frequented indie shops specializing in alternative rock.[18]

Despite the increasing availability of Pärt's music on other labels, its accessibility was curtailed due to ECM's resistance to releasing their products on iTunes, which was dependent on MP3 technology and which ECM openly declared was inadequate in its sound quality. The company withheld their albums until 2004, when they made *The Out-of-Towners* with Keith Jarrett, Gary Peacock, and Jack DeJohnette the first recording to be available on the iTunes downloading system.[19] Pärt's *Tabula rasa* was made available a year later.[20] This meant that younger and newer consumers of Pärt's music were more likely to develop an impression of his music outside of the ECM brand, since trends in music sales overwhelmingly favored downloading rather than the sale of CDs. The company has subsequently fully embraced the commerce of streaming and features a selected list of digital platforms and portals on their web site.[21]

Commercial bonds notwithstanding, the longevity of Eicher and Pärt's partnership is also based on mutual admiration. Pärt's respect for Eicher's project is rooted in an empathetic appreciation for the producer's technical expertise (Pärt also worked as a recording engineer early in his career) and for ECM's practice of encouraging composers to participate in the process of recording their own works. Though Pärt is rarely sectarian in his public statements, he distinguished early on between ECM and other companies, describing other recording projects as having a tendency to be rushed, under-rehearsed, and having poor acoustics.[22] Both composer and producer share a thinly veiled contempt for the frenetic pace of the marketplace. In effect, Pärt's collaboration with Eicher served as a mutual attempt to restrain commercial exploitation and opportunism directed towards his music by other labels. The composer has expressed disappointment that, in the early years of his association with ECM, other companies took advantage of the time it took ECM to produce high-quality recordings. The resultant lag time opened the way for careless releases that were, in his view, "mediocre and immature."[23]

The formative nature of Eicher's impact on Pärt's career virtually ensures that he will be an enduring part of the composer's legacy. Eicher minces no words on the topic of his own historical role, where he openly claims responsibility for introducing the global market to Pärt's music as a part of a "new musical landscape."[24] For decades, Pärt said little about his music and posterity, although his dedication to ECM's mission was synonymous with a process of controlling the dissemination of his work. He has said that he considers the "successful, authorized recording" to be a guide for future interpretations.[25] More recently, the composer's family has taken concrete measures to ensure a comprehensive strategy of documentation and preservation. The impulse to preserve Pärt's work has now become a national endeavor for the Estonian government and has resulted in significant financial support for the development of the International Arvo Pärt Centre in Laulasmaa, Estonia.[26] The center will include a research institute, an education and music center, a museum, and a publishing facility. At the heart of the center is a comprehensive physical and digital archive, developed and managed by Pärt's family. Additional goals of the center include creating opportunities through study and academic research, issuing grants, and publishing, as well as organizing conferences, concerts, and master classes.[27]

The creation of Pärt's public ethos

In the late 1980s the topography of Eicher's new landscape met with a significant and sympathetic audience. Wolfgang Sandner's notes for Pärt's debut album *Tabula rasa* set an example for writing about Pärt's music through its associative style of dialogue, which showcased the composer's provocative statements in tandem with those of a poetic and sympathetic commentator.[28] Sandner's own description of Pärt's compositions as mystical ("hesychastic prayers of a musical anchorite"), the composer's creative well as "secret and unknowable," and his mission as prophetic ("all ages mingle at the break of Arvo Pärt's dawn") have served as leitmotifs in nearly three decades of industry and journalistic commentary.[29] The reissue of *Tabula rasa* (2010) to commemorate Pärt's seventy-fifth birthday revisits these associations. In his essay "Now, and then" which serves as both introduction and reminiscence, Paul Griffiths alludes to the "deep present" in

Pärt's music, music that brings us face to face with something "primordial" and, after a quarter of a century, music that has caused us to have a different relationship to the medium itself, to "this stuff we call music."[30]

Perhaps because it was intended to be the first introduction of Pärt's music to western audiences, *Tabula rasa* was one of the only ECM albums that contained extended commentary. After their next release, *Arbos* (1987), for which Wilfrid Mellers was the contributing writer, ECM largely dropped the practice of including commentary in Pärt's albums. There are only two notable exceptions in the discography that contain editorial material, *Miserere* (1991) and *Alina* (1999), both written by Hermann Conen. Album inserts have included only text and translations for the works and accompanying images.

Sandner's contribution may have been fleeting, given the sum of Pärt's ECM discography, but his rhetoric on the issue of spirituality was eagerly taken up by the English-speaking press. In effect, Sandner offered both a working vocabulary and the license to characterize Pärt's music as embodied worship. His direct parallels between the experience of Pärt's music and Orthodox prayer became a thematic mainstay of subsequent commentary, thus consigning Pärt to an exotic religious ethos. On the issue of religion, the notes to *Tabula rasa* trumped even the composer's own statements, since Part's statements on his religious convictions were few and far between. When pressed for an explanation, he pointed out his reliance on liturgical text, but more often he offered allegorical stories that shifted the interpretive responsibility to his commentators.

The practice of drawing metaphorical ideas from concrete observations about process has been evident in Pärt's statements from the beginning and, in an attempt to provide authoritative commentary, writers have followed his lead. His explanations of the tinntinabuli style are a case in point, which have been recounted in hundreds of instances in both scholarly work and the populist press. Likewise, the documentary film about Pärt entitled *24 Preludes for a Fugue,* written and directed in 2002 by the Estonian filmmaker Dorian Supin, structures its vignettes around metaphorical stories. In one scene, Pärt contemplates how early music informed his work. He describes his encounter with Gregorian chant as an introduction to a new kind of musical thinking. Pärt suggests through his gestures (moving an imaginary score horizontally and then vertically) that chant presented him with a new understanding of the synthesis between the simultaneous and syntactical elements of sound.[31] It is one of Pärt's few early statements on the issue of compositional process, and Supin privileges it by placing it towards the end of the film. As a whole, Supin's documentary is a sympathetic, even reverential, portrait of Pärt, and the brevity of his subject's statements is uniquely suited to Supin's manner of story-telling. In the director's written commentary to the film, he portrays himself as the arbiter of perfectly formed rushes, who has produced a film largely free of authorial intervention. In this sense the film has a special place in the history of Pärt's public ethos. It remains one of the few extended audiovisual documents of Pärt's appeal for "simplicity, clarity, lucidity" and its equation with a priori truth. Supin's film also serves as a historical record of how, nearly two decades after Sandner's initial commentary, the discourse had retained its fundamental approach, in its deferential language and the familiar positioning of Pärt as a prophetic voice.

Although there was a strong impulse to Sandner's approach, the idea that the fabric of Pärt's music embodied a moral authority was not always met with open arms. At times there were vitriolic responses in the American market. After *Tabula rasa* was released, Gregory Sandow of the *Village Voice* wrote that Pärt appeared to be "seized by an almost abject piety, as if he'd transmuted a religious calling directly into his art."[32] In another review in *Downbeat*, Alan Axelrod dismissed Pärt's commitment to musical simplicity as clearly the product of his "puritanical ... Russian Orthodox turn of mind."[33] Further afield, in an ironical twist, critical response to the London Music Festival claimed there was a "growing cult" around the composer.[34]

The utility of Pärt's ethos has been drawn into relief when leaders in spiritual communities have capitalized on its moral and didactic potential. Such was the case with Robert Reilly, a conservative commentator whose self-professed mission is to interpret and shape the direction of contemporary culture through Catholic traditions. Reilly's 1995 commentary in *Crisis* magazine, the most often-cited Catholic publication in the USA, attributes the "recovery of music" from the tyranny and spiritual sickness of atonal procedures to Pärt, Górecki, and Tavener. Here, Pärt is usefully appropriated in the service of Christian humanist teachings and their agenda to solve, as Reilly proposed, the "crisis of modernity."[35]

Despite the most polarized commentaries, it would be fair to say that a larger portion of Pärt's audience has interpreted his religiosity not as a literal prescription but rather an open-ended and suggestive set of values. ECM's branding is largely responsible for these formulations, transcribing Pärt's Orthodox ethos in such a way as to make it palatable on a broad level. Although ECM discontinued the practice of verbal commentary, *Tabula rasa* consumers have had plenty of opportunity to link Pärt's music with ECM's visual cues which have presented the image of a modern monk, one who is devout yet non-partisan. In album after album, the photographs have appealed to his physical presence: his monkish appearance, his pious but generous countenance, and a vocabulary of familiar ritualistic gestures.

Plate 10.2 ECM *Passio* (1988).

The *Passio* album is a case in point, where every aspect of its design supports the image of Pärt as a pious, solitary spiritual seeker who lives in the embodied moment (Plate 10.2). A photographic diptych of the composer is placed at the back of the booklet, after the full translation of the Passion text.[36] The two images focus on his hands, first on their expressive emphasis to his words (left) and then in their singular, silent and prayerful repose (right).[37] The humility of his downward gaze serves as a last word on the project. These gestures participate easily in a broader vocabulary of devotional imagery, one that holds sway in American Protestant material culture where the ritualistic repetition of imagery often serves to mediate or even conceal the disjunctions of its cultural environment. Ritual imagery ensures continuity because it offers focal points for the past, the present, and indications of the future; in the words of David Morgan, it keeps the "chaos and the wasteland at bay."[38] That Pärt's persona is presented as both genuine and approximate in his formal allegiances secures a place for it within the discourse of contemporary visual piety. Moreover, the slippage between Pärt's likeness and any number of historical religious figures reaffirms an underlying unity between the present and the past.[39] Its promise of individual progress defines this slippage as a modern construct. The imagery of *Passio* may be rooted in the past but Pärt's visually constructed identity is an updated and malleable version of the older references. ECM's visual assertions over the years have made the case for its authenticity.[40] The design of *Passio* also describes Pärt both as an individual seeker and as a model for one. The open interlacing of his hands is unmistakably suggestive of prayer, but the gesture is open-ended and interdenominational in spirit. The apparent singularity of Pärt's experience as a modern Orthodox convert, where individual seeking is an integrated component of a modern path and the individual is left to interpret and apply the Word of God on his or her own terms, translates effortlessly onto other types of individualist mentalities of a millennial American audience.[41] In this manner, the *Passio* album conjoins autobiography and reception, a type of remapping of the composer's theological model onto other willing communities such as the American questers' model of religious seeking.[42]

The imagery of *Passio* also poses epistemological questions about the embodied moment, since the photographs are more associative than narrative in their presentation. They can be read backwards as well as forwards as a series of open-ended devotional images.[43] This strategy recurs in other albums such as *Kanon Pokajanen* (ECM 1654, 1997; Plate 10.3). In the center of the booklet, the mysteries of the architectural space where the recording took place are presented not once, but twice, re-formatted and in detail, as if to re-ask the same unanswerable question. In tandem with Pärt's visual persona, ECM's philosophical assertions rework practical narrative frameworks which pose the question "What am I to do?" suggesting instead non-narrative modes that propose a different sort of question, such as "Who am I to be?"[44] The latter question has been central to ECM's ideology, and Pärt's marketable identity has provided a resilient theoretical model.

Recordings and the Western press

After years of steady promotion through the end of the 1990s, Pärt's music had achieved significant success, both in terms of critical favor and its commercial viability. His earliest Grammy nomination (1989) occurred during this period. To date, he has received a total of five Grammy Nominations

Plate 10.3 ECM *Kanon Pokajanen* (1997).

for "Best Contemporary Composition" for *Passio* (1989), *Miserere* (1991), *Kanon Pokajanen* (1997), and the instrumental work *Orient & Occident* in 2003. The latter work was nominated for both individual composition and for its role in the ECM album *Orient Occident*, which was selected for "Best Classical Album" that same year. More recently, *In principio* (2010) was nominated for "Best Classical Contemporary Composition." Despite the odds, Pärt's single winning Grammy was not with ECM, but rather with a Harmonia Mundi recording of *Da pacem* in 2007. The overwhelming majority of this work, including his Grammy-nominated pieces, have been based or at least derived in part from liturgical material. Thus the works which have been most successful critically have been explicitly religious in tone.[45]

In conjunction with ECM's marketing of Pärt and the publicity generated by his awards, the classical music market in the 1990s also experienced an upsurge in the demand for accessible contemporary composition, an impulse that turned many commentators with modernist sympathies into apologists. The surge of Górecki's commercial success with his Symphony No. 3 on Elektra-Nonesuch (1992) ran parallel to Wilfred Mellers's claim of a new "trinity of godly minimalists," which grouped Górecki, Pärt, and Tavener into potent commercial alliance and virtually ensured that Pärt's status as a modern prophet was also shared by a handful of other composers.[46] Reviews of Górecki's Symphony No. 3 and of Pärt's music often avoided discussion of the work's musical traits and instead addressed the work in terms of personal religion.

In Pärt's case, the decade was marked by a second generation of commentary about his music in the form of blogs and social networking sites. Music that had been previously associated with precision and high-minded aesthetics was described on the web and in print as "just plain gorgeously unclassifiable"[47] or "that modern Baltic minimal modern Classical stuff."[48] Like the failed comparisons between the 'holy minimalists,' the associations were less stylistic than commercial and hyperbolic. The variety of claims made on Pärt's behalf, including a "forefather of electronica" and "the Dean of Choral Music composition ... for the Orthodox church," were sustained by a broad range of incongruous communities.[49] At first the language tended to be highly polarized, from critical commentary regarding the composer's fundamentalism to laudatory defense of his music. For professionals who were invested in their own ideological stances, Pärt's music presented challenges to an institutionalized modernist tradition. In the 2010 *Tabula rasa*, Griffiths provides a sympathetic review of Pärt's early critics. His comments, which serve as both defense and historical corrective, identify the mistaken parallel between Pärt's work and what he terms the "early-listening Romantic pastiche" that feigned to devalue "all that had been fought for" in the life of postwar classical composition.[50] In the decade leading to this point Pärt's popularity swelled on the web and in the popular press, where hundreds of sound-bites shaped his American commercial reception. A random albeit humorous slice of 2006 press makes a variety of claims on Pärt's behalf – everything from shaman to therapist:

An article titled "The Shaman of Estonia" by Fred Kirshnit of the *The New York Sun*, in which Pärt's instrumental work *Fratres* is described as "a quivering lamentation of rare power."[51]

A blistering review from Jennifer Dunning of *The New York Times* titled "Druid Types Encounter the New Age" of an experimental dance performance by the Turner Dance troupe at the Danspace Project where Pärt, no doubt suffering from guilt by association, is described in weary terms as a "ubiquitous" presence.[52]

A testament by a crisis worker at an AIDS organization in the mid-1980s, published on Salon.com, who describes *Tabula rasa* as a powerful "balm" for the ill and dying.[53]

An interview in *Daily Variety*, where film producer and director Taylor Hackford discusses his work on the score for the 1995 film *Dolores Claiborne*, where Hackford attributes his own creative inspiration to Pärt's music and then proceeds to describe this music through a visual corollary of the "ever-changing skies" of Nova Scotia.[54]

An entertainment blurb in the *Sun Herald* (August 27, 2006), where the Australian actress Toni Collette, when asked to identify an album or song that "makes her cry," mentions that while other albums make her "feel a lot of things," she can always count on Pärt's *Alina*.[55]

Finally, a mention of the southwest premiere of Pärt's *Berlin Mass* in the 'Religion' section of *The Santa Fe New Mexican*, an event which "members of all faiths are welcome to attend." The announcement is buried in a long list of appeals for participation, along with those by the local kabbalah study group, the local screening of a film about witchcraft trials, a Wiccan orientation session and a lecture by a visiting Sufi teacher.[56]

That Pärt's music has gained a widening and varied base of support in popular music is now actively publicized by the composer's own establishment. In an essay posted on the International Arvo Pärt Centre site, Siim Nestor from *Eesti Ekspress* recounts his conversation with Pärt about his influence on pop musicians and mentions a sample of over fifty individuals and bands.[57]

Since the early 1990s commentary on the web and a variety of popular press continue to describe Pärt's music in relation to the older stylistic practices of musical minimalism.[58] More to the point but less articulated was that Pärt's identity resonated with a kind of social minimalism; in particular, an ethos of voluntary simplicity which the dominant culture of materialism both marginalized and reinforced as a desirable alternative voice. As a counter-culture of self-imposed moral and economic limits, voluntary simplicity represented an historical, and later a commercial, extension of the desire for a simpler life. In millennial America, its commercial realization still appeals occasionally to its nineteenth-century philosophical roots but largely extends to modern equivalencies to propose counterbalances to the feverish consumerism of modern life.[59] In a telling parallel, Griffiths alludes to Pärt's music as a means to "turn through" the elaborate network of modernity and to reveal a *tabula rasa* – a "single, smooth curve." Pärt's own artistic credo resonates metaphorically with these social trends; for example, in the context of his compositional method he has stated how counterpoint creates ideal relations through a kind of "voluntary poverty."[60] That the discourse around voluntary simplicity advocates both aesthetic pleasure and ascetic restraint makes Pärt's stance all the more palatable to some listeners because of their uneasy compliance with a capitalist ideology, while condoning the pleasure they derive from his music.[61] As important as the conventional forms of the concert hall, printed press and web reviews have been for Pärt's reception, since the 1990s his music has had the most exposure through the mediated space of film. It is in relation to the moving image that Pärt's broader engagement with mainstream American liberalism and his role as a symbolic antidote to capitalism, the violence of injustice, and the spiritual fallacy of individual upward mobility takes on a new potency and power of distribution.

Film and new media

In the 1960s and 70s Pärt wrote original music for a variety of film genres. Although this early work includes more than three dozen film projects, he has consistently dismissed the results as inconsequential to his real work as a composer.[62] While this music was written under political control in Estonia and thus largely out of the reach of Western audiences, in the decades after Pärt's move to the west, European and American filmmakers discovered that his music in its preexisting form was an uncommonly effective psychological tool. Substantiated estimates have found the presence of his music in over one hundred film media, which draw from more than twenty of his compositions.[63] These have been produced in Scandinavia (specifically Finland and Sweden) and other parts of Europe (France, Germany, Italy, Spain, and Switzerland), Korea, the United Kingdom and the United States. Most of the films using Pärt's preexisting music have been full-length feature films and to date none of them have been commercial Hollywood productions.

The practice of borrowing Pärt's early tinntinabuli music such as *Spiegel im Spiegel*, *Für Alina*, *Fratres*, and *Cantus* has become so widespread that a few critics claim that Pärt's music has joined the ranks of classical masterpieces given over to soundtrack clichés.[64] *Spiegel im Spiegel* has been one of the most frequently deployed of these works, appearing in over thirteen films as a foil for a wide variety of themes, including war, the Holocaust, terminal illness, terrorism, and 9/11, as well as the altruistic potentials of the human spirit in its compassion and forgiveness. Directors often rely on Pärt's music to describe their protagonist's journey as they navigate forces larger than themselves.

Pärt's music is easily appropriated in part due to its superficial alignment with the conventions of soundtrack instrumentation as well as its pseudo-tonal language, sparse textures, ostinatos, and repetitive rhythms. This belies the fact that Pärt's compositional approach is not easily replicable. For independent filmmakers in particular, the formidable costs of buying the rights to Pärt's music should have resulted in more instances of directors resorting to standard industry practice of creating shadow versions to avoid copyright and licensing. Aside from the few instances of 'Pärt-like' music, noted by some commentators in Jürgen Knieper's non-diegetic music for *Der Himmel über Berlin* (1987)[65] or soundtracks by Nick Cave and Warren Ellis,[66] there is a curious lack of even badly crafted Pärt copies, let alone works that can sufficiently mimic the expressive power of Pärt's individual voice.

Due in part to its non-intrusive formal clarity, Pärt's music has served as an effective canvas for pluralist values and debate and thus is uniquely suited to claims of the documentary genre. In some cases it has played a key role in films that humanize the act of physical suffering, as in the television-play *Wit* (Mike Nichols, 2001), where *Spiegel im Spiegel* critiques the treatment and death of an English literature professor from ovarian cancer. When films address issues of force, Pärt's music serves as both a critical and affective tool in circumscribing different forms of violence. In addition to associating it with the devastation wrought by the attack on the World Trade Towers in New York (*Fahrenheit 9/11*), directors have also situated his music in counterpoint to the destruction of the giant Buddhas of Bamiyan, Afghanistan (*The Giant Buddhas*; Christian Frei, 2005) and the realities of environmental degradation in the American South in Laura Dunn's *The Unforeseen* (2007). Frei's *Giant Buddhas* uses *Für Alina* in its investigation of the complex religious and cultural tensions surrounding the statues and their destruction, while Dunn's *Unforeseen* relies heavily on Pärt's music to contextualize both the tangible harm of economic development and the unpredictable aspects of its resolution.

Aside from its more direct presence on the concert stage or ECM's mediation, Pärt's music has accrued its own audience-generated programs. The works have won new audiences for the visceral qualities of the sound but they have also garnered public attention because they are associated with previous films. A few of Pärt's works, such as *Alina*, have been popularized to the degree that their collective meanings are more complex and textured than other works which have not undergone this type of appropriation. One critic heralds Pärt's banishment to the "canon of the overused" along with other popular precomposed tracks such as Samuel Barber's *Adagio for Strings*.[67] While the story of Pärt's music on the American market and its media distribution differs in significant ways from Barber's, the music of both composers has shared the same affective association, that of physical and existential pain. Barber's work is often characterized in the public vernacular as 'sad' music, through its repeated association with the deaths of important public American figures. In this sense, Barber's work has become a type of sonic memorial and counterpoint to violence and war, in the same way that Pärt's precomposed music has served as a filmic counterpoint.[68]

The question remains whether Pärt's reception will follow the same trajectory as Barber's *Adagio* as an ubiquitous cultural commodity, a path that is ultimately independent of its initial compositional intention or early reception. Directors that value his music for its aural simplicity may be forced to reevaluate in light of his recent music, which departs in sound from the early tinntinabuli works. As Pärt enters the latter part of his career and his legacy as a major voice in twentieth-century composition seems assured, the majority of his American audience may never have heard his music in concert or approached it from the context of classical contemporary music. Filmmakers such as Moore, who set Pärt's music front and center in the public consciousness, have stated that it is their encounter with Pärt's sound first that has fueled their consumption of it. Similar kinds of encounters are mediated through the practices of new media cultural production.

Besides musicians and other artists, it is the individual creative labor of listeners, consumers, and other cultural producers who engage with the sound of Pärt's tintinnabuli music. The modality of this work includes user-generated content on social media platforms (e.g. YouTube, Vimeo, Dailymotion), discussion on social networking platforms (e.g. Facebook), and sample-based hip-hop production (e.g. Lupe Fiasco).[69]

At the very least, Morris's style of appropriation has highlighted a dormant but nonetheless real potential for Pärt's music to serve political causes. After so many years of mercurial political pressures, the composer is able to publicly align his creative process with the mission of alleviating worldly injustice. For example, he was outspoken about the Symphony No. 4 "Los Angeles" (2010), which is dedicated to Mikhail Khodorkovsky, a Russian oil executive with political ambitions who was accused of fraud and was imprisoned in Siberia during its composition. The composer has called Khodorkovsky a "great man" and has said Russia would have been a better country if Khodorkovsky had become its leader.[70] Pärt expresses the desire that his message will reach to out "all those imprisoned without rights in Russia."

In his seventh-fifth year, Pärt's marketable identity is a complex complement to his music. It has also become a useful ideological tool in the hands of a variety of communities. While the rigorous expressions of Orthodoxy and those of American pluralists may seem to be unlikely bedfellows, the concept of Pärt has proven to be a profitable and inspiring haven for the consumers and the commercial interests who aspire to engage it.

Further reading

Bruce David Forbes and Jeffrey H. Mahan (eds.), *Religion and Popular Culture in America* (Berkeley: University of California Press, 2005).

Paul Hillier and Tõnu Tormis, *On Pärt* (Copenhagen: Edition Samfundet, 2005).

Steve Lake and Paul Griffiths (eds.), *Horizons Touched: The Music of ECM* (London: Granta Books, 2007).

Jonathan Ritter and J. Martin Daughtry, *Music in the Post-9/11 World* (New York: Routledge, 2007).

Robynn Stilwell and Phil Powrie, *Changing Tunes: The Use of Pre-existing Music in Film* (Aldershot: Ashgate Publishing, 2006).

Lloyd Whitesell, "White Noise: Race and Erasure in the Cultural Avant-Garde," *American Music* 19 (2001), 168–89.

Linda Williams, "Passio," *Film Quarterly* **60** (2007), 16–18.

Appendix A
Radiating from silence: the works of Arvo Pärt seen through a musician's eyes

ANDREAS PEER KÄHLER

In his famous book *The Little Prince*, the French writer Antoine de Saint-Exupéry writes: "I have always loved the desert. You can sit on a dune. You see nothing. You hear nothing. Yet something is still radiating in the silence."[1] The desert – or possibly in a metaphoric sense, *tabula rasa* – is presented here as a magnificent yet unpeopled space that facilitates this "radiating from silence."

> The desert's beauty – said The Little Prince – lies in a well buried somewhere there.

Arvo Pärt's longing for the purity of sound and his craving to draw closer to it through tintinnabulation is a lot like searching for a well in the desert. Similarly, the conviction that 'radiation from silence' may be attained exclusively by reduction of means and personal spiritual denial is shared by both artists. Saint-Exupéry's drawing at the end of the book is moving – two straight lines at the bottom symbolizing the desert and a small awkward starlet at the top; the words Pärt uses to describe the bell style are similarly significant: "Tintinnabuli is an amazing moment – the escape into a self-imposed asceticism: holy men have left behind all their wealth and are heading for the desert. Similarly, the composer wishes to leave behind the entire modern arsenal and save himself through naked monophony carrying only that which is crucial – the triad."

We shall dwell a little on Pärt's "self-imposed asceticism." Let us not imagine it to be so easy or painless for the composer! Looking from the outside at his historic decision to adopt the tintinnabuli style, we are aware of the price that he paid: Pärt divested himself of inconceivable resources such as the many recognized structural novelties of contemporary music. For instance, the principles of tintinnabulation do not allow for a systematic use of the instrument's technical and timbral capacities, nor for a differentiated and opulent instrumentation. In the 'poor' world of tintinnabuli, instrumentation such as the string orchestra 'color' is not unwelcome (even Pärt's newer works sound very sensual), but it is not the most important attribute of this music. For that reason it is often relatively easy to transcribe works for other instruments: just as, in pre-classical music, melody or counterpoint is more vital than the choice of instrument.[2]

After more than twenty-five years of acquaintance with the wonderful results of this stylistic reduction we take Pärt's music almost for granted, but which vales of tears did he have to cross on his way to the tintinnabuli style?

This is how Pärt verbalizes his new creed: "I have discovered that it is enough to play only one note beautifully." This is not a sort of modest understatement but a radical and determined artistic statement. Interpreters of his music find this radical simplicity anything but simple. Here, to play "beautifully" means to play perfectly – disarmingly simple notation becomes a source of irritation rather than help (remember the image of the desert). Of course, seeing a score like this, musicians often expect they will be able to play the composition straight from the page. The usual result of such an approach is a painful awakening (my own attempts to use the piece *Für Alina* for beginners' piano classes were a complete failure …).

The extreme simplicity of musical means in Arvo Pärt's works reveals the technical or musical deficiencies of some musicians. An average opera singer may rescue their performance by identifying themselves with the role; a violinist who does not boast great legato or appropriate intonation will resort to virtuosity; and a conductor with no clear concept for the interpretation of a work will be grateful for the possibility to give cues constantly. Does this apply to Pärt's music? Let us take the eighteen-minute "Silentium" from the second movement of the concerto *Tabula rasa*: in an infinitely luminous, velvet entanglement of long and very long, quiet and very quiet tones, there is not even a single point to lean on if one cannot cope – technically or mentally – with the interpretive requirements; such a musician, completely powerless, is prey to that which he or she cannot master. Simply put, the famous second part of *Tabula rasa* is something of a musical lie-detector – indeed, I have met musicians who could not count to six by the end!

On the other hand, there are some musicians who, thanks to being exposed to Pärt's works, take up practicing long notes again. Even if they have performed everything else in their careers – sight-reading most of it – they are discovering now that it is all about playing just one note beautifully.

As far as the relationship between the simplicity of the scores and their astonishing potential for peril is concerned, it is hard not to notice that the simplicity of the notes is an unconscious protection of delicate music from incompetent, remorseless interpreters – just as Russia did not meet Napoleon's army at the border but drew it deep into the country in order to ultimately dispose of it. An encounter with the score, which seems quite simple, and in reality turns out to be so infinitely difficult, brings to mind Saint Christopher, who certainly faced greater challenges in his life than carrying a baby across a river – yet the weight of this task almost crushed him.

I believe that for musicians the decisive point in experiencing Pärt's music is whether in interpreting a work they succeed in shifting their own perception from the subjective to the quasi-objective level. In Pärt's music, it is not about thoughts or emotions that feed the performance and ultimately determine the interpretation, but the pure 'it' of musical coordinates. Such issues as balance between triads (T) and melody line (M), a controlled vibrato, dynamics without accidental crescendo and diminuendos (which are often due to bowing technique), and others, have to be subjected to careful self-observation and control. In contrast, 'expression' is irrelevant to the interpreters of Pärt's music; it cannot be directly planned but, in favorable conditions, namely when 'it' is attained, it is created, as a result, by itself. Recall Saint-Exupéry:

> You see nothing. You hear nothing. Yet something is still radiating in the
> distance.

The priority of 'it' often requires the performer to make unusual sacrifices. For instance, a cellist (we are back to the second part of *Tabula rasa*) who, in order not to destroy the delicate balance of T- and M-voices, is not allowed to bring out the legato melody in the octave above C', the instrument's best register, has to constantly hold back his or her sound. Similarly, from the instrumental point of view, this is the case with the extreme one-sidedness of some solo lines. For instance, throughout the ten minutes of *Spiegel im Spiegel* only long tones are required of the violinist, and in the *Fratres* version for string quartet the entire voice of the second violin consists of open-string G and B, which have to be quietly sustained for ten minutes. It requires 'beautiful tone' as an epitome of eternity, against which time is refracted in the movement of other voices.

Due to the compositional extremes, it is of principal importance for a performer of Pärt's music not to be misled by the simplicity of the notes but to take time to get close to the sound with reverence and inner calm. And, just as the power of Pärt's music originates in the beauty of individual tones, an interpreter's way outside, towards artistic articulation, always commences inside, with concentrated self-contemplation and control. Therefore, playing Pärt's music without preparation is problematic not so much for the notes themselves, but for the difficulty of creating in oneself this inner peace, which his works demand. (As the fox in *The Little Prince* said cleverly: "It is because you have given so much of your time to it that your rose is so important to you.")

However, careful listening to your inner self leaves space for some freedom. It can be experienced as a blessing when certain practical interpretational mechanisms are questioned; for example, the indication *espressivo* immediately produces the standard vibrato of the left hand; or that final notes or lengths in iambic rhythms are always played vibrato, and so on. (Sadly, as far as vibrato is concerned, few musicians have adequate perception or can control the movement and intensity of their vibrato, even if the majority are convinced they actually do.) Alternating rapid vibrato and non-vibrato – as required, for example, in *Orient & Occident* – poses a great technical challenge to many musicians.

What, then, takes the place of the typical *espressivo*? Ultimately it would be unwise to question a beautiful sound or vibrato as such – *Tabula rasa* and *Fratres* are good examples of how in a composition all possible shades of sound and specifically vibrato should be presented. Is there maybe something like a specific 'Pärt sound?' Skepticism is advisable here; I am more inclined to think that such can exist: an encounter with Pärt's music is rather an opportunity for an interpreter to seek the right solution or proportions out of listening deeply. Also, violinists performing *Spiegel im Spiegel* will not be able to choose any conventional solution to the question of what they are to do with that many long tones – much more likely, they will discover that, as far as vibrato is concerned, less in fact means more.[3] For those who will commit to it, this intuitive moment may be a welcome phenomenon since it increases perception and a sense of one's responsibility and sincerity. For that very reason, Pärt himself is exceptionally sparing about performance directions; often, he just simply presents a musician with naked notes.

The free creative space thus produced also includes issues of tempo. As with timbre, tempo is not a crucial music parameter according to Pärt. The choice of the 'right' tempo (notwithstanding metronome markings in the score) has a lot to do with the intuitive understanding of the interpreter, and there are a great number of wonderful examples of how the same work can develop in very different directions depending on the selected tempo, without losing its identity. In Alexander Malter's *Für Alina* meditations, for example, or in *Wenn Bach Bienen gerüchtet hätte*, where the bee-like counterpoint represents a masterly commotion and intensive labor. I experienced the most extreme form of this creative freedom with *Summa*: the difference of tempo between a 'romantic' legato version and a crisply articulated non-legato one may even amount to 100 percent.

Obviously there are limits to this freedom. Since Pärt's instrumental music is principally oriented according to the ideal of vocal music, the 'singability' of respective voices creates natural upper and lower limits for the choice of tempo. The performer should be very careful about using *rubato* (unless Pärt himself encourages it by giving such directions as 'calm; noble, raptly listening to yourself' as in *Für Alina*). Metric stability is one of the most significant pillars of the quasi-objective impact of Pärt's music. The *giocoso* (joyous, playful) character is also clearly present in such works as *Mein Weg*, or in the first part of *Tabula rasa*; in others, such as *Fratres* or in the second part of *Tabula rasa*, it is hardly noticeable, but equally present and important. And that is precisely where it gets dangerous for the performers: for example, in the second part of *Tabula rasa* maintaining really steady meter for eighteen minutes without any musical 'events' is an enormous challenge.

Exact intonation is another element important for a musician, particularly with the triad notes in the T-voices. It is an acoustical phenomenon that a chord sounds louder when it is perfectly in tune – that is, when overtone spectra overlap perfectly and thus amplify each other. Great conductors such as Sergiu Celibidache have always made use of this phenomenon, achieving maximum orchestral *forte* not through maximum effort but merely by means of precise intonation, whereby the sound has the required power without sounding forced. It is similar in Pärt, but regardless of the dynamic force. Every note in a T-voice makes sense only as a part of the entire triad, and this triad can only contribute to a homogeneous blend of the T- and M-voices if it is perfectly in tune.

Needless to say, the conventional vibrato of violinists is a hindrance in this context. No doubt, bigger intervallic leaps without vibrato are risky as far as intonation is concerned, but experienced musicians should approach this calmly instead of following the line of least resistance (i.e. choosing the intonationally dubious sphere of vibrato). The acoustic stability of triads bears so much significance in Pärt's music because triads constitute a system of reference to everything that is going on in the melody.[4]

To summarize, it is possible to say that a process of desubjectivization of music takes place in Pärt's tintinnabuli compositions. The sacrifice that interpreters of Pärt's music have to make from the technical-instrumental point of view, or from the point of view of 'expression', is the price that is to be paid for this exceptional kind of music. The reward will be an increase of 'intersubjectivity': Pärt's drive towards purity of sound and relentless demand for balance and uniformity inexorably leads the musician's (and the listener's) consciousness to wholeness and inviolability – a bewildering phenomenon in the context of the twenty-first century![5] It may be observed also in group dynamics: few orchestral musicians have any illusion left about the role of the orchestra as a social institution, yet the unifying effect of Pärt's music is obvious and, when a performance is successful, it produces surprising results in the form of orchestral solidarity and shared positive emotions.

Although this observation is not significant from a scholarly point of view, I would like to point out that there are few vain interpreters of Pärt's music – or at least that vanity is barely present during the performances of his compositions. Music of such expression of purity and credibility really seems to have a good effect on musicians (and listeners).

For professional musicians, the encounter with Pärt may have a cleansing effect. Pärt's almost ritual-like use of scales and triads, as well as the obviousness with which they are presented in their innocent nakedness, provide a somewhat concealed appeal to hear differently, anew, what appears to be already known: a scale, which has been worked at thousands of times, may suddenly become a conscious experience of rising and falling; a triad is again perceived as individual notes, abandoning their individuality in order to create a higher entity.

To a medieval or renaissance musician, being astonished by such phenomena might have been perfectly normal. In this day and age, in which, according to the poet Nelly Sachs, "How long have we forgotten how to listen!", it is like a rediscovery of a musical axiom.[6] I can easily imagine that, for many musicians, getting to know Pärt's music may lead to a more conscious and caring attitude towards music altogether. Can anything more beautiful be said about a contemporary composer?

The desert's beauty – said The Little Prince – lies in a well buried somewhere out there.

Appendix B
Greatly sensitive: Alfred Schnittke in Tallinn[1]

ARVO PÄRT

Even though we did not have much opportunity to see each other, Alfred Schnittke and I had a long friendship. In February 1976, Schnittke came to Tallinn for recording sessions of his *Requiem*; our encounters on those February days were very important for me. In 1976, I was in a long phase of searching for a new direction and for my own musical language. I had spent years in a sort of seclusion, experimenting as a composer. At this time, I felt like the fruit of my long search was ready to open itself for me at any moment.

It was a time of great inner tension for me; I was bursting with a feeling of anticipation, and I felt anxious and ready for the birth of something completely new. Yet, at the same time, I felt desperate and helpless about how I should embody the New. I was like a pick-up note that hangs in the air, ready to be resolved at any second.

Alfred was the first person I opened up to about this. It was not easy to tell someone about something so vague, a thing that, for me, had neither form nor substance, name nor addressee. I could only share this with someone who was very close to me, someone greatly sensitive. This someone was Alfred.

Alfred reacted very wisely. He did not attempt to evaluate the material I had shown him, but he perceived the situation very astutely and accurately identified this developing phase of my search.

The only advice he gave me was to leave the experimental stage on paper for real sound. He was very insistent that I should make my many filled notebooks into sound instead of staying behind closed doors with all my sketches.

His words were like midwifery – the scales fell from my eyes. Soon thereafter, I went public with my new system of composition, the tintinnabuli style. After a short time, I dedicated one of my first works from those years to Alfred Schnittke, *Calix* (*Dies Irae*), which was written for the same instrumentation as his *Requiem*. Later on, *Dies Irae*, in a new version, became part of my larger work *Miserere*.

At a concert in Tallinn one year later, in 1977, Alfred played the prepared piano part in both his *Concerto Grosso* and the premiere of my *Tabula rasa*.

Appendix C
Remembering Heino Eller[1]

ARVO PÄRT

It is with profound gratitude that I think of my composition teacher Heino Eller and of the time I spent studying with him. It is difficult to say just what impressed me more, his way of teaching or his charismatic personality. Over the decades, Heino Eller's generosity and nobility of spirit, as well as his work, have merged in my mind to create an overall picture that has continued to influence me up to the present day.

As a pedagogue he was always open to modern movements in art, allowing his students to go their own ways and respecting their personal decisions, even where they diverged substantially from his own ideals. He taught a sense of responsibility towards our own work and to always remain true to ourselves. Eller once said that his aim as a teacher was to help students develop their individual musical language and personality. The works of more than fifty of his students, ranging from Eduard Tubin to Lepo Sumera, offer the best possible proof of his success.

Through him, a personality from a different generation, we came into contact with the pre-revolutionary aristocracy and its cultural heritage. Soviet ideology was incapable of dimming his insight into human and cultural values. After his training in St. Petersburg, with its centuries-old musical tradition, he was able to establish totally new standards in small Estonia, and thereby build the basis for a professional music scene.

Heino Eller's oeuvre is typified by strict logic, a cultivated sense of style, subtle and masterly orchestration, and a significantly personal compositional voice. These qualities position him firmly alongside the great Nordic composers. Over the years, Heino Eller's *Homeland Song* has arguably gained similarly symbolic status for Estonia as Sibelius's famous composition *Finlandia* has for Finland.

Now that I am approximately the age my teacher was at the time, I have discovered a pronouncement I never personally heard from Eller in his lessons: "Finding a single suitable note is far more difficult than bringing a mass of notes to paper." Although he never conveyed this message to me in so many words, he appears nonetheless to have succeeded in rooting a similarly tormenting search for the "single suitable note" in my soul.

Appendix D
Acceptance speech for the International Bridge Prize of the European City of Görlitz

November 9, 2007,
in Görlitz, Germany

Dear honored guests, dear friends,

To be the center of attention for politicians and scientists is an unusual affair for a musician. Today, I hear words about my music and myself which sound rather excessive to me, as the goals I have set for myself were never as grandiose as they were stated here. My goals and standards were and are much more modest and simple. Back then, when what is today considered my music was just coming into being, I had my hands full with making sure to get myself going and solve my own problems. I had to get to a state where I could find a musical language that I wanted to live with. I was searching for a small island of sound, for a 'place' inside me, where – let's call it – a dialogue with God might occur. To find this place was a vital task for me. I am sure that this kind of desire is a part of every human being, whether consciously or unconsciously, and maybe many of you know that and realize what it is I am talking about.

To clarify my thoughts I would like to describe a picture for you: if we look at some sort of substance or object through a scanning, tunneling microscope, the thousandfold enlargement obviously looks different than the millionfold one. If one moves through the different states of enlargement, one can discover hitherto unimaginable and fairly chaotic 'landscapes' in every material. At one point, however, there is a limit, at just about three-millionfold enlargement. There, the curious landscapes have disappeared and all we see is a strict geometry, a kind of net that is very clear and very specific.

The astonishing fact is that this geometry looks very similar even with completely different substances or objects.

Is something similar true for a human being?

Let us dream a little bit. Let us try to quasi-observe a human soul under such a microscope and gradually increase the degree of enlargement. We will witness how the outer features of a human being with all of his or her peculiarities, weaknesses, and virtues gradually disappear from the picture with the increasing enlargement. It will be an endless process of shortening that will lead us towards the essential. On this 'trip inside,' we will also leave behind all social, cultural, political, and religious contexts. At the end, we will get to a net-like basic pattern. One might call it 'human geometry,' clearly structured, neatly formed – and, most of all, beautiful. In this depth we are all so similar, that we could recognize ourselves in every other person. And it could be that this level is the only one on which a truly functional bridge (of peace) could be imagined, where all our problems – if they still exist then – would be solvable.

I am very much tempted to see this beautiful and neat Ur-substance, this pre-cious island in the inner seclusion of our soul, as the 'place' where, over 2000 years ago, we were told that the Kingdom of God would be – inside us. No matter if we are old or young, rich or poor, woman or man, colored or white, talented or less talented. And so, I keep trying to stay on the path that searches for this passionately longed-for 'magic island,' where all people – and, for me, all sounds – can live together in love. The gates on the way there are open for everyone. But the road there is difficult – despairingly difficult.

Your Brückepreis encourages me to stay on this path and it gives me new strength. For this, I thank you very much!

Arvo Pärt

Appendix E
Acceptance speech for the Léonie Sonning Music Prize 2008

May 22, 2008, in Copenhagen, Denmark.

Distinguished members of the Award Committee, dear friends,

We have to admit: Human beings are imperfect. There is no other knowledge that people have a harder time accepting. Maybe some people think a composer is the exception. I have to tell you: no, he isn't … unfortunately.

In allusion to Pontius Pilate's famous question we ask: But what is perfection? What if we actually knew the answer, would it help us? At first, at least, it might seem that the idea of perfection has no place in our daily life. Somehow it is not current, not relevant. In an artist's creative process, however, this eternal question turns up to its fullest extent. It doesn't leave the creative person in peace. It worries and plagues him, because he strives for perfection with his whole physical and mental being. He searches for it almost to the point of desperation.

Yet very often his goals by far surmount his possibilities, and the huge gap between them painfully shows him his limits. These extreme efforts sometimes lead to a result that exceeds the author's measure and the limits of his potential. And there something happens that does not adhere to the laws of logic: A work of art liberates itself from its intrinsically unfavorable preconditions.

So, in a slightly simplified way, one could say that, in such a case, a successful work of art can be much better than its creator. It overtakes him, and outperforms him and his mundane faultiness. The new dimension of his work – even as it is still far from perfection – is able to transcend its author's imperfection.

A comparable phenomenon can sometimes be observed with top athletes. A record! Even though this doesn't happen every day, and although it might one day be beaten by someone else, or by the same athlete himself: A magic moment has happened, something enduring has been created.

Don't awards mark such magic moments? At least that is how I see it today, in my case. In my opinion, the prize, this great prize honors the music, which has outclassed me as a composer and as the person standing before you here today. And thus, please allow me to thank the Léonie Sonning music prize committee in the name of some of my works. Both of us, my music and I, are very proud to be allowed to call ourselves Léonie Sonning music prize laureates.

Thank you very much!
Arvo Pärt

Appendix F
Works list

Premieres are listed by day/month/year. Titles are given in the language of most common usage.

L'abbé Agathon 2004
Soprano, 8 violoncellos – 15′
Text: English text from "The Desert Christian" by Benedicta Ward
Language: French (alternative version in English)
Premiere: 05/05/2004, Beauvais, France
UE 32767: study score; 33231: piano reduction

— 2004/2005
Soprano, 4 violas, 4 violoncellos
Language: French (English)
Premiere: 10/07/2005, Ossiach, Austria
UE 33004: study score; 33005: piano reduction

— 2004/2008
2 soloists (SA), choir (SA), string orchestra
Language: French (English)
Premiere: 03/11/2008, Richmond, VA, USA
UE 34672: study score; 34673: choral score; 34649: piano reduction

Adam's Lament 2009/2010
SATB, string orchestra – 18′
Text: Saint Silouan
Premiere: 07/06/2010, Istanbul, Turkey
UE 34740: study score; 34741: choral score; 34742: piano reduction

Alleluia-Tropus 2008
SATB, 8 violoncellos (ad lib.) – 3′
Text: Tropus for December 6th (St. Nicholas)
Language: Church Slavonic
Premiere: 20/12/2008, Bari, Italy
UE 34365: score; 34366: vocal score; 34367: piano reduction

An den Wassern zu Babel saßen wir und weinten 1976/1984
SATB, organ – 7–8′
Language: (vocalise)
Premiere: 28/04/1984, Witten, Germany
UE 30159: score = organ part; 30160: vocal score

— 1976/1984
Trombone, chamber orchestra / cl (2), hn, str
Premiere: 19/11/1995, Stockholm, Sweden

UE 30293: score

— 1976/1996
Soloists (SATB), instrumental ensemble
Language: (vocalise)
UE 30161: score; 30160: vocal score

And One of the Pharisees 1992
3 voices or 3-part choir (ct(A)TB) a cappella – 10′
Text: Bible, St. Luke 7: 36–50
Language: English
Premiere: 09/02/1992, Davis, CA, USA
UE 30510: vocal score

Annum per annum 1980
Organ – 8′
Premiere: 12/10/1980, Speyer, Germany
UE 17179

Anthem of St. John the Baptist 2004
SATB, organ – 5′
Text: Bible, St. John 1: 29–34
Language: English
Premiere: 18/03/2004, Oxford, England
UE 32927: score = organ part; 32928: choral score

Arbos 1977
7 (8) recorders, 3 triangles ad lib. – 3′
UE 17443: score and parts

— 1977/1986/2001
8 brass instruments, percussion
UE 31911: study score

The Beatitudes 1990/1991
SATB, organ – 7′
Text: Bible, St. Matthew 5: 3–12
Language: English
Premiere: 25/05/1990, Berlin, Germany
UE 33002: score = organ part; 33003: choral score

— 1990/2001
SATB, organ
Premiere: 24/06/2002, Monza, Italy
UE 31989: score = organ part; 31990: choral score

Beatus Petronius 1990/1996
2 choirs (SATB/SATB), 2 organs – 5′
Text: Unknown origin
Language: Latin
Premiere: 05/10/1990, Bologna, Italy
UE 31156: score = organ part; 31157: choral score

Berliner Messe 1990/2002
SATB, organ – 25′
Text: Kyrie; Gloria; Erster Alleluiavers zum Weihnachtsfest (ad lib.); Zweiter Alleluiavers zum Weihnachtsfest (ad lib.); Erster Alleluiavers zum Pfingstfest (ad lib.); Zweiter Alleluiavers zum Pfingstfest (ad lib.); Veni Sancte Spiritus (ad lib.); Credo; Sanctus; Agnus Dei
Language: Latin
Premiere: 24/05/1990, Berlin, Germany
UE 32989: score = organ part; 32990: vocal score

— 1990/1991/2002
SATB, string orchestra
Premiere: 18/12/1991, Erlangen, Germany
UE 32762: study score; 32761: choral score

Zwei Beter 1998
Female choir (SA) a cappella – 7′
Text: Bible, St. Luke 18: 9–14
Language: German
Premiere: 02/09/2000, Hanover, Germany
UE 31297: choral score

Bogoróditse Djévo 1990
SATB a cappella – 1′
Text: Russian Orthodox Liturgy
Language: Church Slavonic
Premiere: 24/12/1990, Cambridge, England
UE 30414: choral score

Cantate Domino canticum novum 1977/1996
Mixed choir or soloists (SATB), organ – 3′
Text: Bible, Psalm 95 (96)
Language: Latin
UE 31058: score = organ part; 31059: vocal score

Cantique des degrés 1999/2002
SATB, orchestra – 7′
Text: Bible, Psalm 121 (120)
Language: Latin
Premiere: 19/11/1999, Monaco
UE 31468: study score; 31466: choral score

Cantus in Memory of Benjamin Britten 1977/1980
String orchestra, bell – 6′
Premiere: 1977, Tallinn, Estonia
UE 32469: score; PH 555: pocket score

Cecilia, vergine romana 2000/2002
SATB, orchestra – 17–19′
Text: Breviario Romano, 22 novembre, S. Cecilia, terza lettura
Language: Italian

2 2 2 2–4 2 2 1 – perc(2), hp, str
Premiere: 19/11/2000, Rome, Italy
UE 31543: study score; 31719: choral score

Collage über B–A–C–H 1964
Strings, oboe, cembalo, piano – 8′
Premiere: 1964, Tallinn, Estonia
SIK1887: study score

Como cierva sedienta 1998/2002
Soprano or female choir SA (unisone), orchestra – 30′
Text: Bible, Psalms 42 and 43 (41 and 42)
Language: Spanish
Premiere (soprano, orchestra): 03/02/1999, Santa Cruz/Tenerife, Canary Islands
Premiere (female choir, orchestra): 16/06/2000, Stockholm, Sweden
UE 31290: study score; 31370A: solo part
Concerto piccolo über B–A–C–H 1964/1994
Solo trumpet, strings, cembalo, piano – 8′
Premiere: 23/10/1994, Gothenburg, Sweden
SIK1931: pocket score

Credo 1968
SATB, piano, orchestra – 12′
Text: Bible (various parts)
Language: Latin
Premiere: 16/11/1968, Tallinn, Estonia
UE 33344: study score; 33033: choral score; 33497: piano reduction; 34032: solo
piano part

Credo from **Berliner Messe** 1990/2002
SATB, organ (Matzelsdorfer version) – 4′
Language: Latin
UE 33026: score = organ part; 33025: vocal score

— 1990/2005
SATB, string orchestra (Matzelsdorfer version)
Language: Latin
UE 33054: study score; 33053: organ reduction; 32630: choral score

Da pacem Domine 2004/2008
SATB, orchestra – 6′
2 2 2 2–4 2 2 1 – timp, perc, str
Text: Votive antiphon for peace
Language: Latin
Premiere: 01/07/2004, Barcelona, Spain
Premiere (revised version): 27/04/2008, Potsdam, Germany
UE 32999: study score; 32998: choral score

— 2004/2006
SATB a cappella
Language: Latin

Premiere: 29/03/2005, St. Gerold, Austria
UE 32941: vocal score; 32942: piano reduction

— 2004/2006
SATB, string orchestra
Premiere: 18/05/2007, Tallinn, Estonia
UE 33688: study score; 32941: choral score; 32942: piano reduction

— 2004/2006
String quartet
UE 33339: score; 33340: score and parts

— 2004/2006
String orchestra
Premiere: 02/11/2006, Tallinn, Estonia
UE 33664: study score

— 2004/2006
Recorder quartet [S(T)A(B)T(greatbass)B(subbass)]
Arranged by Sylvia Corinna Rosin and Irmhild Beutler (2007)
UE 33704: score and parts

— 2004/2006
8 violoncellos [In preparation]

Darf ich 1995/1999
Solo violin, bell in C♯ (ad lib.), strings – 3′
Premiere: 03/07/1999, Graz, Austria (revised version)
Premiere: 08/08/1995, Gstaad, Switzerland
UE 31486: study score; 30851: piano reduction

De profundis 1980
TTBB, percussion ad lib., organ – 7′
Text: Bible, Psalm 130 (129)
Language: Latin
Premiere: 25/04/1981, Kassel, Germany
UE 32973: score = organ part; 32974: choral score

— 1980/2008
Male choir (TTBB), chamber orchestra
Premiere: 27/04/2008, Potsdam, Germany
UE 34321: study score; 34322: choral score

The Deer's Cry 2007
SATB a cappella – 5′
Text: according to the 'Lorica' of St. Patrick
Language: English
Premiere: 13/02/2008, Drogheda, Ireland
UE 33723: choral score

***Diagramme*, op. 11** 1964
Piano – 4′
Premiere: 1964, Tallinn, Estonia
Published by Sikorski, Hamburg

Dopo la vittoria 1996/1998
Piccola cantata for SATB a cappella – 11'
Text: Dictionary by Archbishop Philaret (St. Petersburg: 1902)
Language: Italian
Premiere: 06/12/1997, Milan, Italy
UE 30429: choral score

Es sang vor langen Jahren 1984
Alto or countertenor, violin, viola – 4'
Text: Clemens von Brentano
Language: German
Premiere: 17/11/1984, Hanover, Germany
UE 18421: performance score

Estländler 2006
Flute – 1'30"
UE 33661

— 2006/2009
Violin
UE 34680

Festina lente 1988/1990
String orchestra, harp ad lib. – 6–9'
Premiere: 26/06/1988, Bonn, Germany
UE 19286: study score

Fratres Three-part music
— 1977
Chamber ensemble – 10'
UE 34174: study score

— 1977/1982
4, 8, 12 … violoncellos
Premiere: 18/09/1982, Berlin, Germany
UE 17710: score; 17711: set of parts

— 1977/1985/1989
String quartet
PH 560: pocket score; UE 19000A/C: parts

— 1977
Wind octet, percussion: ob(2), cl(2), bsn(2), hn(2), perc(1)
Arranged by Beat Briner (1990)
UE 34358: score; 34359: set of parts

— 1977/1991
String orchestra, percussion (1 player: claves, bass drum or tomtom)
UE 17802: study score

— 1977
Brass orchestra
Arranged by Johannes Stert (2004)

Premiere: 12/12/2004, Hilgen, Germany
UE 33036: study score

— 1977
3 recorder players, percussion, violoncello (or viola da gamba)
Arranged by Peter Thalheimer (2009)
[In preparation]

Fratres Three-part music with solo-variations
— 1977/1980
Violin, piano – 11'
Premiere: 17/08/1980, Salzburg, Austria
UE 17274

— 1977
Violoncello, piano
Arranged by Dietmar Schwalke (1989)
Premiere: 30/07/1989, Hitzacker, Germany
UE 19563

— 1977/1992
Violin, string orchestra, percussion (1 player: claves, bass drum or tomtom)
UE 31998: study score; 19898: piano reduction; 19898A: solo part

— 1977
Trombone, string orchestra, percussion (as above)
Arranged by Christian Lindberg (1993)
UE 34829: study score; 34830: piano reduction; 34830A: solo part

— 1977/1995
Violoncello, string orchestra, percussion (as above)
Premiere: 09/12/2001, Rotterdam, Netherlands
UE 31997: study score; 32573: piano reduction; 32573A: solo part

— 1977
Guitar, string orchestra, percussion (as above)
Arranged by Manuel Barrueco (2000)
Premiere: 02/11/2000, Corunna, Spain
UE 32635: study score; 32801: piano reduction; 32801A: solo part

— 1977
Viola, piano
Arranged by Lars Anders Tomter (2003)
UE 32624

— 1977/2008
Viola, string orchestra, percussion (as above)
Premiere: 15/11/2008, Elsinore, Denmark
UE 34375: study score; 34588: piano reduction; 34588A: solo part

— 1977
4 percussion players
Arranged by Vambola Krigul (2006)

Premiere: 09/05/2006, Tallinn, Estonia
UE 33375: study score; 33376: parts

— 1977
Saxophone quartet
[In preparation]

Für Alina 1976
Piano – 2′
Premiere: 1976, Tallinn, Estonia
UE 19823

Für Anna Maria 2006
Piano – 1′15″
UE 33363

Für Lennart in memoriam 2006
String orchestra – 7′30″
Premiere: 26/03/2006, Tallinn, Estonia
UE 33324: study score

Hymn to a Great City 1984/2004
2 pianos – 3′
Premiere: 10/03/1984, New York City, USA (first version)
Premiere: 15/07/2000, Lockenhaus, Austria (revised version)
UE 30439: performance score

I Am the True Vine 1996
SATB a cappella – 6–8′
Text: Bible, St. John 15: 1–14
Language: English
Premiere: 22/06/1996, Norwich, England
UE 30301: choral score

In principio 2003
SATB, orchestra – 20′
Text: Bible, St. John 1: 1–14
Language: Latin
Premiere: 22/05/2003, Graz, Austria
UE 32656: study score; 32655: choral score; 32834: piano reduction

In spe 2010
4 woodwinds, horn, string orchestra – 7–8′
Premiere: 09/09/2010, Glamorgan, Wales
UE 34743: study score
[Based on *An den Wassern zu Babel saßen wir und weinten*]

Kanon Pokajanen 1997
SATB a cappella – 90–110′
Ode I; Ode III; Ode IV; Ode V; Ode VI • Kontakion • Ikos; Ode VII (Memento); Ode VIII; Ode IX (Nïnye k wam); Gebet nach dem Kanon / Prayer after the Kanon
Text: Canon of Repentance by St. Andrew of Crete
Language: Church Slavonic

Premiere: 17/03/1998, Cologne, Germany
UE 31114: study score; UE 31272: choral score

Ode I 1997
7'30"–9'30"
UE 31271: choral score

Ode III 1997
12'–13'30"
UE 31273: choral score

Ode IV 1997
7'–9'
UE 31274: choral score

Ode V 1997
8'–10'
UE 31275: choral score

Ode VI • Kontakion • Ikos 1997
13'30"–16'30"
UE 31276: choral score

Ode VII (Memento) 1994/1997
7'-9'
UE 31277: choral score

Ode VIII 1997
8'30"–10'30"
UE 31278: choral score

Ode IX (Nïnye k wam) 1989/1997
8'–10'
UE 31279: choral score

Gebet nach dem Kanon 1997
11–13'
UE 31280: choral score

Fünf Kinderlieder late 1950s / early 1960s
Children's choir (unison), piano – 10'
Ich bin schon groß; Lied der Glühwürmchen; Lied der Frösche; Lied vom Marienkäfer;
Wie soll die Puppe heißen?
Language: Estonian, Russian, German
[In preparation]

Kyrie 2010
Carillon – 2'30"
For the bells of Trinity Church, 75th birthday celebration in Rakvere, Estonia
Unpublished

Lamentate 2003
Piano, orchestra – 37'
Premiere: 07/02/2003, London, England
UE 32667: study score; 32843: piano reduction; 32843A: solo part

Vier leichte Tanzstücke 1956/1957
Piano – 6'

Der gestiefelte Kater; Rotkäppchen und der Wolf; Schmetterlinge; Tanz der Entenküken
UE 33374

Litany 1994/1996
Soli [alto (countertenor), 2 tenors, bass], mixed choir (SATB), orchestra – 25–30′
Text: Prayers of St. John Chrysostom
Language: English
Premiere: 24/06/1994, Eugene, OR, USA
UE 31116: study score; 30780: choral score

Littlemore Tractus 2000
SATB, organ – 6′
Text: "Wisdom and Innocence," sermon preached on February 19, 1843 in Littlemore
by John Henry Newman
Language: English
Premiere: 21/02/2001, Oxford, England
UE 31595: score = organ part; 31596: choral score

Magnificat 1989
SATB a cappella – 7′
Text: Bible, St. Luke 1: 48–55
Language: Latin
Premiere: 24/05/1990, Stuttgart, Germany
UE 19350: choral score

Sieben Magnificat-Antiphonen 1988/1991
SATB a cappella – 15′
O Weisheit; O Adonai; O Sproß aus Isais Wurzel; O Schlüssel Davids; O Morgenstern;
O König aller Völker; O Immanuel
Language: German
Premiere: 11/10/1988, Berlin, Germany
UE 19098: choral score

Meie Aed 1959/2003
Cantata for children's choir (SSA), orchestra – 10–15′
Text: Eno Raud (in Estonian)
Translations: English: Maarja Kangro; Russian: T. Sikorskaja
2 0 3 2–4 2 3 1 – timp, perc(3), hp(2), str
UE 32636: study score, Italian; 31134: piano reduction; 31135: choral score

Mein Weg 1989/1999/2000
14 strings (vln(6), vla(2), vc(4), cb(2)), percussion – 7′
Premiere: 11/04/1995, Berlin, Germany
Premiere (revised version): 02/07/1999, Graz, Austria
UE 31598: study score

Mein Weg hat Gipfel und Wellentäler 1989
Organ – 8′
Premiere: 09/07/1989, Parainen, Finland
UE 19545

Miserere 1989/1992
Soli (SA(ct)TTB), mixed choir (SATB), ensemble, organ – 30–35′
Text: Psalm 50 (51) (3–5, 6–12) and *Dies Irae* sequence, verses 1–8
Language: Latin
0 1 2 1–0 1 1 0 – perc(3), org, e.guit, e.bass
Premiere: 17/06/1989, Rouen, France
UE 30871: score; 30873: vocal score

Missa brevis 2009
12 violoncelli
Kyrie; Sanctus; Agnus Dei
Premiere: 27/02/2010, Berlin, Germany
UE 34730: study score

Missa Syllabica 1977/1996
SATB, organ – 13–16′
Kyrie; Gloria; Credo; Sanctus; Agnus Dei; Ite missa est
Language: Latin
UE 30430: score = organ part; 30431: choral score

— 1977/1996
SATB a cappella – 13–16′
UE 31151: choral score

— 1977/1996/2010
SATB, string quartet – 13–16′
[In preparation]

Morning Star 2007
SATB a cappella – 3′
Text: Prayer above the tomb of St. Bede in Durham Cathedral
Language: English
Premiere: 10/12/2007, London, England
UE 33718: choral score

Most Holy Mother of God 2003
4 voices (Ct(A)TTB) a cappella – 5′
Text: ?
Language: English
Premiere: 15/10/2003, Durham, England
UE 32622: vocal score

Mozart-Adagio 1992/2005
Violin, violoncello, piano – 6′
Premiere: 06/09/1992, Helsinki, Finland
UE 30456: score and parts
[Based on the second movement of Piano sonata in F major KV 189e (280)]

My Heart's in the Highlands 2000
Countertenor or alto, organ – 8–9′
Text: poem by Robert Burns

Language: English
Premiere: 23/11/2000, Saluzzo, Italy
UE 31541

— 2000/2010
8 violoncellos
[In preparation]

***Nekrolog*, op. 5** 1960
Orchestra – 10'
3 3 4 3–4 4 3 1 – timp, perc, str
Premiere: 1961, Moscow, USSR
BEL 533

Nunc dimittis 2001
SATB a cappella – 7'30"
Text: Bible, St. Luke 2: 29–32
Language: Latin
Premiere: 15/08/2001, Edinburgh, Scotland
UE 31909: choral score

O-Antiphonen 1988/2008
8 violoncellos – 15'
Premiere: 21/10/2008, Amsterdam, The Netherlands
UE 34356: score
[Based on *Sieben Magnificat-Antiphonen*]

Orient & Occident 1999/2000
String orchestra – 7'
Premiere: 30/09/2000, Berlin, Germany
UE 31518: study score

Pari intervallo 1976/1980
Organ – 6'
UE 17480

— 1976/1980
4 recorders
UE 17444: performance score

— 1976/1995
Clarinet, trombone, string orchestra
Premiere: 19/11/1995, Stockholm, Sweden
UE 32398: study score

— 1976/2008
Four-hand piano or two pianos
Premiere: 09/02/2009, New York City, USA
UE 34564

— 1976
Saxophone quartet
[In preparation]

— 1976
8 violoncellos
[In preparation]

Partita, op. 2 1959
Piano – 8'
Toccatina; Fughetta; Larghetto; Ostinato
Premiere: 1959, Tallinn, Estonia
UE 30410

Passacaglia 2003
Violin, piano – 5'
Premiere: 11/10/2003, Hanover, Germany
UE 32738

— 2003/2007
1 or 2 violins, vibraphone (ad lib.), string orchestra
Premiere: 04/06/2007, Saarbrücken, Germany
UE 33693: study score; 33694: piano reduction; 33694A: solo part (V1); 33694B: solo
part (V2)

Passio Domini nostri Jesu Christi secundum Joannem 1982
Soli (SA(ct)TTBarB), choir (SATB), instrumental quartet, organ – 75'
Text: Bible, St. John 18: 1 to 19: 30
Language: Latin
ob, bsn, vln(1), vc(1), org
Premiere: 27/11/1982, Munich, Germany
UE 17568: study score; 17570: choral score

Peace upon you, Jerusalem 2002
Female choir (SA) a cappella – 5'
Text: Bible, Psalm 122 (121)
Language: English
Premiere: 12/02/2003, New York City, USA
UE 32639: choral score

Perpetuum mobile, op. 10 1963
Orchestra – 5–6'
3 3 4 3–4 4 3 1 – perc(6), str
Premiere: 13/12/1963, Tallinn, Estonia
UE 13560: score

Pro et contra 1966
Concert for violoncello, orchestra – 9'
1 1 1 1–1 1 1 0 – alto sax, perc, pno, str
Premiere: 1967, Tallinn, Estonia
SIK1881: study score

Psalom 1985/1991
String quartet – 2'30"–5'
Premiere: 18/11/1991, Vienna, Austria
UE 19980: score and parts

— 1985/1995
String orchestra – 4′–7′
UE 30847: score

— 1985
8 violoncellos – 2′30″–5′
[In preparation]

Quintettino 1964
Flute, oboe, clarinet, bassoon, horn – 5′
Premiere: 1964, Tallinn, Estonia
EP 5774A: Studienpartitur; EP 5774: Stimmensatz

Salve Regina 2001/2002
SATB, organ – 10–12′
Text: Marian antiphons
Language: Latin
Premiere: 21/05/2002, Essen, Germany
UE 31987: score = organ part; 31988: choral score

Sarah Was Ninety Years Old 1977/1990
3 voices (STT), percussion, organ – 25′
Language: (vocalise)
UE 30300: score and parts

Scala cromatica 2007
Trio piccolo for violin, violoncello, piano – 1′45″–2′
Premiere: 29/11/2007, Vienna, Austria
UE 34842: score and parts

Sei gelobt, du Baum 2007
Baritone, violin, quinterne (may also be played on mandolin, mandola, or lute), contrabass – 3′
Text: "Sei gelobt, du Baum"; and text by Viivi Luik
Language: German
Premiere: 27/02/2009, Willisau, Switzerland
UE 34350: score; 34351: set of parts; 34352: piano reduction

Silhouette 2009/2010
Large string orchestra, percussion – 7′
Premiere: 2010, Paris, France
UE 34744: study score
[In preparation]

Silouan's Song 1991
String orchestra – 5–6′
Premiere: 04/07/1991, Rättvik, Sweden
UE 19889: score

La Sindone 2005
Orchestra – 16′
0 0 0 0–0 1 1 0 – timp, perc(4), str
Premiere: 15/02/2006, Turin, Italy

UE 33058: study score

Zwei slawische Psalmen 1984/1997
Soloists (SACtTB) and choir (SACtTB) a cappella – 8′
Text: Bible, Psalms 117 and 131 (116 and 130)
Lobet den Herrn, alle Heiden; Ehre sei dem Vater und dem Sohne; Kindliche Ergebung
Language: Church Slavonic
Premiere: 28/04/1984, Witten, Germany
UE 31115: vocal score

Solfeggio 1964
SATB a cappella – 5–6′
Language: vocalises
Premiere: 1964, Tallinn, Estonia
UE 30455: choral score

— 1963/2008
String quartet
UE 34354: score; 34355: score, parts

— 1963
Saxophone quartet
[In preparation]

— 1963
8 violoncellos
[In preparation]

Two Sonatinen, op. 1 1958/1959
Piano – 6′ + 6′
Sonatine No. 1 (1958); Sonatine No. 2 (1959)
Premiere: 1959, Tallinn, Estonia
UE 30411

Spiegel im Spiegel 1978
Violin, piano – 10′
Premiere: 1978, Moscow, Russia
UE 13360

— 1978
Viola, piano
UE 31257

— 1978
Violoncello, piano
UE 30336

—1978
Clarinet (or bass clarinet), piano
UE 32764

—1978
Horn, piano

UE 32765

— 1978
Contrabass, piano
UE 33057

— 1978
Alto flute, piano
UE 33935

— 1978
Oboe, piano
UE 33863

— 1978
Cor anglais, piano
UE 33864

— 1978
Bassoon, piano
UE 34745

Stabat Mater 1985
Soprano, countertenor (alto), tenor, violin, viola, violoncello – 20–25′
Text: thirteenth-century Catholic hymn
Language: Latin
Premiere: 30/10/1985, Vienna, Austria
UE 33953: study score; 34334: piano reduction; 33955: vocal score; 33954: set of parts

— 1985/2008
Choir (SAT), string orchestra
Premiere: 12/06/2008, Vienna, Austria
UE 34173: study score; 34245: piano reduction; 34172: choral score

Statuit ei Dominus 1990
2 choirs (SATB/SATB), 2 organs – 5–6′
Text: Bible, Ecclesiastes 45: 30
Language: Latin
Premiere: 03/10/1990, Bologna, Italy
UE 19671: score = organ part; 19672: choral score

Summa 1977
SATB a cappella – 5–6′
Text: Creed (Catholic)
Language: Latin
UE 33686: vocal score

— 1977/1990
Violin, 2 violas, violoncello
UE 19675: score and parts

— 1977/1991
String quartet

UE 19099: score and parts

— 1977/1991
String orchestra
UE 19836: score

— 1977
Recorder quartet [S(T)A(B)A(B)T(GB)]
Arranged by Sylvia Corinna Rosin and Irmhild Beutler (2005)
UE 33030: score and parts

— 1977/2008
Trombone quartet
UE 34376: score; 34377: score and parts

— 1977
Saxophone quartet
[In preparation]

— 1977
8 violoncellos
[In preparation]

Symphony No. 1 "Polyphonic" 1963
Orchestra – 16'
1 1 1 1–2 1 1 0 – perc, str
Premiere: 07/02/1964, Tallinn
SIK1885: pocket score

Symphony No. 2 1966
Orchestra – 14'
3 3 4 3–6 4 4 0 – perc, hp, pno, str
SIK1886: pocket score

Symphony No. 3 1971
Orchestra – 21'
3 3 4 3–4 4 4 1 – timp, perc, cel, str
Premiere: 21/09/1972, Tallinn, Estonia
Peters Edition, Hamburg

Symphony No. 4 "Los Angeles" 2008
String orchestra, harp, timpani, percussion (2–4) – 34'
Premiere: 10/01/2009, Los Angeles, CA, USA
UE 34562: study score

Tabula rasa 1977
2 violins, string orchestra and prepared piano – 27'
Ludus; Silentium
Premiere: 30/09/1977, Tallinn, Estonia
UE 31937: study score; 32517: set of solo parts

— 1977
Violin, viola, string orchestra, prepared piano – 27'
UE 31938: study score; 32520: set of solo parts

Te Deum 1984–85/1992
3 choirs (SSAA/TTBB/SATB), prepared piano, string orchestra, tape – 30′
Text: Christian hymn
Language: Latin
Premiere: 19/01/1985, Cologne, Germany
UE 34183: study score; 34184: choral score; 34297: piano reduction

"These Words ... " 2007–2008
String orchestra, percussion (2) – 10–15′
Premiere: 22/05/2008, Copenhagen, Denmark
UE 34177: study score

Tribute to Caesar 1997
SATB a cappella – 7′
Text: Bible, St. Matthew 22: 15–22
Language: English
Premiere: 18/10/1997, Karlstad, Sweden
UE 31137: choral score

Triodion 1998
SATB a cappella – 15′
Text: Orthodox prayer-book
Introduction; Ode I: O Jesus the Son of God, Have Mercy upon Us; Ode II: O Most
Holy Birth-giver of God, Save Us; Ode III: O Holy Saint Nicholas, Pray unto God for
Us; Coda (ad lib.)
Language: English
Premiere: 30/04/1998, London, England
UE 31228: choral score

Trisagion 1992/1994
String orchestra – 12′
Premiere: 18/07/1992, Ilomantsi, Finland
UE 31265: study score

Trivium 1976
Organ – 7′
Premiere: 1976, Tallinn, Estonia
SIK0882

Ukuaru Waltz 1973
Piano – 2′30″
Premiere: 1976, Tallinn, Estonia
UE 34746

Variationen zur Gesundung von Arinuscha 1977
Piano – 4′
Premiere: 1977, Tallinn, Estonia
UE 19823

Vater unser 2005
Boy soprano (or countertenor), piano – 2′30″
May also be performed (in unison) by boys' choirs or children's choirs and piano

Text: The Lord's Prayer
Language: German
Premiere: 11/07/2005, Ossiach, Austria
UE 33028

Veni creator 2006
SATB or soloists, organ – 2′30 ″
Text: Christian hymn attributed to Rabanus Maurus
Premiere: 28/09/2006, Fulda, Germany
UE 33397: score = organ part; 33398: vocal score

— 2006/2010
SATB, string orchestra – 2′30″
[In preparation]

Von Angesicht zu Angesicht 2005
Soprano, baritone, clarinet, viola, contrabass – 4′
Text: Bible, 1 Corinthians 13: 12
Language: Russian
UE 33725: score; 33727: piano reduction; 33726: set of parts

Wallfahrtslied 1984
Tenor or baritone, string quartet – 9′
Text: Bible, Psalm 121 (120)
Language: German
UE 30426: score, parts

— 1984/2001
Male choir (TBar), string orchestra
Premiere: 07/04/2001, Tallinn, Estonia
UE 31876: study score

Wenn Bach Bienen gezüchtet hätte... 1976/2001
Piano, wind quintet, string orchestra, percussion – 6–7′
1 1 1 1–1 0 0 0 – perc(1), pno, str(4 4 4 4 2 or 8 8 8 8 4)
UE 31924: study score

Which Was the Son of... 2000
SATB a cappella – 7′30″
Text: Bible, St. Luke 3: 23–38
Language: English
Premiere: 26/08/2000, Reykjavik, Iceland
UE 31507: choral score

Zwei Wiegenlieder 2002
2 female voices, piano
No. 1: Rozhdyestvyenskaya kolïbyelnaya
Female voice, piano – 2′30″
Text: Bible, St. Luke 2: 7
Language: Russian
UE 32749
No. 2: Eesti hällilaul "Kuus-kuus, kallike"

Female voice, piano – 2'15"
Text: traditional poem
Language: Estonian
UE 32749

— 2002/2006
Female choir or 2 female voices, string orchestra
No. 1
Female choir or one voice, string orchestra – 2'30"
UE 33666: study score; 33623: piano reduction; 33670: choral score
No. 2
Female choir or 2 female voices, string orchestra – 2'15"
UE 33668: study score; 33626: piano reduction; 33669: choral score

— 2002/2009
Female voice, 4 violas, 4 violoncellos
No. 1
Female voice, 4 violas, 4 violoncellos – 2'30"
No. 2
Female voice, 4 violas, 4 violoncellos – 2'15 "

The Woman with the Alabaster Box 1997
2 choirs (SATB) a cappella – 7'
Text: Bible, St. Matthew 26: 6–13
Language: English
Premiere: 18/10/1997, Karlstad, Sweden
UE 31127: choral score

Notes

1 Introduction: the essential and phenomenal Arvo Pärt

1 Cited in *Current Biography Yearbook 1995* (New York: H. W. Wilson Company, 1995), 456 and elsewhere.

2 Geoffrey J. Smith, "Sources of invention: An interview with Arvo Pärt," *Musical Times* 140/1868 (Fall, 1999), 19.

3 *Current Biography*, 458.

4 Alex Ross, "Consolations: The uncanny voice of Arvo Pärt," *New Yorker*, December 2, 2002.

5 Dominic Aquila, "The music of Arvo Pärt," *Image: A Journal of the Arts and Religion* 2 (1992), 110.

6 David Clarke, "Parting glances," *Musical Times*, 134 (December 1993), 680.

7 *Ibid.*, 681.

8 *Ibid.*, 682 and 684.

9 Smith, "Sources of invention," 21.

10 See Paul Hillier, *Arvo Pärt, Oxford Studies of Composers* (Oxford University Press, 1997), p. 96.

11 For details of online resources see the Bibliography section on page 237.

2 A narrow path to the truth: Arvo Pärt and the 1960s and 1970s in Soviet Estonia

1 Veljo Tormis, *Loominguring, Sirp ja Vasar*, June 21, 1957.

2 The other two were Eugen Kapp, rector of the Tallinn Conservatory, and Villem Kapp, his relative, who was also dean of the composition department.

3 From the Estonian weekly *Sirp ja Vasar*, December 27, 1961 (no title, materials of the Communist Party's XXII congress).

4 The National Archives of Estonia, "Heliloojate Liidu Töökoosolekute Protokollid" (Minutes of discussion meetings); ERA.R-1958.1.166, 165–75.

5 *Arvo Pärt 70*, part 3 of 14, a radio series by Immo Mihkelson, 2005: "Teekond heli olemusse. Tööaastad Eesti Raadios toonmeistrina" (Journey to the Essence of Sound. Working in Estonian Radio as Sound Engineer). First aired in September 2005 on Klassikaraadio.

6 For more on Pärt's relationship with ECM Records see Laura Dolp's chapter in this collection, pp. 177–92.

7 *Arvo Pärt 70*, part 3 of 14.

8 *Ibid.*

9 The National Archives of Estonia, *NSVL Heliloojate Liidu Sekretariaadi tööplaanid, otsused, resolutsioonid ja protokollid.* Резолюция 3-го Пленума Правления Союза композиторов СССР от 17 марта 1959 г ERA.R-1958.1.149, 22–8.

10 Arvo Pärt, Eino Tamberg, Veljo Tormis, Jaan Koha, Uno Naissoo, Valter Ojakäär. Pärt, Tamberg, Tormis, and Koha got 'awards' but not always as sole recipient. For example, Pärt's first place was shared with three other people in the same category.

11 Ismene Brown, "Rodion Schedrin," September 18, 2010, TheArtsDesk.com.

12 *Arvo Pärt 70*, part 2 of 14: "Arvo Pärt ja filmimuusika" (Arvo Pärt and Film Music).

13 *Ibid.*

14 *Ibid.*

15 Tatiana Egorova, *Soviet Film Music: An Historical Survey* (London: Routledge, 1997).

16 Enzo Restagno, and others, *Arvo Pärt im Gespräch* (Vienna: Universal Edition, 2010), 30.

17 *Arvo Pärt 70*, part 2 of 14.

18 *Arvo Pärt 70*, part 12 of 14: "Arvo Pärt ja tema muusika seos Eestiga" (Arvo Pärt and Connections of His Music with Estonia).

19 Mihkelson, unpublished interview with Arvo Pärt in October, 2005.

20 The two books were: Herbert Eimert, *Lehrbuch der Zwölftontechnik* (Wiesbaden: Breitkopf & Härtel, 1953); Ernst Krenek, *Studies in Counterpoint: Based on the Twelve-Tone Technique* (New York: Schirmer, 1940).

21 Jamie McCarthy, "An interview with Arvo Pärt," *Musical Times* 130/1753 (March 1989), 134–7. Reprinted in *Contemporary Music Review* 12 (1995), 55–64.

22 *Arvo Pärt 70*, part 4 of 14: "Heliloojaks saamine: Optimistlikud kuuekümnendad" (Becoming a Composer: Optimistic Sixties).

23 The National Archives of Estonia, *Juhatuse koosolekute protokollid* (minutes from a meeting of the Estonian Composers Union board), May 7, 1969, ERA.R-1958.1.292, 25–6.

24 Д.И. Шульгин: *Годы неизвестности Альфреда Шнитке (Беседы с композитором)* Деловая Лига, Москва 1993 (ст 18–19); Yuri Kholopov and Valeria Tsenova, *Edison Denisov* (London: Routledge, 2003), 20–1.

25 *Arvo Pärt 70*, part 4 of 14.

26 Werner Meyer-Eppler, "Statistic and Psychologic Problems of Sound," trans. Alexander Goehr, *Die Reihe* 1 ("Electronic Music," 1957), 55–61; original German edition, 1955, as "Statistische und psychologische Klangprobleme," *Die Reihe* 1 ("Elektronische Musik," 1955), 22–8; see pp. 55 and 22, respectively.

27 *Creation and Time*, a radio program from the seven-part series by Ivalo Randalu, September 11, 1968. ASCDR-1716, Estonian Public Broadcasting Sound Archives. Partly published in *Sirp in Vasar*, November 22, 1968, *Sümfooniakontserdilt* by Merike Vaitmaa.

28 *Ibid.*

29 ASCDR-1716, Estonian Public Broadcasting Sound Archives.

30 The key that unlocks several questions is, in Pärt's words from the broadcast, how he described his goals, moving towards *one*, and in the context of religious paths he chose to continue his search for truth.

31 Холопов Ю.Н.: Аутсайдер советской музыки: Алемдар Караманов "Музыка из бывшего СССР," вып. 1. М. Композитор, 1994, 122–30.

32 *Arvo Pärt 70*, part 6 of 14: "Kadunud heli otsing. 'Credo' ja 'Tabula rasa' vahel" (Searching for the Lost Sound. Between *Credo* and *Tabula rasa*).

33 Dorian Supin, *Arvo Pärt: 24 Preludes for a Fugue*, F-Seitse Films, Estonia, 2002; rereleased by Juxtapositions: 2005, DVD.

3 Perspectives on Arvo Pärt after 1980

1 Many thanks to Kaire Maimets-Volt, Toomas Siitan, Immo Mihkelson, Triin Vallaste, Liisi Laanemets, and Malle Maltis for their invaluable help with this chapter. All translations here are my own.

2 Samuel Wigley, "Is it time to give Pärt a rest?" *guardian.co.uk*, May 29, 2008,www. guardian.co.uk/film/filmblog/2008/may/29/ timetogivepartarest.

3 Including *Repentance* (Tenghiz Abuladze, 1987), *Winterschläfer* (Tom Tykwer, 1997), *Gerry* (Gus Van Sant, 2002), *Swept Away* (Guy Ritchie, 2002), *Notre Musique* (Jean-Luc Godard, 2004), *The Good Shepherd* (Robert De Niro, 2006), and *There Will Be Blood* (Paul Thomas Anderson, 2007).

4 See Kaire Maimets-Volt, *Mediating the "Idea of One": Arvo Pärt's Pre-existing Film Music*. PhD dissertation, Estonian Academy of Music and Theatre, 2009.

5 FotoNuova (http://vimeo.com/3538038); Kurt_Halfyard (http://vimeo.com/ 5125321).

6 For example, Arthur Lubow's "Arvo Pärt: The Sound of Spirit," *New York Times Magazine,* October 15, 2010 and Siim Nestor's "Arvo Pärt: 'Ju me siis salaja armastame üksteist. See on väga ilus,'" *Eesti Ekspress*, September 9, 2010.

7 Other important artists to mention here include Autechre, Nils Frahm, Godspeed You Black Emperor, Jóhann Jóhannsson, Mogwai, and Murcof.

8 Nestor, "Arvo Pärt: 'Ju me siis salaja armastame üksteist. See on väga ilus.'"

9 http://reviews.headphonecommute. com/2009/10/23/hecq-mixtape-one.

10 http://parisdjs.libsyn.com/index.php?post_ id=636121.

11 http://soundcloud.com/studio-irisarri/i30-live-at-triple-door-may-2010-seattle.

12 http://soundcloud.com/the-wick/spiegel-im-spiegel.

13 Alex Ross, *The Rest Is Noise: Listening to the Twentieth Century* (New York: Farrar, Straus and Giroux, 2007); Richard Taruskin, *The Oxford History of Western Music*, Vol. 5: *The Late Twentieth Century* (New York: Oxford University Press, 2005). For other scholarship, see the list for further reading at the end of this chapter.

14 Paul Hillier, *Arvo Pärt*, Oxford Studies of Composers (Oxford University Press, 1997), pp. 58–63; Peter J. Schmelz, *Such Freedom if only Musical: Unofficial Soviet Music During the Thaw* (Oxford University Press, 2009), pp. 231–3.

15 Merike Vaitmaa, "Arvo Pärt." In Helju Tauk (ed.), *Kuus Eesti tänase muusika loojat* (Tallinn: Eesti Raamat, 1970), p. 58.

16 Hillier, *Arvo Pärt*, pp. 118–19.

17 Enzo Restagno, *Arvo Pärt peeglis: vestlused, esseed ja artiklid*, trans. Maarja Kangro and others (Tallinn: Eesti Entsüklopeediakirjastus, 2005), p. 50; Schmelz, *Such Freedom*, pp. 222–33.

18 Leo Normet, "The Beginning Is Silence," *Teater. Muusika. Kino* 7 (1988), 22.

19 *Ibid.*, 20–1.

20 Restagno, *Arvo Pärt peeglis*, p. 50.

21 *Ibid.*, p. 55.

22 Ivalo Randalu, "Arvo Pärt novembris 1978." *Teater. Muusika. Kino* 7 (1988), 48–55.

23 *Ibid.*, 52.

24 Restagno, *Arvo Pärt peeglis*, p. 71.

25 *Ibid.*, p. 72.

26 Toomas Siitan, "Eessõna." In Restagno, *Arvo Pärt peeglis*, p. 10.

27 Restagno, *Arvo Pärt peeglis*, p. 77.

28 *Ibid.*, p. 78.

29 *Ibid.*

30 *Ibid.*, p. 97.

31 Steve Lake and Paul Griffiths (eds.), *Horizons Touched: The Music of ECM* (London: Granta, 2007); Lars Müller, (ed.), *ECM Sleeves of Desire: Edition of Contemporary Music: A Cover Story* (Princeton Architectural Press, 1996).

32 Lake and Griffiths, *Horizons Touched*, p. 381.

33 Paul Griffiths, "Now, and Then." In *Tabula rasa* (Vienna: Universal Edition, 2010), p. 5.

34 Lake and Griffiths, *Horizons Touched*, pp. 375–6.

35 Restagno, *Arvo Pärt peeglis*, pp. 80–1.

36 Paul Hillier and Tõnu Tormis, *On Pärt* (Copenhagen: Theatre of Voices Edition, 2005), p. 62.

37 Restagno, *Arvo Pärt peeglis*, p. 77.

38 *Ibid.*, p. 74.

39 See Hillier and Tormis, *On Pärt*.

40 Arvo Pärt, *Kanon Pokajanen*, ECM 1654/55 (1998), 9.

41 As is customary in the performance of Orthodox canons, the second of the nine odes is omitted, although the numbering of the odes registers its silent presence.

42 Restagno, *Arvo Pärt peeglis*, p. 55.

43 *Ibid.*, p. 87.

44 *Ibid.*, p. 115.

45 Normet, "The Beginning Is Silence"; Randalu, "Arvo Pärt novembris 1978"; and Merike Vaitmaa, "Tintinnabuli: eluhoiak, stiil ja tehnika," *Teater. Muusika. Kino.* 7 (1988), 37–47.

46 Randalu, "Arvo Pärt novembris 1978," 48.

47 Tiia Järg, "Arvo Pärdi kvintetiino," *Teater. Muusika. Kino.* 12 (December 1994), 19–22; Merike Vaitmaa, "Tintinnabuli-elämänkatsomus, tyyli jatekniikka: Arvo Pärtin sävellyksistä," trans. Outi Jyrhämä, *Musiikkitiede* 2(2) (1990), 61–82 and "Arvo Pärdi vokaallooming," *Teater. Muusika. Kino* 2 (February 1991), 19–27.

48 Alo Raun, "Arvo Pärt pühendab oma teoste ettekanded Politkovskajale," *Postimees Online*, October 16, 2006.

49 http://vimeo.com/14923039.

4 Musical archetypes: the basic elements of the tintinnabuli style

1 Carl Gustav Jung, "Archetypes of the collective unconscious." In *C. G. Jung: The Archetypes and the Collective Unconscious*, trans. R. F. C. Hull (Princeton University Press, 1968), p. 3.

2 Jung, "Archetypes," p. 4.

3 Carl Gustav Jung, "The concept of the collective unconscious." In *C. G. Jung: The Archetypes and the Collective Unconscious*, trans. R. F. C. Hull (Princeton University Press, 1968), p. 42.

4 Carl Gustav Jung, "Psychological aspects of the Mother Archetype." In *C. G. Jung: The Archetypes and the Collective Unconscious*, trans. R. F. C. Hull (Princeton University Press, 1968), p. 78.

5 For the text of this speech see appendix D on pp. 200–1.

6 Arvo Pärt, "Dankesrede Arvo Pärts für den Internationalen Brückepreis der Europastadt Görlitz 2007 am 9. November 2007." In Enzo Restagno and others, *Arvo Pärt im Gespräch* (Vienna: Universal Edition, 2010), p. 167.

7 Arvo Pärt, *Werkeinführung zu Silhouette*, www.universaledition.com/Arvo-Paert/komponisten-und-werke/komponist/534.

8 Cited by Saale Kareda, "Zurück zur Quelle." In Enzo Restagno and others, *Arvo Pärt im Gespräch* (Vienna: Universal Edition, 2010), p. 161.

9 Pärt, "Dankesrede Brückepreis," p. 167.

10 The harmonic series are the vibrations of a sound which determine its tone color.

11 Lothar Mattner, "Arvo Pärt: Tabula rasa," *Melos* 2 (1985), p. 98.

12 Paul Hillier, *Arvo Pärt*, Oxford Studies of Composers (Oxford University Press, 1997), pp. 92ff.

13 Nora Pärt, *Introduction to the Tintinnabuli Style*, and references; from typescript in German, UE Vienna Archives.

14 Enzo Restagno, "Mit Arvo Pärt im Gespräch." In Enzo Restagno and others, *Arvo Pärt im Gespräch* (Vienna: Universal Edition, 2010), p. 39.

15 Arthur Lubow, "Arvo Pärt: The sound of spirit," *New York Times Magazine* October 15, 2010.

16 Hillier, *Pärt*, p. 95.

17 Chri-ste = two; Ky-ri-e = three; e-le-i-son = four.

18 Examples of these canons can be found in *Cantus, Arbos*, the second movement of *Tabula rasa* ("Silentium"), *Festina lente*, and *La Sindone*.

19 A detailed analysis can be found in Hillier, *Pärt*, p. 129.

20 Restagno and others, *Pärt im Gespräch*, pp. 88ff.

5 Analyzing Pärt

1 Roeder's analysis is viewable online at: http://theory.music.ubc.ca/~trx/animations/TheBeatitudes.mov and is discussed further below.

2 Roeder refers to his analysis in his introduction to a special issue of *Music Theory Online*, whose title speaks to this in-the-music perspective: "Animating the inside," *Music Theory Online* 15/1 (March

2009), www.mtosmt.org/issues/mto.09.15.1/
mto.09.15.1.roeder_intro.html.

3 Ian Bent with William Drabkin, *Analysis* (New York: Norton, 1987), p. 5.

4 *Ibid.*, p. 5.

5 The term 'historical musicology' is sometimes preferred, so that the broader term 'musicology' can include both historical musicology and music theory.

6 Jan LaRue, *Guidelines for Style Analysis*, 2nd edn. (Warren, MI: Harmonie Park Press, 1992).

7 *Ibid.*, p. 2.

8 *Ibid.*, p. vii.

9 *Ibid.*, p. 37.

10 *Ibid.*, p. 195.

11 See Leonard B. Meyer, *Emotion and Meaning in Music* (University of Chicago Press, 1956) for a study that influenced much of late twentieth-century hermeneutical thought.

12 For a discussion of hermeneutics in the early twentieth century, including some analytical examples, see Lee Rothfarb, "Hermeneutics and energetics: Analytical alternatives in the 1900s," *Journal of Music Theory* 36/1 (Spring 1992), 43–68.

13 Rothfarb, "Hermeneutics and energetics," 46, quoting and translating Hermann Kretzschmar, "Anregungen zur Förderung musikalischer Hermeneutik," *Jahrbuch der Musikbibliothek Peters* 9 (1902), 51.

14 The text of Edmond Jabès's poem, from *Livre des questions*, is reprinted in its entirety, translated by Rosemarie Waldrop, at the beginning of the published score. Also see Andrew Shenton, "Arvo Pärt's organ music," *The American Organist* 45 (December 2010), 76–8.

15 Deryck Cooke, *The Language of Music* (London: Oxford University Press, 1959), p. 115.

16 In figured-bass notation, numerals designate the intervals from the bass note to each of the chord's upper-voice constituents. A '5–3' chord, then, represents a root-position triad.

17 Unlike 'pitch,' which can refer to a specific frequency, 'pitch class' refers to all pitches equivalent at the octave without respect to specific register.

18 Numbers are chromatically assigned to the pitches of the octave starting with C = 0, C♯ = 1, and so on.

19 'Heterophonic' voices have similar, but not identical, melodic contours. 'Homorhythmic' voices have identical rhythms but their pitches may differ.

20 Robert Morris introduced the multiset to music theory in *Composition with Pitch Classes* (New Haven, CT: Yale University Press, 1987).

The exponent '1' is redundant, and pc 11 may be eliminated altogether because its multiplicity is zero. (It could read: {4^2, 5^3, 8, 9^2}.) All numbers are retained here, though, both for clarity's sake and because it is among these exponents that the real action takes place, even the zeros and ones.

21 Paul Hillier, "Arvo Pärt: Magister Ludi," *Musical Times* 130/1753 (March 1989), 134–7.

22 Don Harran, *Word-Tone Relations in Musical Thought: From Antiquity to the Early Seventeenth Century* (Neuhausen-Stuttgart: Hänssler-Verlag, 1986) is a survey of primary sources, compiling widely observed rules of text underlay. A note of caution: analyzing Pärt with tools suited for early music will strike many as an unwarranted and unwelcome reverse anachronism.

23 "I begin to perceive these minute details when I can sustain close attention and a gradual process *invites* my sustained attention" (emphasis added). Steve Reich, "Music as a gradual process." In *Writings About Music* (Halifax, NS: The Press of the Nova Scotia College of Art and Design, 1974), pp. 9–11.

24 In combinatorics, a *composition* is the splitting of a number into a distinct number of *terms*. For example, a two-term composition of 5 is 3+2, a three-term composition of 7 is 4+2+1, and so forth. The latter composition can be ordered into six *permutations*: [1,2,4], [1,4,2], [2,1,4], [2,4,1], [4,1,2], and [4,2,1].

25 This melody (Tenor 2) is harmonized by another tenor (Tenor 1), but their pitch choices are in a one-to-one correspondence with one another so claims of multiplicity in one apply equally to the other.

26 For another example of this compositional technique, see *Trisagion* (1992/1994).

27 The T-suspension shares with the suspension in species counterpoint only its means of production: the metric displacement of one of a pair of voices. The ramifications of each are entirely different.

28 Instead of writing a fully realized keyboard part for accompanists, composers in the seventeenth and eighteenth centuries often used a notational shorthand, a 'figured bass,' whose figures (numerals) dictated the intervallic spelling of a chord from a given bass tone. Once certain patterns and conventions were well established, composers sometimes would provide an *un*figured bass, a bass part with no figures to indicate the chord to be built atop it. Less experienced accompanists likely found Campion's method helpful.

29 François Campion, *Traité d'accompagnement et de composition selon la règle des octaves de musique* (Geneva: Minkoff,

1976 [1716]). Campion was the first to publish but not the first to invent such a technique. See Kevin Mason, "François Campion's secret of accompaniment for the theorbo, guitar, and lute," *Journal of the Lute Society of America* 14 (1981), 69–92.

30 Reich, *Writings*, p. 11.

31 Several of Reich's earliest pieces involved the falling of two voices in and out of phase with one another. Each voice articulates the same motivic cell, but one gradually advances, while the other stays at a constant tempo. See, for example, *Violin Phase* (1967).

32 Ian Quinn, "Minimal challenges: Process music and the uses of formalist analysis," *Contemporary Music Review* 25/3 (2006), 283–94.

6 Arvo Pärt: in his own words

1 Quotations from letters to the author dated March 18 and September 24, 2010.

2 Geoffrey J. Smith, "Sources of invention: An interview with Arvo Pärt," *Musical Times* 140/1868 (Fall, 1999), 22.

3 www.spikemagazine.com/0600arvopart.php.

4 Jamie McCarthy, "An interview with Arvo Pärt," *Musical Times* 130/1753 (March 1989), 130–1.

5 Quoted in Kazimierz Ploskon, "Arvo Pärt – Composer of the 'Borderland': Between Orthodox East and Catholic West," *The 20th Century and the Phenomenon of Personality in Music: Selected Papers / 39th Baltic Musicology Conference* (Riga: Latvijas Komponistu savienība: Musica Baltica, 2007), p. 68.

6 Quoted in Stuart Greenbaum, *Arvo Pärt's "Te Deum": A Compositional Watershed*, PhD dissertation, University of Melbourne, 1999, p. 103.

7 Dominic Aquila, "The music of Arvo Pärt," *Image: A Journal of the Arts and Religion* 2 (1992), 110.

8 Arthur Lubow, "Arvo Pärt: The sound of spirit," *New York Times Magazine*, October 15, 2010.

9 *Ibid.*

10 Wolfgang Sandner, "Arvo Pärt: Tabula rasa," in *Arvo Pärt: Tabula rasa* (ECM New Series 1275 / Universal Edition 35 222, 2010), p. 29.

11 McCarthy, "Interview," 63.

12 *Ibid.*

13 Both of theses pieces exist in alternate versions.

14 Martin Elste, "An interview with Arvo Pärt," *Fanfare* (March–April 1988), 338.

15 McCarthy, "Interview," 63.

16 *Ibid.*, 60.

17 Elste, "Interview," 338.

18 *Ibid.*, 339.

19 Sandner, "Tabula rasa," p. 27 (see also Aquila, "Music of Arvo Pärt," 113).

20 www.arvopart.ee/en/Uudiste-arhiiv/silhouette-world-premiere

21 Paul Hillier, *Arvo Pärt*, Oxford Studies of Composers (Oxford University Press, 1997), p. 201.

22 *Ibid.*, p. 74. Dorian Supin's film *Arvo Pärt: 24 Preludes for a Fugue* shows Pärt reviewing these notebooks and discussing the process, and Nora recounts a similar story for the composition of *Passio* in Enzo Restagno, "Mit Arvo Pärt im Gespräch," in Restagno and others, *Arvo Pärt im Gespräch* (Vienna: Universal Edition, 2010), p. 51.

23 Restagno, "Mit Arvo Pärt," p. 38.

24 Smith, "Sources of invention," 22.

25 *Ibid.*, 19.

26 *Ibid.*, 21.

27 Hillier, *Arvo Pärt*, p. 201.

28 Merike Vaitmaa, "Arvo Pärt." In *Kuus Essti tänase muusika loojat* [Six Estonian creators of modern music], ed. H. Tauk (Tallinn: Eesti Raamat, 1970), p. 58.

29 Transcribed from Supin, *24 Preludes for a Fugue*.

30 Ivalo Randalu, "Arvo Pärt in November 1978," *Teater. Muusika. Kino* 7 (1988), trans. Andres Didrik with Doug Maskew, 1997, from David Pinkerton's *Arvo Pärt Information Archive* (arvopart.org).

31 Greenbaum, *Te Deum*, p. 120.

32 McCarthy, "Interview," 63.

33 Smith, "Sources of invention," 22.

34 Elste, "Interview," 340.

35 Lubow, "The sound of spirit."

36 *Ibid.*

37 Peter Quinn, "Out with the old and in with the new: Arvo Pärt's *Credo*," *Tempo* 211 (January 2000) 16.

38 McCarthy, "Interview," 130.

39 Hillier, *Arvo Pärt*, p. 87. In Supin's film *24 Preludes for a Fugue*, Pärt actually attributes this revelation to a conversation he had with a janitor outside his apartment. "How should a composer write his music?" Pärt asked him. The man replied: "I think he has to love each single sound." Pärt notes how important this concept is: "This is how a composer must understand music. This knowledge opens an entirely new world."

40 Hillier, *Arvo Pärt*, p. 87.

41 Elste, "Interview," 337.

42 Leo Normet, "The beginning is silence," *Teater. Muusika. Kino* 7 (1988), 22.

43 Liner notes for ECM recording of *Tabula rasa*, ECM New Series 1275, 1984.

44 Lubow, "The sound of spirit."

45 Hillier, *Arvo Pärt*, p. 96.

46 Lubow, "The sound of spirit."
47 McCarthy, "Interview," 62.
48 Smith, "Sources of invention," 22.
49 Lubow, "The sound of spirit."
50 *Ibid.*
51 McCarthy, "Interview," 63.
52 Restagno, "Mit Arvo Pärt," p. 66.
53 Elste, "Interview," 339.
54 Nick Kimberly, "Starting from scratch," *Gramophone* 74 (September 1996), 16.
55 Smith, "Sources of invention," 22.
56 Arvo Pärt, *Kanon Pokajanen*, trans. Catherine Schelbert, in accompanying booklet to *Kanon Pokajanen*, performed by the Estonian Philharmonic Chamber Choir, conducted by Tõnu Kaljuste, ECM New Series 1654/55, 1998, p. 9.
57 Restagno, "Mit Arvo Pärt," p. 62.
58 Margaret Throsby, "Interview with Arvo Pärt," Melbourne: Australian Broadcasting Corporation FM Radio, October 4, 1996; quoted in Greenbaum, *Te Deum*, p. 26.
59 See for example Greenbaum's interview with Pärt concerning the *Te Deum* score (Greenbaum, *Te Deum*, p. 10).
60 See Appendix A on pp. 193–7, and Hillier, *Arvo Pärt*, pp. 199–207 for more on performance practice.
61 Elste, "Interview," 340.
62 McCarthy, "Interview," 62.
63 Smith, "Sources of invention," 21.
64 Personal interview with the author, November 20, 2010.
65 Sander, "Tabula rasa," p. 28.
66 McCarthy, "Interview," 57.
67 Arvo Pärt, "David and Goliath," August 20, 2010 available at: www.khodorkovskycenter. com/news-resources/events/london-s-royal-albert-hall-hosts-uk-premiere-arvo-p%C3%A4rt-s-symphony-dedicated-kh.
68 www.arvopart.ee.

7 Bells as inspiration for tintinnabulation

1 Wolfgang Sandner, Program notes for Arvo Pärt's *Tabula rasa*, trans. Anne Cattaneo, ECM New Series 1275, 1984, compact disc.
2 Sandner, Program notes (emphasis added).
3 Dorian Supin, *Arvo Pärt: 24 Preludes for a Fugue*, F-Seitse Films, Estonia: 2002; re-released by Juxtapositions: 2005, DVD.
4 Geoffrey J. Smith, "Sources of invention: An interview with Arvo Pärt," *Musical Times* 140/1868 (Fall 1999), 21.
5 Johannes Kepler reflected on the mathematical relationships of nature and of music as unified harmonic proportions, similar to Boethius' *musica mundana* (music of the spheres) of the sixth century. "The general idea of the world as the visible image of God ... was one that Kepler made his own," *The Harmony of the World (Harmonice Mundi* of 1619), trans. by E. J. Aiton, A. M. Duncan, and J. V. Field (Philadelphia, PA: American Philosophical Society, 1997), p. xiii.
6 According to Bishop Kallistos Ware, in *The Orthodox Church,* new edition (Baltimore, MD: Penguin Books, 1997), p. 21. *Theosis,* or deification, is primarily an Orthodox aim of salvation, based on 2 Peter 1:4: "Through these he has given us his very great and precious promises, so that through them you may participate in the divine nature"; also in John 17: 22–3: "I have given them the glory that you gave me, that they may be one as we are one – I in them and you in me – so that they may be brought to complete unity." New International Version of the Bible, 2010, www.biblica.com/niv.
7 Arthur Lubow, "Arvo Pärt: The sound of spirit," *New York Times Magazine*, October 15, 2010.
8 Paul Hillier, *Arvo Pärt*, Oxford Studies of Composers (Oxford University Press, 1997), p. 21.
9 Ivalo Randalu, "Arvo Pärt in November 1978," *Teater. Muusika. Kino* 7 (1988), trans. Andres Didrik with Doug Maskew, 1997, from David Pinkerton's *Arvo Pärt Information Archive* (arvopart.org).
10 Supin, *24 Preludes for a Fugue.*
11 Hillier, *Arvo Pärt*, p. 97. Nora Pärt is an equal partner during most interviews. She is seen in Supin's documentary giving conducting and interpretive suggestions, and interacting with soloists. In one scene she claims to have drawn the famous flower in the *Für Alina* manuscript.
12 Lubow, "The sound of spirit," 4.
13 Rachmaninov's "Pâcques Russe," from *Fantasy-tableaux (Suite No. 1)*; Rimsky-Korsakov, *Russian Easter Festival Overture*; Mussorgsky, "Coronation Scene" from *Boris Godunov*. Most famous, perhaps, is *Carillon de Westminster* for organ, by Vierne.
14 Some examples: Rachmaninov's *Kolokola (Choral Symphony)*, Meyerbeer's *Les Huguenots*, Puccini's *Tosca*, Ginastera's *Don Rodrigo*, Stravinsky's *Petrushka*, Britten's *Peter Grimes*, Berlioz' *Symphonie fantastique*, Dvořák's *Zlonicke Zvony [The Bells of Zlonic]*, Wagner's *Parsifal*, Liszt's *Die Glocken des Strassburger Münsters [The Bells of Strasburg]*. Schwanter utilizes bells in *Canticle of the Evening Bells*, as does Takemitsu in *From me flows what you call Time*, and they can be heard in *A Ring of Time* by Argento.
15 From *Thirteen Pieces on Estonian Motifs* by Eller. Other examples: Liszt's "La Campanella,"

Debussy's "La Cathédral engloutie," Messiaen's "Noël" from *Vingt Regards sur l'Enfant-Jésus*; Maxwell Davies' *Stedman Doubles*; and Harvey's *Mortuos Plango, Vivos Voco* composed of electronic manipulation of the acoustical spectrum of Winchester (UK) Cathedral's tenor bell.

16 Founded in 2010: www.arvopart.ee.

17 'Greater church' is used in the broad context of 'Christianity,' 'institutional religion,' or perhaps the contemporary 'emergent church' which currently defies definition. Noteworthy composers are the so-called 'holy minimalists': Pärt, Tavener, and Górecki, with Gubaidulina, Shchedrin, Kancheli, Hovhaness, and Moody, among others.

18 Translated as a conductor's 'upbeat.'

19 Among these are Percival Price's *Bells and Man* (Oxford University Press, 1983) and contributions to Oxford Music Online/ Grove Music Online, or "Bell," in *New Grove Dictionary of Music and Musicians*, ed. Stanley Sadie, 2nd edn, vol. 3 (New York: Macmillan Publishers Limited, 2001), pp. 168–82.

20 Paul Hillier, "Arvo Pärt: Magister Ludi," *Musical Times* 130/1753 (March 1989), 134; and Hillier, *Arvo Pärt*, p. 18.

21 During the fourteenth century, Dutch brothers François and Pieter Hemony initiated the 'Golden Age of the carillon.' During the 1890s, clergyman Arthur B. Simpson of Great Britain began an effort to improve the tuning of English peals. By rediscovering the Dutch methods of five-partial tuning, he became known as the 'Father of the modern carillon.' His work was carried on by John Taylor & Co. foundry, and was codified in his publications "On bell tones I & II," *The Pall Mall Magazine* 7 (September–December 1895), 183–94 and 10 (September–December 1896), 150–5.

22 E. V. Williams, *The Bells of Russia* (Princeton University Press, 1985), p. 174.

23 Patriarchate of Moscow, *Typikon for Church Bell Ringing*, trans. Blagovest Bells (St. Anselmo, CA: Russian Orthodox Church 2002), www. stlukeorthodox.com/files/bellringingtypikon. pdf.

24 Information on surviving classic *zvoni* in the former Soviet Union was compiled with assistance of Mark Galperin of Blagovest Bells.

25 Hillier, *Arvo Pärt*, p. 22, n.35.

26 Rostislav Rumjantsev of Saint Alexander Nevsky Cathedral, e-mail message to author, June 22, 2006: "During the Soviet years bells is continued rung [*sic*] – by Sundays and church holidays."

27 According to the World Carillon Federation.

28 Irina Aldoshina and A. Nicanorov, "The investigation of acoustical characteristics of Russian bells," paper presented at the 108th Convention of the Audio Engineering Society, New York, February 19–22, 2000.

29 Terminology of M- and T-voice as structural elements originated with Hillier, and have become standardized.

30 Hillier, *Arvo Pärt*, p. 96.

31 Smith, "Sources of invention," 24; and the *International Arvo Pärt Centre*.

32 Williams, *Bells of Russia*, p. 244.

33 Kurt Sander, "The musical icon," DMA research project: Northwestern University, 1998, p. 3.

34 Sander, pp. 10, 65. Sander's "human quest for Divine perfection" is another affirmation of *theosis*.

35 Lubow, "The sound of spirit," 4.

36 Personal conversation, September 24, 2011, at the Arvo Pärt: Soundtrack of an Age Conference, London, UK.

37 Transcribed from Supin, *24 Preludes for a Fugue*.

8 Arvo Pärt and spirituality

1 For more on the origins of this differentiation see William James, *Varieties of Religious Experience* (London: Penguin, 1983) [originally published in 1902]. More recently, Ann Taves has attempted to create an intellectual framework for and understanding of the processes of spiritual or religious experiences, drawing from narratives of neurology, psychology, and sociology. See Ann Taves, *Religious Experience Reconsidered: A Building-Block Approach to the Study of Religion and other Special Things* (Princeton University Press, 2009). My thanks to Stephen Schloesser for his comments on this study.

2 Charles Taylor, *A Secular Age* (Cambridge MA: Harvard University Press, 2007), p. 302.

3 Charles Taylor describes this phenomenon as the "Age of Authenticity." *A Secular Age*, pp. 473–504. In *The Search for Spirituality: Our Global Quest for Meaning and Fulfilment* (Norwich: Canterbury Press, 2009), the theologian Ursula King characterizes the ramifications of this counter-cultural ideology when she opines that "An immense spiritual hunger exists to find a life of deeper significance than that of material goods, consumerism, and exploitative capitalism. The current global situation with its deep injustices, numerous wars, and threats of ecological disaster calls for new creative thinking and for transformative ways of living. This requires a more reverent attitude towards people and the planet; it also calls for a spirituality that will

lead to the reorganisation of world economics, politics, education, business, and world governance," p. ix.

4 Richard Dawkins, *The God Delusion* (New York: Houghton Mifflin, 2006); Christopher Hitchens, *God Is Not Great: How Religion Poisons Everything* (New York: Twelve, 2007); for a response to these works, see David Bentley Hart, *Atheist Delusions: The Christian Revolution and its Fashionable Enemies* (New Haven, CT and London: Yale University Press, 2009).

5 For more on this see Gordon Lynch, *The New Spirituality: An Introduction to Progressive Belief in the Twenty-First Century* (London: I. B. Tauris, 2007).

6 The idea of art as spirit, or that art provides access to the self, and the soul, is an ancient but ever relevant philosophical issue. For more on this, see Daniel K. L. Chua's *Absolute Music and the Construction of Meaning* (Cambridge University Press, 1999), and also Jonathan Harvey's *Music and Inspiration* (London: Faber and Faber, 1999).

7 Pärt's own thinking is evidenced in a small number of interviews, quotes from liner notes, and most significantly, from Paul Hillier's *Arvo Pärt*, Oxford Studies of Composers (Oxford University Press, 1997).

8 At the end of "An interview with Arvo Pärt," *Contemporary Music Review* 12/2 (1995), 55–64, Jamie McCarthy asks if the composer's Russian Orthodox faith has influenced his music, and Pärt replies: "Religion influences everything. Not just music, but everything."

9 Hillier, *Arvo Pärt*, p. 96. In a discussion with Hillier, Pärt describes the relation of the two voices: "the M-voice always signifies the subjective world, the daily egoistic life of sin and suffering; the T-voice, meanwhile, is the objective realm of forgiveness … This can be liked to the eternal dualism of body and spirit, earth and heaven; but the two voices are in reality one voice, a twofold single entity. This can be neatly though enigmatically represented by the following equation: $1 + 1 = 1$."

10 The first fifty phrases of the Evangelist's narrative in *Passio* form a section that builds from a single voice to eight voices and then back again, creating a clear arch of sound.

11 Robert Fink, *Repeating Ourselves: American Minimal Music as Cultural Practice* (Berkeley: University of California Press, 2005), p. x.

12 Hillier, *Arvo Pärt*, pp. 2–5.

13 See Alain Besançon, *The Forbidden Image: A History Of Iconoclasm*, trans. Jane Marie Todd (University of Chicago Press, 2000).

14 Pärt has written a great deal of religious choral music. I have deliberately chosen to restrict the present discussion to his wordless instrumental (absolute) music, and the way it configures spirituality.

15 For more on the iconostasis see Leonid Ouspensky and Vladimir Lossky, *The Meaning of Icons*, trans. G. E. H. Palmer and E. Kadloubovsky (New York: St. Vladimir's Seminary Press, 1982), pp. 59–72.

16 When the diamond-shaped notes are placed a fourth above the main note, the sound is two octaves above the ordinary pitch, and when placed a fifth above, the sound is a twelfth above the ordinary pitch.

17 Much of the harmonic tension, and character of the music, in measures 3–5, 11–13, 19–21, and 29 is caused by the proximity of $B_\flat$ and $B_\natural$ (for instance in the violin I and viola in m. 3).

18 In modal theory (for example) Mode 1 (the Dorian mode) is D–D on the white notes of the piano. Mode 2 is the hypo-Dorian mode, which is A–A on the white notes again. But the tonic of this mode is still D even though the final note (*finalis*) is A. It is this sense of a shifting *finalis* with a stable tonic that Pärt is playing with in *Fratres* to create a sense of development and narrative.

19 Marcel Cobussen's *Thresholds: Rethinking Spirituality through Music* (Aldershot: Ashgate, 2008) is concerned with the ways in which music opens up or inspires alternative spaces or discourses that can be understood as spiritual. On page 149 (footnote 8) he reveals the raison d'être of his haunting monograph: "That empty space between the two spheres, not here and not there – that space *is* the spiritual; spirituality is the intimacy of the gap."

20 Interview with James MacMillan, June 1998, during the second annual Vancouver new music festival, quoted in Jeremy S. Begbie, *Resounding Truth: Christian Wisdom in the World of Music* (Grand Rapids, MI: Baker Academic, 2007), p. 179.

21 In Christian theology these two types of time meet in the person of Christ (God made man).

22 Begbie, *Resounding Truth*, p. 261.

23 Laurence Rees, *Auschwitz, the Nazis and the 'Final Solution'* (BBC Worldwide Ltd, 2005). The Nazi massacre described occurred at Ostrog, Ukraine on March 4, 1941. *Fratres* is also used throughout this documentary.

24 In Pärt's *Sarah Was Ninety Years Old* (1977/1990), silence implies a contingent and unfulfilled state of being, of expectation, that implies tension and release, waiting and receiving. Silence also embraces a sense of discomfort, non-identity and a resistance to the realization of becoming and being. In a

more positive vein, the potential of silence in Pärt's music often seems to provide a mirror to ourselves, to the quality of our own being and hearing, that may therefore promote a sense of spiritual awareness without recourse to Christian discourse. See also Cobussen, *Thresholds*, pp. 109–24.

25 T. W. Adorno, "Cultural criticism and society," in *Prisms [Prismen*, 1967], trans. Samuel and Shierry Weber (Cambridge, MA: The MIT Press, 1995), p. 34.

26 The "disenchantment of the world" is proposed by Max Weber in "Science as Vocation" (1917) in *From Max Weber*, ed. H. H. Mills and C. Wright Mills (New York: Oxford University Press, 1946), p. 155. See also Chua, *Absolute Music and the Construction of Meaning*, pp. 12–22. Weber identifies the way in which the modern world denudes itself of the illusions created by superstition and the sacred. Chua states: "The modernisation of society is therefore its secularisation; humanity, by disenchanting the world, needs believe in no other god than itself," p. 12.

27 Arnold Schoenberg, "Composition with twelve tones (I)," in *Style and Idea*, ed. Leonard Stein, trans. Leo Black (Berkeley: University of California Press, 1984), p. 216.

28 For more on this see Daniel K. L. Chua, "Adorno's metaphysics of mourning: Beethoven's farewell to Adorno," *The Musical Quarterly*, 87/3 (2005), 523–45.

29 Alex Danchev (ed.), *100 Artists' Manifestos: From the Futurists to the Stuckists* (London: Penguin, 2011).

30 Other composers, such as Stravinsky, Webern, Messiaen, and Tavener, for instance, had made extensive study of renaissance music and absorbed this study into their own music. The challenge to form and coherence mentioned here is a problem faced by early twentieth-century composers (and indeed those that came after), and it can be put like this: In the absence of tonality, how is it possible to create large-scale coherent musical structures? This is a question that has been answered in many ways. Pärt's music belongs to the formal tradition of using superimposed blocks of material, and this has been one consistent compositional answer to the problem of how to create musical narrative and continuity.

31 Friedrich Nietzsche, "The madman," *The Gay Science* (1882), trans. Thomas Common (New York: Dover, 2006), pp. 90–1.

32 Chua, "Adorno's metaphysics of mourning," 523–4.

33 The literary critic George Steiner states: "I believe the modulation of music towards our apprehension and sufferance of death to be of the essence. Without the truths of music, what would be our deficit of spirit at the close of day?" *Real Presences* (Chicago: The University of Chicago Press, 1991), p. 63. For the French Catholic composer Olivier Messiaen, what Steiner describes as a "deficit" is fulfilled by music as faith: a panacea to the disenchantment of modernity. See Olivier Messiaen, 'Introduction to the programme booklet for Paris, 1978,' in Almut Rössler, *Beiträge zur geistigen Welt Olivier Messiaens* (Duisberg: Gilles und Francke, 1984), trans. Barbara Dagg and Nancy Poland as *Contributions to the Spiritual World of Olivier Messiaen* (Duisberg: Gilles und Francke, 1986), p. 10. Both positions are sedimented in Pärt's musical aesthetics.

34 Michael Saler, "Modernity and enchantment: A historiographic review," *The American Historical Review*, 111/3 (June 2006), 692.

35 In an interview, the composer told Jamie McCarthy that "When things are simple and clear, they're also clean. They are empty; there is room for everything." McCarthy, "An interview with Arvo Pärt," 62.

36 Arvo Pärt (from the sleeve-note to the ECM recording of *Tabula rasa*), quoted in Hillier, *Arvo Pärt*, p. 87.

37 Francisco J. Varela, Evan Thompson, and Eleanor Rosch, *The Embodied Mind: Cognitive Science and Human Experience* (Cambridge, MA and London: The MIT Press, 1991), p. 23.

38 Hillier, *Arvo Pärt*, p. 96.

39 Begbie, *Resounding Truth*, p. 261.

40 *Ibid.*, p. 262.

41 The descriptions of transcendence in Albert L. Blackwell's *The Sacred in Music* (Cambridge: The Lutterworth Press, 1999), pp. 202–23, are religiously configured, and tend to minimize the role of the body. In *The Idea of the Holy*, trans. John W. Harvey (Oxford University Press, 1923), Rudolf Otto's *mysterium tremendum et fascinans* again focuses on certain aspects of the experience of transcendence – mystery, fear, dread, expectation, awe – that imply that the body is a kind of puppet of an external stimulus (music), rather than a participant or even a co-creator of the experience.

42 Varela, Thompson, and Rosch, *The Embodied Mind*, p. 27.

43 *Ibid.*

44 See Roger Scruton, *The Aesthetics of Music* (Oxford University Press, Clarendon Press, 1997), pp. 354–7, and Begbie, *Resounding Truth*, p. 299.

45 See Arnie Cox's fascinating discussion of what he calls "mimetic motor imagery," in "Embodying music: Principles of the mimetic hypothesis," *Musical Theory Online*, 19/2 (July

2011), www.mtosmt.org/issues/mto.11.17.2/mto.11.17.2.cox.html.

46 Pärt describes the idea of 'the neutral,' which I interpret as a space outside the implications of the historical development of musical language, in Dorian Supin's film *24 Preludes for a Fugue* (2005).

47 See for example Richard Taruskin's "Sacred entertainments," *Cambridge Opera Journal* 15 (2003), 109–26, and Robin Holloway, "Beware the pitfalls of sincerity," *Essays and Diversions 1963–2003* (Brinkworth: Claridge Press, 2003), pp. 294–6.

48 See Kiene Brillenburg Wurth, *Musically Sublime: Indeterminacy, Infinity, Irresolvability* (New York: Fordham, 2009).

49 See Mihaly Csikszentmihalyi, *Flow: The Psychology of Optimal Experience* (London: Harper Perennial Modern Classics, 2008), and relevant parts of Aaron Williamson (ed.), *Musical Excellence: Strategies and Techniques to Enhance Performance* (New York: Oxford University Press, 2004).

50 Music has both an exploratory and a therapeutic role in our society. It is, as George Steiner puts it: "a phenomenon without the which, for innumerable men and women, this plagued earth and our transit on it would probably be unbearable." George Steiner, *Errata: An Examined Life* (London: Weidenfeld and Nicolson, 1997), p. 65.

51 At the end of McCarthy, 'An interview with Arvo Pärt', 63–4, Pärt states: "the last moments before death are very precious – very important – for at that time things can happen which have not come about during a whole lifetime."

9 The minimalism of Arvo Pärt: an 'antidote' to modernism and multiplicity?

1 Jim Samson, "Genre," in *The New Grove Dictionary of Music and Musicians*, ed. Stanley Sadie and John Tyrell, second edition, vol. 9 (London: Macmillan, 2001), p. 657.

2 Leonard Meyer, *Style and Music: Theory, History and Ideology* (Philadelphia: University of Pennsylvania Press, 1989), p. 3.

3 *Ibid.*, p. 5.

4 *Ibid.*

5 Wolfgang Sandner, CD note to *Tabula rasa* (ECM, 476 3878).

6 Josiah Fisk, "The New Simplicity: The music of Górecki, Tavener and Pärt," *Hudson Review*, 47/ 3 (Fall 1994), 394–412.

7 Timothy Johnson, "Minimalism, style, or technique?" *The Musical Quarterly*, 78/4 (Winter 1994), 748.

8 Elaine Broad, "A new X? An examination of the aesthetic foundations of early minimalism," *Music Research Forum* 5 (1990), 51–2; emphasis in original.

9 Keith Potter, "Minimalism," in *The New Grove Dictionary of Music and Musicians*, ed. Stanley Sadie and John Tyrell, second edition, vol. 16 (London: Macmillan, 2001), p. 716.

10 Milton Babbitt, "Who cares if you listen?" in *Contemporary Composers on Contemporary Music*, ed. Elliott Schwartz and Barney Childs (New York: Da Capo Press, 1978), p. 248.

11 Michael Nyman, *Experimental Music: Cage and Beyond* (Cambridge University Press, 1999), p. 1.

12 Quoted in Jonathan Cross, *Harrison Birtwistle: Man, Mind, Music* (London: Faber, 2000), p. 246.

13 Babbitt 'Who cares if you listen?' pp. 246–7.

14 Andrei Zhdanov, "Concluding speech at a conference of Soviet music workers, 1948," in *Essays on Literature, Music and Philosophy* (London: Lawrence and Wishart, 1950), pp. 57–8.

15 Jürgen Habermas, "Modernism versus postmodernity," *New German Critique*, 22 (Winter 1981), 8.

16 IRCAM (Institut de Recherche et Coordination Acoustique/Musique) is one of the largest public research centers dedicated to both musical expression and scientific research, and is the world's leading center for computer-music training.

17 Robin Holloway, *Essays and Diversions 1963–2003* (Brinkworth: Claridge Press, 2003), p. 296.

18 *Ibid.*, p. 300.

19 "Modernism and After," in *Reviving the Muse: Essays on Music after Modernism* (Brinkworth: Claridge Press, 2001), p. 110.

20 Quoted in Robert Fink, *Repeating Ourselves: Music as Cultural Practice* (Berkeley: University of California Press, 2005), p. 63.

21 David Matthews, "Renewing the past: Some personal thoughts," in *Reviving the Muse*, p. 203.

22 Jamie McCarthy, "An interview with Arvo Pärt," *Musical Times*, 130/1753 (March 1989), 133.

23 Quoted in *The Daily Telegraph*, October 23, 2010.

24 Introduction to Robert Beauregard and Sophie Body-Gendrot (eds.), *The Urban Moment: Cosmopolitan Essays on the Late-20th Century City* (Thousand Oaks, CA: Sage Publications, 1999), p. 3.

25 See Fisk, "The New Simplicity," 344.

26 These musical trends are most likely reflections of their shared experience of Orthodox worship, and particularly of the *troparia* and *oktoehos* that lie as a foundation of Orthodox chant. See Andrew Wilson-Dickson,

The Story of Christian Music: From Gregorian Chant to Black Gospel (Oxford: Lion Publishing, 1992), p. 151.

27 Alex Ross, *The Rest is Noise: Listening to the Twentieth Century* (London: Fourth Estate, 2008), p. 531.

28 Tavener's comment on "Buy cleverness, sell wonder: The music of John Tavener," on www.beliefnet.com.

29 Brian Morris, *Religion and Anthropology: A Critical Introduction* (Cambridge University Press, 2006), p. 274.

30 *Ibid.*, p. 34.

31 Tavener, "Buy cleverness, sell wonder."

32 See Liz Todd, "Prince Charles's favourite composer John Tavener in fight for life," *Daily Mail*, March 9, 2008.

33 K. Robert Schwarz, *Minimalists* (London: Phaidon, 1996), p. 216.

34 See Paul Hillier, *Arvo Pärt*, Oxford Studies of Composers (Oxford University Press, 1997), p. 8.

35 *Ibid.*

36 Quoted in Don Saliers, *Music and Theology* (Nashville, TN: Abingdon Press, 2007), p. 14.

37 Andrew Wilson-Dickson, *The Story of Christian Music* (Oxford: Lion Publishing, 1992), p. 159.

38 Quoted in Martyn Barrie, *Rachmaninoff: Composer, Pianist, Conductor* (Aldershot: Scholar, 1990), p. 222.

39 Wilfrid Mellers, "Arvo Pärt, God and gospel: *Passio Domini Nostri Iesu Christi Secundum Iohannem* (1982)," *Contemporary Music Review* 12/2 (1995), 40.

40 Hillier, *Arvo Pärt*, p. 2.

41 McCarthy, "Interview," p. 131.

42 Hillier, *Arvo Pärt*, p. 14.

43 *Ibid.*, p. 74.

44 Saliers, *Music and Theology*, p. 59.

45 *Ibid.*, p. 60.

46 Fisk, "The New Simplicity," 402–3.

47 Mervyn Cooke, *A History of Film Music* (Cambridge University Press, 2008), p. 478.

48 The version of *Spiegel im Spiegel* employed in the film is that which is most commonly known – the version for violin and piano. This is only one of a number of arrangements that Pärt has sanctioned, which include versions for viola, cello, clarinet, horn, contrabass, alto flute, oboe, cor anglais, and bassoon. The availability of such arrangements might imply that Pärt understands the market only too well; that, as with any labour-saving businessman, he possesses an ability to increase revenue from the development of one product. Alternatively, one can understand these multiple versions as proof of the integrity of the formal design which allows itself to operate successfully across a range of timbres. In this Platonic reading, they become embodiments of a single, transcendental idea whose depth and perfection of form allow it to be universally realized in a variety of simulacra. For a more in-depth discussion of these issues (although not specifically relating to Pärt) see Roger Scruton, *The Aesthetics of Music* (Oxford University Press, 1997), especially chapter 4, "Ontology."

49 Margaret Edson, *Wit* (London: Nick Hern Books, 2000).

50 Jonathan Harvey, Maxwell Steer, and Michael Tucker, "Music and inner meaning," *Contemporary Music Review* 14/3–4 (1996), 9–23, p. 10.

51 Saliers, *Music and Theology*, p. 67.

52 Theodor Adorno, *Introduction to the Sociology of Music*, trans. E. B. Ashton (New York: Continuum, 1989), especially Chapter 1, "Types of musical conduct," pp. 1–20.

53 Babbitt, "Who cares if you listen?" p. 245; Saliers, *Music and Theology*, p. 68.

54 Saliers, *Music and Theology*, p. 63.

55 *Ibid.*, p. 21.

56 John Barth, "The literature of replenishment, postmodernist fiction," *Atlantic Monthly* 245 (January 1980), 67–72.

10 Arvo Pärt in the marketplace

1 The *Fahrenheit* soundtrack (Warner Music, 2004), was followed by another release by Sony BMG (Epic Records, 2004) that included an expanded collection of songs by Moore. Pärt's *Cantus* is included in the first but not in the second collection. Moore's comments are included in the *Songs that Inspired* album. Various Artists, *Songs and Artists that Inspired Fahrenheit 9/11* (Epic Records, 2004); Jeff Gibbs, *Fahrenheit 9/11* (2004).

2 Kaire Maimets-Volt, *Mediating the 'Idea of One': Arvo Pärt's Pre-Existing Film Music*, PhD thesis, Estonian Academy of Music and Theatre, 2009, p. 11.

3 Jeff Leeds, "Deal is struck for two albums related to 'Fahrenheit 9/11," *New York Times*, September 9, 2004.

4 [80.1 million] Nielsen EDI compiles their statics by compiling data from fifty American theaters where the film earned the most money. Waxman also notes that *Fahrenheit* was most popular at a national level on both coasts and the 'Rust Belt' cities, and in the New York metropolitan area, largely in Manhattan. Sharon Waxman, "Urban moviegoers for anti-Bush documentary, suburban audience for religious epic," *New York Times*, July 13, 2004.

5 Maimets-Volt, *Mediating the 'Idea of One,'* p. 188.

6 Out of the group, Pärt, Tavener, and Górecki are often more closely associated with one

another, perhaps because their commercial success coincided (Pärt's *Miserere* [1991] and Tavener's *The Protecting Veil* [1992] had prefaced Górecki's success in the American and British markets). Pärt, Górecki, and Kancheli were born within two years of each other; Górecki in Czernica, Silesia (Poland) on December 6, 1933 and Kancheli in Tbilisi, in the former Soviet republic of Georgia, on August 10, 1935 (the same year as Pärt). John Tavener and Pēteris Vasks were born after the war in the mid-1940s: Tavener on January 28, 1944 in Britain and Vasks in Aizpute, Latvia in 1946. Individuals within this group have been linked generationally and cast in terms of artistic legacy; for example, the British press has touted Vasks as "the next Górecki." Stephen Jackson, "Out of Latvia on a snowball, Peteris Vasks, an obscure Latvian composer, is set for international stardom," *Sunday Telegraph*, February 26, 1995.

7 *Morimur: The Bach Project, Haydn: The Seven Words, Janáček: A Recollection, Holliger: Schneewittchen and Verklärte Nacht*, with compositions by Veress, Schoenberg, and Bartók.
8 Stewart Nicholson, "It's hard to put a label on it," *The Irish Times*, March 17, 2001.
9 Geoff Andrew, "DVD of the week: Jean-Luc Godard and Anne-Marie Miéville: four short films," *Time Out London*, July 19, 2006.
10 Steve Lake, "Looking at the cover," *Sleeves of Desire: A Cover Story* (Baden: Lars Müller Publishers, 1996), p. 257.
11 Catalog, *Sleeves of Desire*, p. 308.
12 This minimalist aesthetic strategy was assumed by other marketing endeavors as well, including the Nonesuch releases in the early 1990s that featured Górecki recordings. See Luke Benjamin Howard, "Packaging Górecki's Symphony No. 3," in '*A Reluctant Requiem': The History and Reception of Henryk M. Górecki's Symphony No. 3 in Britain and the United States*, PhD, University of Michigan, 1997, pp. 161–9.
13 Lake, "Looking at the cover," p. 263.
14 Lars Müller, "It is the second sight that counts," in *Sleeves of Desire*, p. 47.
15 In 2007, the British publisher Granta issued another comprehensive history of the label: Steve Lake and Paul Griffiths (eds.), *Horizons Touched: The Music of ECM* (London: Granta, 2007).
16 Bradley Bambarger, "Retail eagerly awaits ECM's Arvo Pärt set," *Billboard* 108/36 (September, 1996), 1, 119, 120.
17 *Ibid.*
18 *Ibid.*
19 www.ecmrecords.com/News/ Diary/61_Jarrett_Billboard_Charts. php?cat=&doctype=Diary&we_start=8.
20 This event was announced on several blogs,

including Tim Jarrett, www.jarretthousenorth. com/2005/10/18/ecm-hits-the-itunes-music-store-go-get-some-prt.
21 www.ecmrecords.com/About_ECM/FAQ.
22 Bambarger, "Retail eagerly awaits ECM's Arvo Pärt set."
23 *Ibid.*
24 *Ibid.*
25 *Ibid.*
26 More specifically, in addition to the Pärt family, the Estonian Cultural Endowment and from 2011 onwards the Estonian state.
27 www.arvopart.ee/en.
28 Cizmic describes her own experience of ECM's "eye-catching, elegant" visuals to construct "an aural experience perhaps as elegantly spare as the CD cover aims to invite." Granted the anecdote clearly is meant to function as an entry point into a series of observations about sparseness of Pärt's compositional style, but it also borders on an example of how, even within a scholarly context, consumers can be seduced into the synergic relationship between packaging and contents with little pause to interrogate the relationship. Maria Cizmic, *Performing Pain: Music and Trauma in 1970s and 80s Eastern Europe*, PhD, University of California Los Angeles, 2004, pp. 134–6.
29 Wolfgang Sandner, *Tabular rasa* liner notes [ECM 1275], 1984.
30 The book includes previously unpublished manuscript scores of *Tabula rasa* and *Cantus*, and study scores of the album's four works, as well as Wolfgang Sandner's 1984 liner essay. At the back is a discography of Pärt's works on ECM with corresponding publishing details. Paul Griffiths, "Now, and then," *Arvo Part: Tabula rasa*, Special Edition (Munich: ECM and Universal Edition, 2010), pp. 5, 7.
31 Part states that he is not sure where this encounter took place but he believes it happened in a Tallinn bookshop. The scene 'Meeting' occurs late in the film, after twenty-seven other montage-like snapshots of the composer's life. *Arvo Pärt: 24 Preludes for a Fugue*, written, directed, and filmed by Dorian Supin, F-Seitse Films, Estonia, 2002; rereleased by Juxtapositions: 2005, DVD.
32 Gregory Sandow, "Music: Tasting the new era," *The Village Voice* 30/5 (1985), 72.
33 Alan Axelrod, "Record reviews: *Tabula rasa*," *Downbeat* 28/52 (1985), 28.
34 Susan Bradshaw, "Arvo Pärt: Emerging light," review of concerts at the Southbank Centre, London, April–May 1995, *Musical Times* 136/1830 (August 1995); Oliver Kautny, *Arvo Pärt zwischen Ost und West: Rezeptionsgeschichte* (Stuttgart: Metzler Verlag, 2002), p. 206.

35 www.ecm.com.

36 Photographs by Roberto Masotti and cover design by Barbara Wojirsch.

37 The associations are explicit in a Christian context. For example, prayer with fasting and almsgiving is stated as one of the three "pillars of piety" (Matthew 6:1–18).

38 David Morgan, *Visual Piety: A History and Theory of Popular Religious Images* (Berkeley: University of California Press, 1998), pp. 10, 9, 5.

39 Morgan, *Visual Piety*, p. 206. Oliver Kautny draws a parallel between the rhetoric of Pärt's critical reception and two intellectual traditions: the Palestrina myth and the writings of early nineteenth-century philosophers on Christian iconography and Nature topoi. Kautny, *Arvo Pärt zwischen Ost und West*, pp. 233–8.

40 Morgan, *Visual Piety*, p. 207. Kautny appropriates the rhetoric for purposes of analysis, characterizing the composer as priest ("Geistlicher"), his music as liturgical service ("Gottesdienst") and his audience as the congregation ("Gemeinde"). *Arvo Pärt zwischen Ost und West*, pp. 210–33.

41 This neo-Orthodox model of the individual seeker is part of a system that sets itself apart from the liberalism that underestimates human sinfulness but does not extend to a literalistic reading of scripture. God is seen neither as the gentle Jesus of the liberals, nor as an evangelical figure prone to interventionist action, but rather one that leaves only His word as a guide for daily life.

42 See C. D. Batson, P. Schoenrade, and W. L. Ventis (eds.), *Religion and the Individual* (New York: Oxford University Press, 1993).

43 Cizmic poses the idea that the manner in which ECM and other Western record companies market, produce, package, and sell Pärt's music is aligned with Fredric Jameson's critique of antinomies in the postmodern discourse. For Cizmic, these paradoxes are suggested (though not directly consciously reflective of these political realities) in the music by "regular change [that] no longer appears like change at all; change turns into its opposite: stasis." Cizmic, *Performing Pain*, pp. 139–41.

44 Alisdair MacIntyre asks a similar question in his essay "The virtues, the unity of a human life, and the concept of Tradition," in *Why Narrative? Readings in Narrative Theology*, ed. Stanley Hauerwas and L. Gregory Jones, (Grand Rapids, MI: W. B. Eerdmans, 1989).

45 These include *Passio*, on the Passion of St. John; *Miserere*, on Psalm 50 of the Vulgate text with an interpolated "Dies Irae"; *Kanon Pokajanen*, on the Greek and Russian Orthodox canon of repentance; and *Orient &*

Occident, whose structure is derived from the Credo.

46 The history of its premiere and subsequent marketing through Elektra-Nonesuch records is outlined in detail by Howard. See Luke Benjamin Howard, "Motherhood, Billboard, and the Holocaust: Perceptions and receptions of Górecki's *Symphony No. 3*," *The Musical Quarterly* 82 (1998), 131–59; Howard, "A Reluctant Requiem"; Wilfred Mellers, "Reviews: Arvo Pärt," *Musical Times* 134 (December 1993), 714.

47 Stephanie von Buchau, "Notable choral music," *The Oakland Tribune*, October 7, 2005.

48 Justin Sullivan (from the band New Model Army), "New Model Army's cult of notoriety," *Scunthorpe Evening Telegraph*, May 11, 2006.

49 C. Michael Bailey, *Arvo Part: In Principio* [Review] (2009 [cited March 20, 2009]), available from www.allaboutjazz.com/php/article.php?id=32051; Robert Baird, *Recording of March 2009: Arvo Pärt: In Principio* [Review] (2009), www.stereophile.com/recordingofthemonth/recording_of_march_2009_arvo_p196rt_iin_principioi/index.html.

50 Griffiths, "Now, and then," p. 6.

51 Fred Kirshnit, "The shaman of Estonia," *New York Sun*, May 17, 2006, p. 15.

52 Jennifer Dunning, "Druid types encounter the New Age," *New York Times*, October 3, 2006, p. 5.

53 Maria Cizmic uses this as a case study for her discussion of trauma and narrative in Pärt's music; see Cizmic, *Performing Pain*, pp. 164–5. For the original source see Patrick Giles, *Sharps & Flats* (1999) available from www.salon.com.

54 Anthony D'Alessandro, "In their own words; Sonnenfeld, Hackford talk about working with Elfman," *Daily Variety*, September 14, 2006, p. A8.

55 Christine Sams, "Entertainment," *Sun Herald*, August 27, 2006, p. 12.

56 "Religion: in briefs," *Santa Fe New Mexican*, May 27, 2006, p. D4.

57 www.arvopart.ee/en/Valik-artikleid/arvo-paert-qi-suppose-secretly-we-love-one-another-it-is-very-beautifulq.

58 Howard makes a similar point in relation to Górecki's Symphony No. 3, which met with a cooler reception in Britain. Howard, "A Reluctant Requiem," p. 130.

59 Henry David Thoreau, *Walden*, ed. J. Lyndon Shanley (Princeton University Press, 1971), p. 91. Thoreau's plea for "simplicity, simplicity, simplicity" in earlier eras of American modernization continues to be the model for the ethos of voluntary simplicity advocated by contemporary activists. Duane

Elgin, *Voluntary Simplicity: Toward a Life That Is Outwardly Simple, Inwardly Rich* (New York: William Morrow & Co, 1993); David E. Shi (ed.), *The Simple Life: Plain Living and High Thinking in American Culture* (Athens: University of Georgia Press, 2001). For example, on www.simpleliving.net's list of recommended books *Walden* is still a featured item.

60 Griffiths, "Now, and then," pp. 6, 7; Jurg Stenzl, "Misterioso near and far away," trans. J. Bradford Robinson, liner notes, *Misterioso* (ECM, 2006), p. 19.

61 Lawrence Buell, "Downwardly mobile for conscience's sake: Voluntary simplicity from Thoreau to Lily Bart," *American Literary History* 17/4 (2005), 656.

62 Pärt's own dismissal of this music has been confirmed by both Paul Hillier and Kaire Maimets-Volt. By current estimates, he produced thirty-seven original scores for feature films, documentaries, cartoons, and other animated films. Pärt's music for film (both original scoring and the process of appropriation) has received far less scholarly attention than other aspects of his work. Some notable exceptions include Maimets-Volt's quantification and subsequent study of the early film scores, referenced in her study of the films which use Pärt's preexisting music. Paul Hillier, *Arvo Pärt*, Oxford Studies of Composers (Oxford University Press, 1997), p. 74; Maimets-Volt, *Mediating the 'Idea of One*,' pp. 9–10, see n. 8.

63 Maimets-Volt has done close studies of the role of *Für Alina* and *Spiegel im Spiegel* in five films (*Heaven*, *Gerry*, *Wit*, *Bella Martha*, and *Swept Away*), and has accounted for approximately one hundred films that incorporate his music. Maimets-Volt, *Mediating the 'Idea of One*,' p. 9; David Pinkerton's Arvo Pärt Information archive (1997–2009), available from: www.arvopart.org.

64 David Ng, *When Classical Music Masterpieces Become Soundtrack Cliches* (2008), http://latimesblogs.latimes.com/culturemonster/2008/09/when-classical.html; Samuel Wigley, "Is it time to give Pärt a rest?," *Filmblog* (*The Guardian*, 2008), www.guardian.co.uk/film/filmblog/2008/may/29/timetogivepartarest.

65 Annette Davidson, *Hollywood Theory, Non-Hollywood Practice: Cinema Soundtracks in the 1980s and 1990s* (Aldershot: Ashgate, 2004), pp. 155–6.

66 www.arvopart.ee/en/Valik-artikleid/arvo-paert-qi-suppose-secretly-we-love-one-another-it-is-very-beautifulq.

67 David Ng, *When Classical Music Masterpieces Become Soundtrack Cliches.*

68 Luke Benjamin Howard, "The popular reception of Samuel Barber's *Adagio for Strings*," *American Music* 25 (2007), 50–80.

69 See Jeffers Engelhardt's chapter on pp. 29–48.

70 Mark Swed, *Review: A Mystic in La La Land – Arvo Pärt's "Los Angeles" Sympony* (2009), http://latimesblogs.latimes.com/culturemonster/2009/01/review-a-mystic.html.

Appendix A Radiating from silence: the works of Arvo Pärt seen through a musician's eyes

1 Excerpts from *The Little Prince* are translated from Kähler's German version of Saint-Exupéry in order to give the best reading of Kähler's intention: Antoine de Saint-Exupéry, *Der kleine Prinz* (Düsseldorf: Karl Rauch).

2 Pärt's opinion on that issue is as follows: "In my opinion the value of music is beyond its color. Although idiosyncratic instrumental timbres of instruments are a part of the music they are not its most crucial one. That would be my capitulation to the mystery of music. Music must exist in itself … two, three tones. There has to be a mystery, regardless of the instrument."

3 By the way, I agree with Paul Hillier that experience in playing early music is very positive for performing Pärt. See Paul Hillier, *Arvo Pärt*, Oxford Studies of Composers (Oxford University Press, 1997).

4 A very good example can be found in the piano piece *Für Alina*: sound and expression of the top line (M) are predominantly dependent on the way it is supported by notes and overtones of the bottom line (T).

5 This is what Pärt says on this subject: "It is like breathing in and out. One cannot only breathe in the air, it has to be breathed out too."

6 Nelly Sachs, *Collected Poems*, trans. Michael Hamburger, Ruth and Matthew Mead, and Michael Roloff (Los Angeles, CA: Green Integer, 2011).

Appendix B Greatly sensitive: Alfred Schnittke in Tallinn

1 First published in *MusikTexte 78*, March, 1999, 41.

Appendix C Remembering Heino Eller

1 First published in liner notes, ECM 1745, Heino Eller – *Neenia*.

Select bibliography

Web sites

Arvo Pärt works list compiled by Onno van Rijen: http://home.wanadoo.nl/ovar/
part.htm

David Pinkerton's Arvo Pärt Information Archive: www.arvopart.org

ECM Records: www.ecmrecords.com

International Arvo Pärt Centre: www.arvopart.ee

Pärt information: www.arvopart.info

Universal Edition Pärt catalogue: www.universaledition.com/tl_files/
Komponisten/Paert/Paert_Catalogue.pdf

Universal Edition Pärt page:
www.universaledition.com/Arvo-Paert/composers-and-works/composer/534

Books and articles

Adamov, Norbert, "Specifika kompozicnej vystavby Janovych pasii Arvo Parta," in
*Zbornk prspevkov z muzikologickej konferencie Duchovna hadba v premenach
casu: Hudobne druhy a zanre*, ed. Jana Lengova and Frantisek Matus, Presov:
Suzvuk, 2001, pp. 117–22.

Agamennone, Maurizio, "Risonanza interiori nella musica di Arvo Pärt," *Arte
Organaria e Organistica* (April–June 1997), 8–11.

Aquila, Dominic, "The music of Arvo Pärt," *Image: A Journal of the Arts and
Religion* 2/110 (1992), 110–19.

Artner, Alan G., "Religious chords: Arvo Pärt's spirituality shines through his compositions," *Chicago Tribune*, April 3, 1994, Arts: 8. Reprinted as "Spirituality of
Arvo Pärt is international," *Calgary Herald*, April 17, 1994: F5.

Asch, Kenneth, "Underground composer," *Choir & Organ* 9/1 (January/February
2001), 26–9.

Aumere, Helga and others, *Eesti heliloojad ja Muusikateadlased: Biograafiline
Leksikon*, Tallinn: Eeesti Raamat, 1966.

Bambarger, Bradley, "Retail eagerly awaits ECM's Arvo Pärt set," *Billboard*, 7
(September 1996), 1, 119, 120.

Banks, Frederick W., "Arvo Pärt's expression of crisis: An analysis of Credo (1968),"
Master's thesis, University of Washington, 1995.

Beck, Jeremy, "Arvo Pärt: Notes from Oregon," *SCI Newsletter* (The Society of
Composers) 25 (April 1995), 1–2, 7.

Becker, Peter, "Review of Oliver Kautny's *Arvo Pärt zwischen Ost und West.
Rezeptionsgeschichte*," *Neue Zeitschrift für Musik* 165 (January 2004), 83.

Behne, Klaus-Ernst, "Musik mit Minuszeichen? Anmerkungen zu Arvo Pärt
Collage über B–A–C–H," *Musik und Unterricht* 2 (July 1991), 37–8.

Berger, Lyubov, "Arvo Pyart, Perpetuum mobile (Interferentsiya):
Khudozhestvennyi obraz i kompozitsionnaya ideya," *Sovetskaya Muzyka* 2
(February 1991), 59–63.

Bernhardt, Ross, *The Interrelationships of Text, Musical Form, and Tintinnabuli Technique in Arvo Pärt's* Berliner Messe *and* Litany, *and their Implications for Choral Rehearsal and Performance*, DMA Document, Michigan State University, 1997.

Blaszkiewicz, Teresa, "Aleatoryzm w wybranych utworach kompozytorów radzieckich," *Panstwowa Wyzsza Szkola Muzyczna w Gdansku* 8 (1975), 207–29.

Bradshaw, Susan, "Arvo Pärt," *Contact* 26 (Spring 1983), 25–8.

Brauneiss, Leopold, *Zahlen zwischen Struktur und Bedeutung: Zehn analytische Studien zu Kompositionen von Josquin bis Ligeti und Pärt*, Frankfurt am Main: Peter Lang-Verlag, 1997.

  "Grundsatzliches zum Tintinnabulistil Arvo Pärts," *Musiktheorie* 16 (2001), 41–57.

  "Arvo Pärt's Tintinnabuli-Style: Contemporary Music Toward a New Middle Ages?" In *Studies in Medievalism*, vol. 13, *Postmodern Medievalism* Woodbridge: Boydell & Brewer, 2005, pp. 27–34.

Broda, P. M., "Dum emisit spiritum: Passionsmusik bei Pergolesi, Pärt und Bruckner," *Singende Kirche* 37 (1990), 4.

Brotbeck, Roman, and Roland Wächter, "Lernen, die Stille zu hören," *Neue Zeitschrift für Musik* 151 (March 1990), 13–16.

Byrd, Margaret Erwin, *Teaching Post-minimalist Piano Literature by John Adams, Tom Johnson, and Arvo Pärt*, DMA thesis, University of South Carolina, 1997.

Canning, Hugh, "A passion for purity," *Manchester Guardian*, March 21, 1989, 37.

Carrara, Vittorio, "Dare calore al suono freddo dell'organo: A colloquio con Arvo Pärt," *Arte Organaria e Organistica* (April–June, 1997), 12–13.

Caux, Daniel, "Arvo Pärt, Dadaista cristiano?" *Pauta: Cuadernos de teoria y critica Musical* (July–September 1992), 65–7.

Church, Michael, "Don't bring all your noise into my silence," *Independent*, August 24, 1996, Arts, 3.

Clarke, David, "Parting glances," *Musical Times* 134 (December 1993), 680–4.

Conen, Hermann, ed. *Arvo Pärt: Die Musik des Tintinnabuli-Stils*, Cologne: Dohr-Verlag, 2006.

Cowgill, Rachel, *Sacred Music in Secular Times: Arvo Pärt, an anachronism in the twentieth century?* BMus. thesis, Goldsmiths College, University of London, 1989.

Crittenden, Stephen, "Arvo Pärt: Music dug out of the earth," ABC Radio 24 Hours (Australian Broadcasting Corporation), February 1, 1993, 26–8.

Danuser, Hermann, "Neue Innerlichkeit in der zeitgenössischen Musik," *Dissonance* 22 (November 1989), 4–10; reprinted as "Innerlichkeit und Äußerlichkeit in der Musikästhetik der Gegenwart," in *Die Musik der achtziger Jahre*, ed. Ekkehard Jost, Mainz: Schott, 1990.

Dermann, Peter, "Un-er-hort: Johann Sebastian Bach's Präludium C-Dur im Credo von Arvo Pärt," *Musik & Bildung: Praxis Musikunterricht* (March–April 1997), 22–6.

Dobbs, Quincy Oad, *"Holy Minimalism": A Performer's Analysis and Guide to the Solo Organ Works of Arvo Pärt*, DMA thesis, Arizona State University, 2000.

Dolp, Laura, *The Silent Garden: inventive procedure and ancient principle in the Berlin Mass of Arvo Pärt*, Master's thesis, Boston University, 1997.

Drakeford, Richard, "Review of *Summa for Violin, Two Violas and Cello*," *Musical Times* 134/1801 (March 1993) 141.

Durbin, Karen, "Amazing grace," *Mirabella* (April 1990), 68.

Eelhein, Ela, Eha-Pilvi Jõgi, Jüri Kallasmaa, Endel Pajula, Urve Tammjarv, Helgi Tuksammel, and Tiiu Viires (eds.), *Eesti Muusika Biograafiline Leksikon*, Tallinn: Kirjastus Valgus, 1990.

Eichert, Randolf G., "Satztechnik: Form und Harmonik in der Musik von Arvo Pärt," *Musiktheorie*, 1 (1999), 47–63.

Elste, Martin, "An interview with Arvo Pärt," *Fanfare* 11 (March/April 1988), 337–41.

Everett-Green, Robert, "Arvo Pärt searches for echoes of Eden," *Globe and Mail*, January 22, 1996, C1, C2.

Fanselau, Rainer, "B–A–C–H – didaktisch buchstabiert," *Musik und Bildung* 17 (January 1985), 18–32.

Ferguson, Marijke, "Musique pauvre: Arvo Pärt en de klank van mystiek," *Mens en Melodie* 50 (April 1995), 256–8.

Finkelshteyn, Tracy Engman, *From J. S. Bach to Arvo Pärt: Six Pieces from the Violin Repertoire Dating from 1720–1980*, DMus. thesis, Northwestern University, 1999.

Fischer, Kurt von, "Zur Johannes-Passion von Arvo Pärt," *Kirchenmusikalisches Jahrbuch* 75 (1991), 133–8.

Fisk, Josiah, "The new simplicity: The music of Górecki, Tavener and Pärt," *Hudson Review* 47/3 (Fall 1994), 394–412.

Frink, Christina and Frauke M. Hess, "Die tonende Stille der Glocken: Arvo Pärts Tintinnabuli-Stil – Emanation oder Technik?" *Neue Zeitschrift für Musik* (May–June 1997), 38–41.

Gerlach, Hannelore, "Musik in der Estnischen SSR," *Musik in der Schule* 28 (December 1977), 402–5.

Gojowy, Detlef, "Sowjetische Avantgarde: Zur Neuer Musik nach dem Zweiten Weltkrieg," *Neue Zürcher Zeitung* 185 (August 12–13, 1989), 61–2.

"Arvo Pärt im sowjetischen Umfeld," *Symposion Arvo Pärt: Rezeption und Wirkung seiner Musik*, Osnabrück, Germany: Electronic Publishing, 2001. www.epos.uos.de/music/templates/buch.php?id=3&page=/music/books/k/kauo001/pages/

Goldberg, Clemens, "Text und Liturgie bei Arvo Pärt," in *Musik als Text*, ed. Danuser Hermann and Tobias Plebuch, Kassel: Barenreiter, 1998, pp. 416–22.

Golianek, Ryszard Daniel, "Miedzy metafizyka a nuda," *Ruch Muzyczny* 26 (1998), 20–1.

Griffiths, Paul, "Radiant calm," *The Times*, June 10, 1986, 15.

Modern Music and After: Directions since 1945 (Oxford University Press, 1995).

Gröhn, Constantin, "Klangideale von Arvo Pärt und La Monte Young," *Positionen: Beitrage zur neuen Musik* 64 (August 2005), 25–7.

Dieter Schnebel und Arvo Pärt: Komponisten als "Theologen," Berlin; Lit, 2006.

Guillot, Matthieu, "Musique et métissage," *Revue d'esthetique* 24 (1993), 123–5, 127, 129–40.

"Look at the voice in the music of Arvo Pärt," *International Choral Bulletin* (October 1993), 11; reprinted as "Arvo Pärt and the human voice," *Anacrusis* 14 (Winter 1995), 7–10.

Hatzis, Christos, "Towards a new musical paradigm," *MikroPolyphonie*, 2/1 (July–December 1996).

Hebort, Heinz Josef, "Wohlklang und Stille," *Die Zeit,* February 1, 1985, 44.

Helbig, Adriana, *Arvo Pärt: The Search for the Eternal Silence at the Heart of Sound,* BA thesis, Drew University, 1997.

Hentig, Hartmut von, "Musik wahrnehmen: Zu einem Stück Arvo Pärt," *Musik und Unterricht* 2 (July 1991), 35–6.

Hillert, Richard, "The liturgical choral music of Henryk Górecki and Arvo Pärt," *Cross Accent: Journal of the Association of Lutheran Church Music* 7 (January 1996), 16–25.

Hillier, Paul, "Arvo Pärt: Magister Ludi," *Musical Times* 130/1753 (March 1989), 134–7.

Arvo Pärt, Oxford Studies of Composers (Oxford University Press, 1997).

"The Passion of Arvo Pärt," *BBC Music Magazine* 5 (February 1997), 35.

"Minimalism in music," *Schwann Opus* 8/3 (Summer 1997), 14A–16A.

Hillier, Paul, and Tõnu Tormis, *On Pärt*. Copenhagen: Theatre of Voices: 2005.

Hoek, Klaas, "Orgelmuziek van Arvo Pärt," *Het Orgel* 88/4 (1992), 121–5.

Holcroft, Reuben F. P., *The Art of Simplicity: Design, Sentiment, and Value in Non-Developmental Music, Studies in Works by Satie, Pärt and Poulenc*, Master's thesis, University of Otago, 1995.

Holm, Thomas Robert, *Analysis and Comparison of Three Major Vocal/ Instrumental Works of Arvo Pärt*: Passio, Miserere, *and* Litany, DMA thesis, University of Illinois at Urbana-Champaign, 1998.

Järg, Tiia, "Arvo Pärdi kvintetiino," *Teater. Muusika. Kino* 12 (December 1994), 19–22.

Johnson, Stephen, "An expression of faith," *Gramophone* 66 (February 1989), 1263.

Kälvemark, Torsten, *Arvo Pärt: Om musiken vid tystnadens gräns*, Skellefteå: Artos & Norma, 2002.

Kareda, Saale, "'Dem Urknall entgegen': Einblick in den Tintinnabuli-Stil von Arvo Pärt," *Kirchenmusikalisches Jahrbuch* (2000; 2001), 59–67.

Kautny, Oliver (ed.), *Arvo Pärt. Rezeption und Wirkung seiner Musik. Vorträge des Wuppertaler Symposiums 1999* (University of Osnabrück, 1999), www.epos. uni-osnabrueck.de.

"Arvo Pärts *Passio* und Johann Sebastian Bachs *Johannespassion*: Rezeptionsästhetische Perspektiven," *Archiv für Musikwissenschaft* (March 1999), 198–222.

Arvo Pärt zwischen Ost und West: Rezeptionsgeschichte, Stuttgart: Metzler Verlag, 2002.

"Dem Himmel ein Stück näher … : Der neoromantische Mythos 'Arvo Pärt,'" *Neue Zeitschrift für Musik* (May 2002), 24–7.

"'Alle Länder, in ihrer Verschiedenheit, sind eins ...': Der Schein des Orientalischen bei Arvo Pärt," *Neue Zeitschrift für Musik* (February 2003), 24–7.

Kenyon, Nicholas, "Ritual simplicity," *The Listener*, April 2, 1987, 29.

Kimberley, Nick, "Starting from scratch," *Gramophone* 74 (September 1996), 14–16.

Kirnarskaya, Dina, "Arvo Pärt restores the link of times," *Moscow News Weekly*, April 21–27, 1995, 12.

Kosak, Gerard J., *Arvo Pärt's Summa: An Example of Systematic Construction*, MMus. thesis, Northern Arizona University, 1994.

Kostelanetz, Richard, "A mystic's music: Arvo Pärt's quiet revolution," *Connoisseur* 220 (April 1990), 66, 68–70, 72, 76.

Langager, Graeme, *The Tintinnabuli Compositional Style of Arvo Pärt*, MM thesis, California State University, Long Beach, 1997.

Lesle, Lutz, "Glockchenspiel und heiliges Staunen: Zum 65. Geburtstag des estnischen Komponisten Arvo Pärt," *Musik und Kirche* (July–August 2000), 238–45.

Lovisa, Fabian R., *Minimal-music: Entwicklung, Komponisten, Werke*, Darmstadt: Wissenschaftliche Buchgesellschaft, 1996.

Lubow, Arthur, "Arvo Pärt: The sound of spirit," *New York Times Magazine*, October 15, 2010.

Macek, Petr, *Die Musickentwicklung nach 1968.69: im Vorzeichen einer Uberlebensphilosophie der neuen Musik?* Brno: Masarykova univerzita; Prague: vE spolupraci s Barenreiter, 1999.

Maimets-Volt, Kaire, *Mediating the 'Idea of One': Arvo Pärt's Pre-existing Film Music*, PhD thesis, Estonian Academy of Music and Theatre, 2009.

Marstal, H., and O. Jegindoe Norup, "Arvo Pärt: Fra Konstruktivisme til Konstruktivisme," *Dansk Musik Tidsskrift* 70 (1995–96), 46–52.

Mattner, Lothar, "Arvo Pärt: Tabula Rasa," *Melos* 2 (February 1985), 82–99.

McCarthy, Jamie, "An interview with Arvo Pärt," *Musical Times* 130/1753 (March 1989), 130–3. Reprinted in *Contemporary Music Review* 12 (1995), 55–64.

Meleshin, P., *Asketicheskii stil' Arvo Pyarta*, diploma work, Gorky Conservatory, 1990.

Mellers, Wilfrid, "Round and about Górecki's Symphony no. 3," *Tempo* (March 1989), 24.

"Arvo Pärt, God and gospel: *Passio Domini Nostri Iesu Christi Secundum Iohannem (1982)*," *Contemporary Music Review* 12/2 (1995), 35–48.

Mohr, Chris, "Arvo Pärt in Oregon," *On the Air* 5 (October 1994), 33–4.

Monita, Rafal, "Muzyczny fin de siècle," *Ruch Muzyczny* 26 (1998), 21–2.

Morton, Brian and Pamela Collins (eds.), *Contemporary Composers* (Chicago and London: St. James Press, 1992).

Mosch, Ulrich, "Tönende Stille - stilles Tönen. Zur Musik von Arvo Pärt," *Positionen: Beiträge zur neuen Musik* 10 (January 1992), 17–23.

Motte-Haber, Helga de la, "Wenn Bach Bienen gezüchtet hätte ... Über das Verhältnis von neuer und alter Musik im Werk on Arvo Pärt," *Positionen: Beiträge zur neuen Musik* 24 (March 1995), 18–21.

"Struktur als Programm: Analytische Bemerkungen zur Komposition Summa von Arvo Pärt," in *Nahe und Distanz: Nachgedachte Musik der Gegenwart*, ed. Wolfgang Gratzer, Hofheim: Wolke, 1996, pp. 14–25.

"Helga de la Motte-Haber im Gesprach mit Arvo Pärt: Klang und Linie als Einheit," in *Controlling Creative Processes in Music*, ed. Reinhard Kopiez and Wolfgang Auhagen, Frankfurt am Main: Lang, 1998, pp. 229–41.

Nestyeva, Marina, "Pärt, Arvo," *The New Grove Dictionary of Music and Musicians*, 6th edn., ed. Sadie, Stanley, London: Macmillan, 1980.

Nicholl, Sarah C. Wrathall, *Arvo Pärt's Six Versions of Fratres: An Analysis and Comparison*, BEd. thesis, Brigham Young University, 2000.

Nikezic, Jelena, "Muzika stvara vreme – Muzika zahteva vreme: Povodom dela Tabula rasa Arva Parta," *Novi Zvuk* 17 (2001), 49–52.

Nordwall, Trygve, "Arvo Pärt – religioes mystiker eller excentrisk naivist eller," *Nutida Musik* 31 (1987–88), 10–13.

Normet, Leo, "Pyarti i Tormis pishut dlya khora," *Sovetskaya Muzyka* 25 (July 1961), 40–2.

"Erfolgreiche zeitgenössische Musik in Estland," *Musik und Gesellschaft* 13 (July 1963), 433–4.

Normet, Leo and Artur Vahter, *Soviet Estonian Music: Ten Aspects of Estonian Life*, Tallinn: Eesti Raamat, 1967.

Olt, Harry, "Musikens rättigheter och rätt musik," *Musikern* 4 (April 1969), 14–15.

Modern Estonian Composers, Tallinn: Kodumaa, 1972.

Estonian Music, Tallinn: Perioodika, 1980.

Overbeeke, E, "De nieuwe spiritualiteit: expressie zonder dubbele bodem," *Mens en Melodie* 50 (May 1995), 294–6.

Pärt, Arvo, "Tintinnabuli – Flucht in die freiwillige Armut," in *Sowjetische Musik im Licht der Perestroika: Interpretationen, Quellentexte, Komponistenmonographien*, ed. Hermann Danuser, Hannelore Gerlach, and Jürgen Köchel, Laaber Verlag, 1990, pp. 269–70.

"Über Arvo Pärt," *Neue Zürcher Zeitung* (September 27, 2003), 38.

Piatak, Richard Daniel, *The Tintinnabulation of Arvo Pärt: A Study of Style and Aesthetics*, MM thesis, Ohio University, 2000.

Pinkerton, David, *Minimalism, the Gothic Style, and Tintinnabulation in Selected Works of Arvo Pärt*, Master's thesis, Duquesne University School of Music, 1996.

Pisarenko, Olgierd, "Sluchac ciszy," *Studio* 11 (1997), 8–11.

Pitts, Anthony, "A brief introduction to Pärt-writing," *Church Music Quarterly* (March 2004), 6–9.

Pociej, Bohdan, "Arvo Part czyli duchowosc muzyki," *Sycyna* 3/4 (1999), 5.

Quinn, Peter, *Arvo Pärt, Cantus in memory of Benjamin Britten: A Study of the First Major Work of the Tintinnabuli Period, its Links with Russian Orthodoxy through the Use of the Bell, and its Creation Based on the Evidence of the Sources*, MM thesis, University of London, Goldsmiths College, 1991.

"Out with the old and in with the new: Arvo Pärt's *Credo*," *Tempo* 211 (January 2000), 16–20.

Raggi, Enrico, "Arvo Pärt," *Rivista Internazionale di Musica Sacra* 1/4 (1990), 356–74.

Randalu, Ivalo, "Arvo Pärt in November 1978," *Teater. Muusika. Kino* 7 (1988), trans. Andres Didrik with Doug Maskew, 1997, from David Pinkerton's *Arvo Pärt Information Archive* (arvopart.org).

"Muutumised: Andres Mustonen Arvo Pärdist ja iseendast," *Teater. Muusika, Kino* (November 1995), 33–40.

Restagno, Enzo, *Arvo Pärt allo specchio: Conversazioni, saggi e testimonianze*, Milan: Il Saggiatore Collana Biblioteca, 2004.

Arvo Pärt peeglis: vestlused, esseed ja artiklid, trans. Maarja Kangro, and others, Tallinn, Eesti Eesti Entsüklopeediakirjastus, 2005.

Restagno, Enzo and others, *Arvo Pärt im Gespräch*, Vienna: Universal Edition, 2010.

Revol, Patrick, "Arvo Pärt et la polarization modale," *Analyse Musicale* (4th trimester 2001), 103–8.

Rey, Anne, "Pärt le pur," *Le Monde*, November 18, 1986, 16.

"Arvo Pärt, le saint excentrique," *Le Monde*, June 2, 1987, 11.

"L'énigme Arvo Pärt," *Le Monde de la musique* (October 1987), 69.

Rienäcker, Gerd, "Review of 'Arvo Pärt zwischen Ost und West: Rezeptionsgeschichte' by Oliver Kautny," *Musik & Asthetik* (April 2004), 107–10.

Robison, Clayne B., *Elements of Ethos and Pathos in Two Modern Choral Pieces, Arvo Pärt's Magnificat and Dominick Argento's Gloria*, BA thesis, Brigham Young University, 1993.

Roeder, John, "Transformational aspects of Pärt's tintinnabuli music," *Journal of Music Theory* 55/1 (2001), 1–41.

Sabbe, Herman, "Music makes time – music takes time: Apropos of Arvo Pärt's Tabula Rasa," *New Sound* 17/1 (2001), 47–51.

Saeterbakken, S., "Alt jeg behøver aa vite: 4 notater under innflytelse av Arvo Pärt's musikk," *Ballade Tidsskrift for Ny Musikk* 14 (1990), 13ff.

Salvadori, Luca, "Le geometrie spirituali di Arvo Pärt," *Arte Organaria e Organistica* (April–June 1997), 14–18.

Sandner, Wolfgang, "Der stille Ton," *Frankfurter Allgemeine Zeitung*, September 1, 1984.

"Der stille Ton: Zu den Orchesterwerken von Arvo Pärt," in *Studien zur Instrumentalmusik: Lothar Hoffmann-Erbrecht zum 60. Geburtstag*, ed. Anke Bingmann and others, Tutzing: Hans Schneider, 1988, pp. 509–13.

Sandow, Gregory, "Tasting the new era," *Village Voice* 31 (June 17, 1986), 79.

Savenko, Svetlana, "Strogiy stil' Arvo Pyarta," *Sovetskaya Muzyka* (October 1991), 15–19.

Schatt, Peter W., "'Wir mussen der Musik eine Chance geben …': Vom Musikpadagogischen umgang mit dem Werk Arvo Pärts," in *Kultur – Bildung – Politik: Festschrift fur Hermann Rauhe zum 70*, ed. Hermann Rauhe, Hanns-Werner Heister, and Wolfgang Hochstein, Hamburg: Von Bockel, 2000, pp. 537–52.

Schenbeck, Lyn, "Discovering the music of Estonian composer Arvo Pärt," *Choral Journal 34* (August 1993), 23–30.

Schlee, Thomas Daniel, "Komponisten zu 'Ordnung und Freiheit,'" in *Ordnung und Freiheit: Almanach zum Internationalen Beethovenfest, Bonn 2000*, ed. Thomas Daniel Schlee, Laaber Verlag, 2000, pp. 188–200.

Schubert, Werner, "Die lateinische Sprache in der Musik des 20. Jahrhunderts. III: Arvo Pärt," *International Journal of Musicology* 6 (1997), 413–27.

Schwartz, Elliot and Daniel Godfrey, *Music Since 1945: Issues, Materials and Literature*, New York: Schirmer Books, 1993.

Shenton, Andrew, "Arvo Pärt's organ music," *The American Organist* (December 2010), 76–8.

"De orgelcomposities van Arvo Pärt: Minimal music met een spirituele laag," *Timbres* (Autumn 2011), 38–43.

Shimbo, Amy M., *Analyses of Works by the Twentieth-Century Composers John Cage, Arvo Pärt, and Brian Wilson of the Beach Boys*, MA thesis, University of Washington, 1999.

Simon, Allen H., "Deterministic techniques in Arvo Pärt's Magnificat," *Choral Journal 37* (October 1996), 21–4.

Smith, Geoffrey J., "Sources of invention: An interview with Arvo Pärt," *Musical Times* 140/1868 (Fall, 1999), 19–25.

Soomere, Uno, "The symphonies of Arvo Pärt," in *Composers of the Union Republics*, Moscow, 1977.

Spohr, Mathias, "Mit 'freiwilliger Armut' Geld verdienen," *Dissonanz* 36 (May 1993), 20–2.

Stapert, Calvin, "A meadow of wildflowers: The music of Górecki, Pärt, and Tavener," *Perspectives* (January 1997), 9–13.

Stenger, Alfred, "Dur-Stellen innerhalb der geistlichen Musik von Arvo Pärt," in *Festschrift fur Winfried Kirsch zum 65. Geburtstag*, ed. Winfried Kirsch and others, Tutzing: Schneider, 1996, pp. 560–2.

Stenius, Caterina, Pentti Ritolahti and Kalevi Kuosa, "Monastery moods: Arvo Pärt," *Finnish Music Quarterly* 2 (1989), 36–7.

Sussmann, Franz, "Am Rande der Stille: Eine Begegnung mit Arvo Pärts *Sarah was Ninety*," *Musik & Bildung: Praxis Musikunterricht* (November–December 1998), 46–9.

Szwarcman, Dorota, "Arvo Pärt o Drodzé," *Ruch Muzyczny* 33 (December 3, 1989), 5–7.

"Jak krysztal," *Gazeta Wyborcza* 253 (1998), 16–17.

Tarakanov, Mikhal, "Novaya zheizn' staroy formi," *Sovetskaya Muzyka* 32 (June 1968), 54–62.

Teachout, Terry, "Holy minimalism," *Commentary* (American Jewish Committee) 99 (April 1995), 50–3.

Topman, Monika, *An Outline of Estonian Music*, trans. Aino Jõgi, Tallinn: Perioodika, 1978.

Tuisk, Ofelia, "Arvo Part-kilka słów o niektórych pracach," *Res Facta* 6 (1972), 133–9.

Turner, Geoffrey, "Sounds of transcendence," *Cross Currents* 45 (Spring, 1995), 54–67.

Vahter, Artur, and Leo Normet, *Music in the Estonian SSR*, trans. G. Liiv, Tallinn: Eesti Raamat, 1965.

Vaitmaa, Merike, "Arvo Pärt," in *Kuus Eesti tänase muusika loojat*, ed. H. Tauk, Tallinn: Eesti Raamat, 1970, pp. 35–60.

"Tintinnabuli-elämänkatsomus, tyyli ja tekniikka: Arvo Pärtin sävellyksistä," trans. Outi Jyrhämä, *Musiikkitiede* 2/2 (1990), 61–82.

"Arvo Pärdi vokaallooming," *Teater. Muusika. Kino* 2 (February 1991), 19–27.

van den Brand, H., "Arvo Pärt (1935): Te Deum ('84–'86)," *Gregoriusblad: Tijdschrift tot Bevordering van Liturgische Muziek* 119 (1995), 173–5.

van der Hilst, Rob, "Een alternatieve Johannes," *Mens en Melodie* 44 (March 1989), 144–5.

von Fischer, Kurt, "Zur Johannes-Passion von Arvo Pärt," *Kirchenmusikalisches Jahrbuch* 75 (1991), 133–8.

Die Passion: Musik zwischen Kunst und Kirche, Kassel: Bärenreiter, 1997.

Wallace, Helen, "Review of Fratres," *Musical Times* (February 1993), 87.

Walljasper, Jay, "Mystical minimalists," *Utne Reader* 66 (November/December 1994), 22, 24.

Wallrabenstein, Wolfram, "Arvo Pärt: *Cantus in memoriam Benjamin Britten*. Zur Bedeutung von Assoziativität und Subjektivität im Erkenntnisprozeß – Beispiele aus der Unterrichtspraxis," *Zeitschrift für Musikpädagogik* 31 (October 1985), 13–31.

"Schüler interpretieren die Collage über B–A–C–H von Arvo Pärt. Sinnerschließung von Musik durch kontemplatives Hören (Alle Schulformen der Sekundarstufe I und II)," in *Spiel-Räume fürs Leben: Musikerziehung in einer gefährdeten Welt*, ed. Karl Heinrich Ehrenforth, Mainz: Schott, 1989, pp. 137–9.

"Arvo Pärt hören: Texte und Materialien zur Hörbegegung mit Pärts Collage über B–A–C–H," *Musik und Unterricht* 2 (July 1991), 31–5.

Whiteman, Carol L. Matthews, *Passio: The Iconography of Arvo Pärt*, City University of New York, 1997.

Whiteman, Michael, "'Holy minimalists' and the logic of musical styles," *South African Music Teacher* 124 (June 1994), 6–8, 29–31.

Wilms, Bernd, "'Ein Bild von der Unendlichkeit': Arvo Pärts *Spiegel im Spiegel* im Unterricht der Sekundarstufe I," *Musik & Bildung: Praxis Musikunterricht* (November–December 1997), 26–9.

Witherden, Barry, "Pärt, the Essentialist," *Classic CD* 63 (July 1995), 63.

Wolverton, Vance D., "Breaking the silence: Choral music of the Baltic republics. I: Estonia," *The Choral Journal* (February 1998), 21–8.

Wong, Hoi Sze Susanna, *Timbre and Tintinnabulation in the Music of Arvo Pärt*, MPhil. thesis, Chinese University of Hong Kong, 2001.

Wright, Stephen, *Stylistic Development in the Works of Arvo Pärt, 1958–1985*, Master's thesis, University of Western Ontario, 1992.

"The organ music of Arvo Pärt," *American Organist* 29 (April 1995), 56–7.

Wuthe, Cortina, "Arvo Pärt (1935–): Ein Verzeichnis der in offentlichen Musikbibliotheken der Bundesrepublik Deutschland vorhandenen Werke," *Forum Musikbibliothek: Beiträge und Informationen aus der Musikbibliothekarischen Praxis* 1 (1998), 105–14.

Zech, Karl Ferdinand, "Arvo Pärt und der Tintinnabuli-Stil," *Musik in der Schule* (October 1998), 234–5.

Index

Cambridge Companions to Music

Instruments

Printed in the United States
By Bookmasters